Why
I Am Still a
Catholic

Why
I Am Still a
Catholic

Edited by
Kevin and Marilyn Ryan

RIVERHEAD BOOKS

•

NEW YORK

Riverhead Books
Published by The Berkley Publishing Group
A member of Penguin Putnam Inc.
200 Madison Avenue
New York, New York 10016

Copyright © 1998 by Kevin Ryan and Marilyn Ryan
Book design by Omega Clay
Cover design by Elizabeth Sheehan

First edition: May 1998

The Penguin Putnam Inc. World Wide Web site address is
http://www.penguinputnam.com

Library of Congress Cataloging-in-Publication Data

Why I am still a Catholic / edited by Kevin and Marilyn Ryan.—1st
    ed.
        p.   cm.
    Includes bibliographical references.
    ISBN 1-57322-677-7
    1. Catholics—United States—Biography.   2. Christian biography—
United States.   I. Ryan, Kevin.   II. Ryan, Marilyn.
BX4651.2.W48   1998
282'.092'273—dc21
    [B]   97-32061
                                                                         CIP

Printed in the United States of America

10   9   8   7   6   5   4   3   2   1

Contents

Preface

THIS BOOK is the product of curiosity and concern. As a couple settled and happy in the Church (one a cradle Catholic and the other a convert), we have been interested for years in what holds others in the Church. We know why we are still Catholics. Still, we have regularly wondered what moves others to get out of bed on Sundays, keep Lenten rules, and try—in a world of wrap-around noise—to hear the voice of God. Why do they remain with a faith so at odds with the prevailing culture? What has happened in their spiritual lives? What are their stories?

We worry about the next generation of young Catholics. Surely, it is a reflection on our own faith that we worry about our Church in the face of Christ's promise to Peter that "the Gates of Hell shall not prevail against it." Yes, the Church will last, but will this generation of young Catholics gain the support and grace from it that they need? Amid the demands of career and the siren songs of materialism and sexual pleasures, will the message of Christ break through? Or will they see a version of the Church which has been packaged by those indifferent or hostile to the Church of Rome? Will their mental map of Christ's Church be the one portrayed by television sitcoms and by the arched brows of our nightly news commentators?

Missing often from the common picture of the Church is the presence of successful adults doing secular work and living a life of faith. Other than their parents and a few neighbors and relatives, young Catholics see few examples of people who though successful by the world's standards draw from the Church their strength. Of course, they once saw glimpses on their television sets of an eighty-seven pound Albanian nun cleaning the sores of Calcutta's sick and dying, and they regularly get snippets of an aged Slavic Pope waving to the crowds. We believe images of accomplished Americans who love and publicly affirm their Church are missing. Our hope in this volume is to present such images.

So, while our book is for the curious, those who want to know why others stay in this gnarled, old Church, it is primarily for the young. We hope it will be read by those who are in high school and college, those who are, in effect, coming of age as Catholics. They have inherited "the faith of their fathers," but are now beginning to take seriously the world beyond their parents. Typically, they are in schools and colleges which all but sanctify our tripartite governmental system of executive, legislative, and judicial branches, but indirectly (and sometimes directly) suggest that religion is a relic of a pre-scientific era. Like quill pens and wooden plows, it will soon slip into the deleted files of history. When not in school, American youth spent vast amounts of time in a media culture dominated by a McDisney commercialism and a toxic sexual ethos. The role models they regularly encounter are not Dorothy Day or the sandaled St. Francis of Assisi, but the cast of *Friends* clad in Nikes and Tommy Hilfiger gear. The self-denial and prayer of Catholicism are an anomaly today. What could be more out of step with our culture than fasting, pre-marital chastity, and meditation on the mysteries of the most holy rosary? How can our young be attracted to the spiritual exercises of Ignatius of Loyola when their daily fare rocks? The good life screams out, "Party hearty!", "You deserve a break today!", and "Just do it!" And from the Church door escapes the whisper, "Follow Christ."

The main purpose behind this book, then, is to present all Catholics, young and old, with living pictures of Catholics who have listened to the whisper. We wanted to see more clearly how our fellow Americans who have grown up in a particular tradition have gone on personal journeys and, as adults, have fallen in love with the Catholic Church and know her joy. We are, all of us, people of the story. We learn primarily from the human examples we encounter. Abstract principles, whether they be scientific or theological, have value, but often they don't have the power to move the mind and heart as a good story. *Why I Am Still a Catholic*, then, is not a set of arguments. Rather it is a storybook of personal journeys. We wanted to compile a legacy of faith that is essentially a teaching tool to pass on to the next generation. We selected our twenty-five storytellers from among the famous, the near-famous, and the soon-to-be famous. While it was not part of their marching orders from us, we wanted their stories to show how people who are making contributions to the larger society were, also, living lives of faith. We hoped, too, to show that their spiritual lives and commitment to the Church were not empty and ritualistic, but rather joyful and deeply satisfying. We wanted to demonstrate, especially to the young, that one can be a success, can do good work in the world, and still be a vital Catholic.

Let's face it. Many of our fellow Americans, particularly among our academic and cultural elites, wish Catholics would just go practice somewhere else. Or, that we would simply let our odd rituals and offensive doctrines recede out of sight. They are offended by our stubborn opposition to abortion and to euthanasia. They are piqued that, in the face of massive American opinion poll data, the Church insists on denying women their natural right to be ordained as priests. Then, we appear to reverse ourselves and have such devotion to Christ's mother. They are suspicious of our allegiance to this aged, white-haired Pole who is capable of generating so much love around the world. There are, also, the little annoyances like calling those men in funny collars "Father," and all those foreheads smudged with ashes. Their teeth are really put on edge by our outrageous claim that when we take a white wafer into our mouths, we are receiving God into our own bodies.

Therefore, we feel an enormous debt of gratitude to each author, each brave soul who committed his or her own history and beliefs to paper.

They are comrades in this struggle to maintain a true Catholic presence in this country. They have inspired and moved us, as we hope they will move you. This willingness to organize one's own faith into a coherent account and then sweat it out word by word is an act of courage. In proclaiming their faith to the world, they remind us of the young and shy Flannery O'Connor, dining with a group of sophisticates at the table of Mary McCarthy. McCarthy, at the top of her fame as a literary figure, dominated the conversations. As a quite lapsed Catholic, she began to expound on Church matters and at one point referred to the Eucharist as "only a symbol." At that point, Flannery, who hadn't said a word until then, burst out with characteristic bluntness, "If It's just a symbol, then to Hell with It!" And our authors might add, "So, too, with the primacy of our Pope, with our Catholic sense of man as both sinner and salvageable, with our sacramental life, and with our social teachings of responsibilities to the poor, to the forgotten, and to the unborn." Their lives witness that these are not arbitrary ideas that we can put on or take off to suit the social coloration of the moment. Our Catholic sacramental life and our doctrine are the truest parts of our existence. And they should inform and direct our every act.

Readers may wonder how we compiled our list of authors. It was a rather grueling process, but it had its light moments. For instance, when we wrote a letter to a famous star of film and television asking her to write about why she was still a Catholic, only to receive a warm and gracious response, informing us that she was Episcopalian, thank you very much. The very first response we received brought tears to our eyes. One of our favorite entertainers, who for years has been raising money for various Catholic schools and other causes, wrote us that while he loved the Church deeply, he was separated from the Church for over four decades when he married his current wife. His pain leapt off the page.

Nonetheless we found a broad variety of Catholics who were each willing to contribute a personal reflection—try it once and see how difficult it is—of their backgrounds and their faith. Some stories have the ring of familiarity; the themes of cozy family and church lives should resonate with many readers. But there are more complicated stories as well. Several contributors recount how they returned to the church after falling away, and others examine the struggles inherent in conversion. Some authors have remained with the Church despite having serious disagreements with individual church policies, while others are determined to defend the Church's positions throughout their work and their lives. Almost all of the writers note how they have relied on the exemplary strength of friends, nuns, priests, and parents to teach and sustain them. The iridescent power of example shines through these reflections. For all of us, sainthood prods the sinner.

Two final comments. First, "labor of love" is a tired old cliché, but it fits here. We have loved gathering and editing this collection. We love the "smells and bells" of our old Church and the openness of the new Church. We love the traditions and the sense of belonging to a long line of imperfect, dented, and sometimes broken souls struggling together along with some radiant saints. We love the heroic heritage which comes with being a member of the Catholic Church. A wonderful bonus, though, has been the opportunity of getting to know our authors. What generous souls they are!

Second, we want to thank all our friends whom we have tormented for the last three years with endless talk about this book. There was a method to our madness. In sheer self defense they came up with names and addresses of observant Catholics for us to contact. Among these dear souls are Karen Bohlin, Marie Oates, Hilary and Jeff Tucker, Richard Griffin, Walter and Eileen Connor, Fr. David Murphy, Kay Meyer, Julia and Alfie Graham, Joe Astirita, William Schmitt, Fr. James Gilhooley, Pat Shay, James Lee Burke, Tom and Sally O'Keefe, Maura Daly, and Margaret Sullivan. Special thanks go to several of our authors who not only wrote wonderful essays and gave us steady support, but went to great lengths to help us recruit other authors.

Kevin and Marilyn Ryan

Remembering Churches
Jon Hassler

BUNDLED IN a snowsuit, scarf, and blanket, I'm gliding happily along the icy sidewalk in the box sled my father has built and my mother is pulling. It doesn't occur to me that this daily trip downtown in all weather is a measure of my parents' devotion to one another; I'm only four and too self-involved to understand any but their equally strong devotion to me. I have begun to sense, however, that my father has a competitor—somebody named God—for my mother's attention, because whenever it's below zero and the north wind bites at her exposed calves (this is about five years before the first respectable woman in this town will wear slacks in public) it's always at Sacred Heart Church that we stop for a few minutes' shelter. But not in the church proper. This is the Depression, and the cost of heating the vast reaches of the upper church through a Minnesota winter is more than this congregation can afford. We enter the vestibule and descend into the whitewashed, low-ceilinged basement, where Father Donnay has fashioned an altar and brought in a variety of cast-off kneelers and pews and slatted folding chairs that creak when you squirm, and it's here my mother takes out her rosary and gives herself up to her Maker. She talks with Him, she says. So does old Mrs. Crouch, apparently, whom we inevitably find kneeling at the Communion rail with her alarm clock ticking loudly at her elbow and her tall son sitting behind her in the front pew, looking alert and idiotically happy.

These visits don't do much for my relationship with God. I don't like it down here. It's not Sonny Crouch who repels me; I can tell by his constant smile that he's harmless. Nor is it particularly gloomy in the basement; the ground-level windows are large enough to catch a good bit of the southwest-sinking sun and bounce its pink light off the far wall, where a couple of old ladies are praying in the vicinity of the votive candles. It's the ticking clock I dislike, and the tedium it measures out. It's terribly dull down here. I've had my nap and I want to be on my way. I've long since given up trying to have a conversation with God. I used to listen, but He never said anything. I'm eager to get to the grocery store and see my father in his apron. I'm hungry for the piece of candy he'll give me.

After what seems eternity we're suddenly stirred to life by the shrill alarm of Mrs. Crouch's clock—it's ten minutes before *Jack Armstrong*, which she claims is Sonny's favorite radio show. Mother knots my scarf tightly under my chin and Mrs. Crouch zips up Sonny's jacket. The two old ladies grunt and sigh, rising arthritically to their feet. These are the Macklin sisters-in-law, who come every day to pray for the repose of the soul of their brother and husband, who died, says my mother, in a farm accident. That these two women resemble each other greatly amuses my mother. The Macklins were married so long, says Mother, that Mrs. Macklin came to resemble not only her husband but also his sister. Outside, Mother joins the three women in a brief knot of gossip under the smiling gaze of Sonny Crouch. I can't stand to wait another minute. I break free and run to my sled.

And yet now, sixty winters later, when I go back in memory to Sacred Heart, I go eagerly into the basement. It's only with effort that I picture Father Donnay and his acolytes in the upper church—at Easter, say, engulfed by the lilies festooning the raised sanctuary with its hand-carved high altar imported from France. Upstairs there's too much color and space to take in, too much mystery to puzzle over, too many people crowded into the waxed and polished pews. All but faded from memory are the gigantic and resplendent saints in the window glass and the sculpted saints looking patiently down from their niches over the side altars. Pardon me while I slip down into the basement where my initial, ascetic impression of Catholicism was formed, down under that low ceiling where the Crouches, the Macklins, my mother, and I watched the dying daylight play over the whitewashed walls, and we listened for God in the tick of the clock.

✝

The nuns of Sacred Heart School were my teachers in the primary grades. In the first grade Sister Simona taught us the Apostles' Creed, Ramona Overby wrote me love notes, and Leo Kranski, whenever Sister was out of the room, displayed his penis. In the second grade (same room, same sister) Ricky Burke told me he'd quit smoking; Father Donnay, on his name day (December 6, the Feast of St. Nicholas), presented each of us with a small red apple; and I, on December 7 or 8, beat up Billy Shelver. What made Billy culpable, to the best of my memory, was his large vocabulary. We were playing at war in the alley between our houses, putting our toy soldiers and planes and ships through a reenactment of Pearl Harbor, when Billy, a year younger than I, uttered the word "weapons." It was a word I didn't know, so I gave him a bloody nose. I was both thrilled and terrified by the sight of his blood and tears. My memory of this event will forever be tied up with my memory of Father Donnay's apple, a frightening experience unmitigated by any sort of thrill. I carried the apple home from school and forgot it until, weeks later, I found this sacred gift turning black with rot at the back of the refrigerator. Here was a sacrilege too serious to be forgiven, and I lived for weeks with the dread of the hellfire awaiting me when I died. I might have sought consolation from my confessor if he weren't the man who'd given out the apples.

In the third grade, under Sister Constance, we went deeper into theology. Why did our guardian angels insist on remaining invisible? In fasting from solid food during Ember Days, could we have a thin milkshake? Was I guilty of a serious sin when, standing in line at the confessional, I overheard Ricky Burke confess that he fought with his brothers? Sister was stumped by the first question, declared no to the second, and found both Ricky and me guilty in regard to the third.

I was a champion believer in those days. I believed every fact, myth, and holy opinion taught me during those first years of parochial school. I believed in the Communion of Saints, the Knights of Columbus, the multiplication tables, and life everlasting. I believed in the efficacy of prayer, fasting, phonics, scrap metal drives, and war bonds. The one thing I had trouble believing was Sister Constance's prohibition of the word "leg." She said we must always say "limb" because "leg" had improper connotations. I never believed that.

Then we moved. After a decade of managing a store for the Red Owl Corporation, my father got a job in a munitions plant in Minneapolis, where we lived with my mother's parents on South Aldrich, a pretty avenue shaded by a canopy of elms and all but devoid of traffic because of the wartime shortage of tires and gasoline. Our house was a dozen long blocks from the Church of the Incarnation, a handsome Romanesque structure with white marble statuary standing out against the dark brick, but without (it seemed) a basement. Here, in 1930, my parents had been married, and here, on Easter Sunday 1933, I had been baptized.

Surely our household of five went to Mass every Sunday (a serious strain of religious devotion came down to me out of Bavaria on my father's side of the family, out of Ireland on my mother's side), and yet I don't recall a single Mass at Incarnation. What I do remember are the rather sparsely attended Tuesday evening devotions my mother and I walked to throughout the spring and summer of 1943 (my father, on night shift, went to work at suppertime), and how earnestly we prayed for victory followed by world peace. I remember the coolness of the vast empty spaces between the faithful during May and June, and then, during August, the heat trapped inside as the days shortened and cooled. This was the year I came to love, under my mother's guidance, singing "Tantum Ergo" and lighting votive candles. This was also the year, I believe, that my sainted grandmother, in that very church, was refused absolution and cast out of the confessional by a roaring priest whose name we never learned and whose form of insanity we speculated about for years after we left the city.

+

Which we did, eventually, moving to a village surrounded by fields of corn and cattle, where my parents had purchased a Red Owl Store of their own. Among my first memories of this town are ones in which I attempt to derail a train and another in which I befriend a saint.

When, at the end of our first week in Plainview, I conspired to derail a train—a thrilling and terrifying experience—I felt very little, if any, guilt because I was merely following directions. That the director, Timmy Musser, was only eight years old seemed immaterial to me. While my parents and the nuns of Sacred Heart had trained me in the art of willing obedience, they hadn't gotten around to discernment, so I had no mind of my own. Whenever I was allowed to attend one of the thrilling and terrifying mobster movies of that era, I seldom identified with either the chief detective or the gang leader, but recognized myself in the role of some stupidly obedient henchman.

The Mussers, a Greek-or Latin-looking family of four, lived across the street from us in a small house that sat very low, as in a ditch, its threshhold below street level and its back door pushed up against the oil tanks beside the railroad embankment. They were given to odd behavior. Mrs. Musser, for example, spoke in broken English, never left her house or yard except to attend Mass at St. Joachim's, and preserved meat the way I had seen my mother put up peaches and tomatoes—in jars to store in the cellar. Mr. Musser, unlike my own father, never lifted a finger to help around the house. Evenings he divested himself of his work clothes down to his pants and suspenders and reclined on the couch, ignoring the loose door hinges and cracked windowpanes and droning on about his job at the canning factory. His wife may have listened to this boring recital, but certainly no one else did. Not I, who lay on the floor with Timmy, trying to teach him the game of checkers. Not Timmy, whose conniving, criminal mind had no room in it for games or make-believe or whimsy of any sort. Not Lou, his older sister, a dark-eyed beauty who busied herself with her high school homework under the dim and only lamp in the room. Lou's odd behavior was tied up with her holiness. She never went out with boys or read magazines, her mother told me proudly. She saw only religious movies such as *Song of Bernadette*. What's more, she went to confession every week. Lou was preparing herself to follow in the footsteps of an older sister who was a nun in California. God had called her, said her mother.

If God was leading Lou into convent life, then Satan surely had prison in mind for her little brother. Already as a third grader, Timmy Musser had the instincts of a hardened gangster. He wore on his swarthy little face an unchanging expression of great seriousness, and by the unceasing movement of his eyes—deliberate rather than shifty—he seemed always to be planning his next heist while checking to see if he was being followed.

Train Derailment Day began with Timmy calling to me as we ran after Axel Johnson's cattle truck, "C'mon to the stockyards, you can hear Old Man Johnson swear!" It was a lovely Saturday in September. I remember climbing a fence in the sun-drenched stockyards and sitting beside Timmy on the top rail, where we concentrated on the spectacular curses falling from the lips of the trucker as he drove a squealing mass of medium-sized pigs down a chute and into a corral, where they would await rail transportation to the next stage of their unhappy lives. "GOD-DAMN YOU ASSHOLE PIGS!" thundered Axel Johnson, whipping and poking the bewildered creatures with a sharp stick, "GIT YOUR GODDAMN GOOD-FOR-NOTHING ASSHOLES DOWN THE GODDAMN CHUTE!" Whenever these poor creatures, frightened by his shouting and his stick, wedged themselves into tight knots in the narrow chute, Axel grew hysterical. "YOU SHIT HEELS!" he raged, jabbing them repeatedly in the rump, "GIT DOWN THERE, YOU GODDAMN GOOD-FOR-NOTHING ASSHOLE SWINE!" Even now, sixty years later, I don't recall a richer or more comprehensive recital of this sort. Very few of the words were new to me, for Timmy had spent the first week of our acquaintance briefing me on definitions, but it was nonetheless shocking to hear them put to such intense and furious use. By the time Johnson followed the last pig out of the truck, his face was scarlet and running with sweat. From a thermos in the cab, he poured himself a tin cup of coffee, drew a sandwich out of a sack, and leaned on the fence to eat and watch the snorting animals scurry across the hard-packed dirt, looking for shade.

"Hey Axel," shouted Timmy, "How many them fuckers you bring in, all told?"

Axel Johnson ignored this inquiry. He was busy kicking pigs away from the narrow strip of shade at his feet.

"C'mon," said Timmy, jumping down from the fence. I respectfully followed him around to the passenger side of the truck cab and found him digging carefully and quietly through a toolbox bolted to the running board. He took out an enormous crowbar and threw it into the tall weeds. "We'll need that to tip over the train this afternoon," he said.

This train, consisting of a caboose, two or three boxcars, a coal tender, and a locomotive, came to town only when summoned to carry away a car of canned peas or corn from Lakeside Packing, a few head of livestock from the stockyards, or a load of grain from the J. D. Dill elevator. The pigs were an indication that it would show up today.

We were hidden among the gigantic oil tanks overlooking the tracks when in midafternoon the train arrived together with a few drops of rain from a sky grown overcast. "Those shit asses," murmured Timmy when the train stopped short of our hiding place. "Don't tell me they ain't coming all the way into town." We tensely watched the fireman uncouple the locomotive and coal tender, and the engineer switch them onto a spur running behind the warehouse of the canning factory. After a very long time they reappeared, pulling a boxcar. Then the train, reassembled, proceeded to the stockyards, where the crew took half an hour to get the evasive pigs up a chute and into the cattle car. Then it chugged below us and beyond us, rounding a curve toward the grain elevator at the center of town.

As soon as it was out of sight, we slithered down the wet curve of the oil tank we'd been lying on and descended a series of ladders to ground level. I watched for traffic at the railroad crossing while Timmy planted the crowbar in a switch. Then we scrambled back up to our perch. This being the highest point of land for miles around, I could see clear across town to the athletic field, where a bunch of kids who looked about my age were playing football. I could see the bell towers of the two biggest churches in town—St. Joachim's Catholic and Immanuel Lutheran—standing like sentinels at opposite ends of Main Street. I could see the roof of the Red Owl, and wished I were there instead of shivering in the damp wind at the top of a rusty oil tank and waiting to see a disaster I helped to bring about.

Timmy, suddenly alert to the ding of the bell and the chuffing of steam, said, "Damn to hell," and pointed down at the switch. The sun had reappeared and the crowbar, worn shiny from use as a tire iron, was glistening brightly in the sun. "They'll see it, goddammit, they'll see it."

"No, they won't," I said, hoping they would. Now, with the train backing lazily around the bend, I was terrified. Someone would die. We would be caught and put in prison.

On chugged the train, neither slowing down nor speeding up. "Damn them fartblossoms," seethed Timmy, "they ain't going fast enough to tip over." With my heart in my throat I watched the caboose hit the switch and teeter. Fearful as I was, I felt triumphant as well, inasmuch as the scene below me proved that one could work one's will on the world. It required only that you were calculating enough and sneaky enough to carry it out. Choosing a weaker victim was essential, of course, the way I had chosen Billy Shelver on Pearl Harbor Day, the way this third grade prodigy at my side had chosen a mere railroad train and its crew.

The caboose didn't tip over or slip off the rails. It stopped, still rocking, and the brakeman stepped out on the back platform and looked every direction except up. The engineer and fireman came running.

"We better go," I said, shrinking back from the edge of the oil tank we lay on.

Without taking his eyes from the tracks, Timmy asked why.

"We'll get caught," said I, finding with my foot the top rung of the ladder.

I understood why Timmy wanted to stay—what was the good of an act of violence if you weren't around to study the consequences?—but I'll never understand where he got the courage to do so, to keep poking his head over the edge to take it all in, right up to the point where the crew climbed aboard and the rest of the train drew slowly across the switch and then, with a triumphant toot and ding-dong, chugged off between the fields of corn. I wasn't there for that part.

Within a month of our arrival in town, and completely untutored, I began to serve Mass at St. Joachim's. This being a nunless parish and its old and ascetic pastor, Father O'Connor, being too far removed from the mundane to bother instructing a mere child of ten, I apprenticed myself to the only other server in the parish, a boy named Jackie.

Jackie was the good-natured youngest child of a widow who cleaned houses for the two or three well-to-do families in town. He was two years older than I, and the object of my great admiration, not only because he was a faultless altar boy—dedicated, devout, punctual, and obedient—but also because he seemed smarter than a lot of Catholics I knew, and he had a wry sense of humor. (At this point in my life, it seemed to me that I had met, among the truly religious, an over-abundance of humorless types, and I'd begun to wonder if slowness of mind might be a prerequisite to holiness.) Whenever Father O'Connor lost his way in the pulpit and followed an irrelevant path into private musings, Jackie would turn his wise little grin in my direction as if to say "How pathetic," and hope, I'm sure, for an answering grin from me.

Outside of church, however, we saw very little of one another—such is the age gap between a fifth grader and a seventh grader—and yet, when at the end of our first year in town we moved from the stockyards neighborhood to a house near the athletic field and I found myself living just a few doors down the block from Jackie, I imagined we might become chums at last. But it was too late for that. By this time Jackie was dying.

I was perhaps his only regular visitor. I went every Saturday after lunch. His mother had converted the front room of their small house into Jackie's bedroom, so he could watch the passing traffic on Highway 42 from his bed. What did we do or say during my visits? We may have played a hand or two of rummy, and maybe we looked over the assignments I brought him from his homeroom teacher, but I have no memory of anything but making small talk. It's a characteristic of anyone growing up in a happy household, I've found, this ability to wring every possible remark out of an unremarkable topic. Around people we're fond of, our urge to converse is far greater than our need to do so, and therefore we talk at length about little, stringing out our words the way spiders emit the filament of their webs. In the grocery store, imitating my parents, I was growing proficient at small talk, particularly with old people, and Jackie was about as old as he was going to get.

At first I went to see him under orders from my mother. Visiting the sick was a corporal work of mercy, after all, and she was eager for me to start building up some credit in eternity. Besides, rheumatic fever, unlike polio, was said to be noncontagious. But soon I found myself making these weekly visits of my own accord, for I was finding more and more about Jackie to be fond of. "This seeing the sick endears them to us," says Gerard Manley Hopkins, and of course it's true. He seemed to be changing. He was going through the same shrinking stages we witness now and then in a public figure who will allow himself to waste away on the television news—recently Cardinal Joseph Bernardin of Chicago, Vice President Hubert Humphrey twenty years ago—but I'm not talking about this physical transformation so much as a change from within. His illness seemed to relax him. It had a kind of purifying effect on him, taking away his tendency to be ironic and leaving in its stead the sort of transparency through which I could see quite plainly the sweetness that permeates the soul of a saint.

One sunny day in late autumn, for example, gazing out the window of the front parlor that had been converted into his bedroom, Jackie's eyes settled on the distant athletic field and he remarked, "I can see you guys playing football over there after school." He said this without a trace of envy in his voice, no hint of anguish or despair. Whereas I, with my obsessive love of football, would doubtless have been bitterly frustrated in his position, Jackie seemed to be speaking out of sheer pleasure.

Or again: one of his older sister's husbands, dismayed by Jackie's loss of weight, stopped by with a quart of ice cream one day and demanded that he eat all of it nonstop. This was shortly before my arrival, and I found Jackie looking bloated and amused as he slowly spooned up the last of the ice cream. His brother-in-law stood over him, looking smugly full of himself—believing, I suppose, that he'd just discovered the cure for rheumatic fever. And Jackie's sublime smile said that he believed it, too, but of course this was for his brother-in-law's benefit only, for when he turned to look at me, I saw a flicker of the old wryness in his eyes. "We'll get some meat on that kid's bones yet," the brother-in-law explained to me on his way out. "I'm coming back tomorrow with another quart." With his savior safely out of the way, Jackie asked me to bring him the basin from the drainboard in the kitchen, then he asked me to please go outside and come back later. As I left, I heard him begin to vomit.

God knows how many quarts of ice cream Jackie put down and later brought up in order to sustain his brother-in-law's hope. I only know that the more I saw of Jackie's self-abnegation, the more fascinating it became. Wasn't this the sort of God-pleasing humility the Church of Rome had been urging on me since the first grade? But with this difference: Jackie wasn't being humble for God's sake, or the Church's, or even his brother-in-law's; he was being simply himself.

Here, then, was virtue in its pure form, and I found it every bit as attractive as Timmy Musser's evil bent. I longed to be as good as Jackie, and yet, at the tender age of ten or eleven, I somehow knew that to reach Jackie's level of virtue, I would need to drop my pride, my self-regard, the very idea that I was being virtuous. I was much too self-aware to be as good as Jackie.

Or as bad as Timmy, for that matter. For isn't it this same lack of self-regard that allows the thief, the terrorist, the train derailer to carry out his mischief? No, I would never be a candidate for sainthood or prison. With my proclivity for patient watchfulness, I would always play the role of bystander. I could thrill to tales of derring-do, and I could admire goodness, but I'd never come close to either end of the scale. My place was at the intersection, watching for traffic while the crowbar was inserted in the switch. My place was in the chair beside the bed.

Jackie died, and I made one last trip to his house, this time in the evening, with my parents, to view the body. We found the kitchen crowded with Jackie's brothers (one in uniform) and mother and sisters and their families. Jackie, in his coffin, had the front room practically to himself while we the living ate his mother's homemade cookies and made cheery small talk. We were reluctant to leave each other's company for more than the few seconds it took to step through the open doorway and mumble a prayer. I didn't do even that. I, who had given him a part of every week for several months, had no time for him now.

It was a dark, rainy morning when most of the eighth grade, and I from the sixth grade, were released from class and hurried down the street to St. Joachim's, where I put on my black requiem cassock and my white surplice, and then, bearing the crucifix on a staff, I led Father O'Connor down the middle aisle to meet the coffin and the drenched mourners in the vestibule. After the priest's prayer and a sprinkling of holy water, I turned around and led the procession into the crowded church as the organ and choir broke out in their lament. But more sorrowful than the organ and choir was that other noise we heard whenever there was a pause in the music—the relentless pounding of rain on the roof.

I didn't feel the sting of Jackie's death that day. I was too full of myself as an altar boy, imagining how I must look to my classmates, particularly the Protestants and the nonchurchgoers. How admirably I went about my duties at the altar, how amazing and mysterious were the phrases I cried out in sharp contrast to Father O'Connor's mumbled prayers. "Dominuuuuu vobiscuuuuuu," droned the priest. "ET CUM SPIRITU TUO!" shouted I, eleven years old and St. Joachim's lone surviving altar boy. That's nothing, folks, just wait till we get to the cemetery and I display my mastery of the sprinkler and censer.

There was rainwater standing in the grave. Although nobody mentioned it afterward, there must have been others besides me who were secretly horrified to think of lowering Jackie into eight or ten inches of chill water. And he'd better be lowered soon, before the grave filled itself up with the small mudslides that were coming loose around its perimeter. When the priest finally finished commending Jackie to God, he closed his wet book, and I handed him the sprinkler. He mixed a couple shakes of holy water with the raindrops drumming on the coffin. Then I handed him the censer, which he waved in the direction of the grave as though it still held fire. Then a mighty gust of wind swept the cemetery with a fresh squall of rain, prompting most of the mourners and schoolchildren to run for their cars while the undertaker, with the help of Jackie's brothers and brothers-in-law—no time for decorum now—dropped the coffin into the grave. That's when it finally hit me—the finality of Jackie's death—when the coffin, hitting bottom, made a splashing noise.

Summers, during my high school years, I was the parish groundskeeper, for my parents by that time had purchased, for $110, the first postwar power mower seen in that town, a magnificent, self-propelled, reel-type Toro, green and yellow and heavy as an army tank. I began by cutting a few lawns for our neighbors, an enterprise my parents encouraged in order to keep me busy during the slow weekdays when most of the farmers and their families were busy in their fields and trade in the store was slack, and before long, I found myself cutting and trimming not only the wiry grass around the church and the rectory but the wild groundcover of the cemetery as well. And every Saturday morning from early May until Labor Day, I knocked on the door of the rectory, which Father O'Connor kept hermetically sealed against the summer heat, and I stood there until an inner door opened and then the front door and finally the porch door, and the old priest looked down at me in his distracted manner and said, "Yes?"

"I've come for my pay, Father."

"Ah, the grass," he said, his cold blue eyes momentarily alight with a glimmer of recognition, and I followed him into his office, where he sat down at his desk, put on his glasses, opened the parish checkbook, dipped his pen in an ink bottle, and asked me—I swear to God—the same question week after week, year after year: "What's your name?"

Odd as it may seem, I wasn't bothered by this man's detachment. After all, hadn't I been brought up to think of religion as a kind of secret room the individual entered to find his God, and wasn't one's parish priest merely the faceless mortal who unlocked the door? He was holy, to be sure, and smart enough to learn all that Latin, but a mortal like the rest of us and easy to overlook when you were communing with the Being that created him. And, besides, wasn't this the demeanor of all priests? Wasn't the aloof Father Donnay, the pastor of my childhood at Sacred Heart, seen only at morning Mass and never in the chapel in the basement?

✠

Father O'Connor, already too old for parish duty, remained our pastor for the next seven years. He was a tall, pious man, austere in appearance and habits, and oblivious to the lives being lived around him until they ended; then I picture him backing his gleaming black 1926 Oldsmobile out of its narrow brick garage and raising a cloud of gravel dust as he hightailed it through town to the bedside of some dying parishioner. On Saturday afternoons he heard confessions on the hour from two o'clock until five, and I picture him praying on his knees before Our Lady's altar between his stints in the box. I was once allowed into his spare kitchen—I may have been delivering one of his meager orders of groceries—and found him reading his breviary as he dawdled over a dinner composed of sugar cookies and boiled carrots.

✠

For a long time I was happily oblivious to the strong current of religious animosity running under the surface of daily life in that town. How silly we must have looked to the smaller congregations—the Congregationalists, the Methodists, the Church of Christers—we Catholics and Lutherans competing for power on the village council, trying to outvote one another in school board elections, patronizing only those merchants whose theology matched our own, and burying our dead in cemeteries a mile apart. The mind-bending damage must have been done years before our taking up residence there, for not once did I hear our infirm and inward-looking old priest condemn Luther or Lutheranism, nor did the the pastor of Immanuel Lutheran, to the best of my knowledge, disapprove of the friendship I struck up with his son Donald.

It was a school board election that brought this ugly religious feuding to my attention. In my novel *Grand Opening*, it is Brendan's mother who is defeated for the school board, whereas in actual fact it was my father, but the method was the same in both cases. After serving two successful terms on the board, my father was drubbed by an uprising of Lutherans who, apparently deciding that four years of service to the community was enough for any Papist, conducted a secret phone campaign resulting in a last-minute write-in vote amounting to twice the number of his supporters.

This experience loosened that town's hold on my father, who until then, blissfully busy in his thriving store, had helped me resist my mother's desire to go back to the northern town we'd come from and live among the circle of friends she missed so sorely. And so, three days after my high school graduation, we moved. Or I should say my parents moved. I stayed behind and worked in the canning factory until it was time for me to start college in the fall. My father moved back into the less rewarding store he had managed when I was little, while my mother, at age fifty, moved into a curious phase of trying to rebuild the life she'd known as a younger woman.

Half a century has gone by since then, and I'm still a Catholic. Holy Mother Church is ailing these days. She suffers from a kind of paralysis that threatens to atrophy her. Her heart shrinks. She calls out, not for help but to scold. There's an unattractive hint of paranoia in her eye. But I'm still a Catholic.

She's had spells like this before, of course, some lasting centuries. She'll outlive us all—we have that on the highest authority. What makes this relapse so alarming is the swiftness of its coming on. Scarcely thirty years ago, having undergone a treatment called Vatican II, she was fresh and frisky as a girl, full of promise and optimism, with courage enough to let go of her dead old language and with brains enough to learn a hundred new ones.

I didn't always hold this opinion. Thirty years ago I was certain the Church had betrayed me, had lost her soul. I fought the changes. Long after she began speaking in the vernacular, for example, I carried my dear old thousand-page missal to church and took comfort in the double columns, Latin and English. But then, in 1976, in the process of writing my first novel, I transferred that reactionary part of myself into one of my characters, Agatha McGee by name, and the moment I sent her off to Mass with her thousand-page missal, I was free to move ahead with the times.

I have given readings to a number of Protestant audiences lately— mostly Lutheran audiences, this being Minnesota—and I've been infected by the exuberance of their clergy. Young ministers, men and women alike, married and single, speak of their calling with zeal. I sense very little zeal among our aging priests; they're overworked and weary. Luther Seminary in St. Paul has full enrollment this year, while our Catholic seminaries are emptying out, and the candidates we do have are not the vigorous men of past generations. "Seminarians make up 2 percent of the student body on this campus," I was recently told by a medical doctor at a Catholic college, "and they use up 98 percent of our counselors' time."

Of course the Church will continue to exist without women and married men at the altar, but where will that existence be? In a cave? For some years I imagined a dozen faithful gathered around the last priest in the world, a shaky old bishop saying Mass in a cave somewhere. I'm still haunted by this pathetic vision, but lately the setting has changed to a storefront in an abandoned shopping mall.

But never mind, I'm still a Catholic. And why is that?

I'm still a Catholic because I love the Mass. It punctuates my life like a semicolon; it's a pause, a breather, in my week, my day. I don't pray very well at Mass; in fact, I often don't pay much attention, yet sixty years of churchgoing has left me with a need—it's more than mere habit; it's a deep-seated need—to be lifted up and carried along, time after time, by the familiar words and rubrics. It's like boarding a boat and standing out from the shore of my life for a half-hour or so, viewing it through the refreshing air of a calm and scenic harbor.

I'm still a Catholic because I want to be identified with the institution that, despite her dark ages and her lightweight popes, her blind alleys, her blood lust, her hypocrites in high places, has welcomed people of all classes and nations to its altars; because once, around the time of the last millennium, it preserved our Western civilization from oblivion; because it has left its traces in the cathedrals of Europe, in the scraps of prayers in our memories, in the bridges between continents and generations; and, above all, because it has delivered Jesus' message safely across twenty centuries and is placing it now on the doorstep of the third millennium.

I'm still a Catholic because I believe this message is the most powerful, revolutionary, and sensible cure for human strife and anxiety ever conceived. It's a message so simple that no mere human being could have thought of it, a three-word message so all-encompassing that the Son of God had to come to earth to utter it: "Love one another."

Dreams and Visions, Fits and Starts
Susan Dodd

If I had not known you, I would not have found you.
—PASCAL, *Notebooks*

MY SECOND grade teacher was six feet tall. Her profile was a precipice. A leather pouch fitted with tools and writing instruments dangled from her belt beside a rosary whose beads were as big and shiny as ripe olives. Her black broadcloth habit showed a greenish tint in sunlight.

"Faith," Sister Virgina said, "is a gift. Sometimes we must wait for it for a very long time. God asks some to suffer for it. Many people have been punished, even put to death, for their belief. But faith is always a gift from God."

And you have to deserve it—did Sister say that, too? Did she throw down the gauntlet then, claiming faith not only could be, but had to be, earned? Was it at that very moment that my heart and soul began to give up on themselves?

The Catholicism I knew as a child, frightening as it was beautiful, was more than I could live up to. It never occurred to me that I might not be expected to. Somehow the good news of forgiveness never penetrated the way the promise of punishment did. As I grew up, my heart seemed to grow punier. What I wanted, I thought, was for God to stop taking notice of me. I couldn't bear how I disappointed Him, so I took myself out of the running. I threw the first draft of my faith in the wastebasket.

The Catholicism I now embrace feels new. It comes with a joy that amazes me. It has a lot more give in it than the original did.

As a little girl, I dreamed of having a vocation. My father's only sister was a nun. Sister Cletus and the other sisters at St. John Bosco convent in Chicago were Dominicans. They seemed, in their white linen habits and long black veils, a gentler tribe than the Franciscans who taught me. The Dominican Sisters smelled—I swear every one of them did—like lavender soap.

I used to stay at my aunt's convent when my mother and father went away. I believe I was five and my parents were at The Escape in Fort Lauderdale when Sister Cletus and Sister Theophane hand-sewed a habit for me. It was exactly like theirs, even the underneath parts that didn't show. I was, of course, much photographed as the little Sister. The rapture in my smile foretells limited potential for poverty, chastity, or obedience.

If I was not given to the vocation I expected, a vocation is mine nonetheless. The life I have fashioned for myself as a writer has something of the cloister about it. I live with mystery, rite, and ritual—the Word. There is devotion in it, and deprivation. Self-mortification, too. My sister, Gael, and I continue to seek a lavender soap that precisely duplicates the fragrance we both so clearly recall as the essence of St. John Bosco convent.

Today, the second Sunday in Lent, my mind is startled to attentiveness by the Word. The Gospel is according to Mark: *"Suddenly looking around, they no longer saw anyone with them—only Jesus."*

Standing with Jesus on a mountaintop, they all—Peter, James, and John—heard it, the voice they'd have sworn came out of a cloud. I'm nearly as thunderstruck as the men on the mountain: *No longer anyone with them. . . .*

That is what it's like to die, I think. Mark is talking about death. There you are daydreaming, and before you know it, everybody's taken off. . . .

The notion, the shock of it, stays with me. The King James version, as usual, struts poetry's stuff, heightening the wonder: *"And suddenly, when they had looked round and about, they saw no man any more, save Jesus only with themselves."*

Yes, dying must be very much like that . . . everyone gone, nobody left but you and God. The God Who loves you, has always loved you . . . *what on earth are we afraid of?*

Poor souls, working ourselves into a lifelong lather over a Heaven and Hell we can imagine only by way of what on *earth* we are afraid of.

But thinking, even imagining, has little to do with what the soul already knows: *Save Jesus only with ourselves* . . . my soul so sure of it.

Is that faith? Or just hope talking again?

Is there a difference?

✝

Faith is always a gift from God. A gift—imagine! Can you? Can you imagine the child of six or seven who could imagine herself *deserving,* ever, of such a lavish gift? Or what it would take to *earn* it?

After the age of reason befell me, after Sister Virgina's stern initiation, I continued for another dozen years or so to go to daily Mass, to receive the Eucharist. Though my motivations may have been somewhat murky, I chose a Catholic university, and into my sophomore year, at least, I received the Sacraments in the very church where John Fitzgerald Kennedy had knelt and prayed. Now and then I worked up the monumental nerve to send the Lord hints that faith was a gift I would not be averse to receiving . . . my unworthiness instantly implicit in the hubris of the appeal, even the hope: Who was *I* to think something so rare and precious and sacred might drop into her grubby hands? Faith! Might I, confronted with such a miracle, have found it in myself to die for it? It was not a question I dared entertain.

By the time I reached nineteen or twenty, I no longer found the Sacraments alluring, as they'd seemed when I was a child. I wish I could remember why. I only know that by the time I entered adulthood, the Church felt like a dreary and forbidding tribunal where, week after obligatory week, I was charged with my own worthlessness. *Lord, I am not worthy, but only say the word* . . . it appeared the Lord was no longer speaking to me. I did not blame Him. My attendance at Mass grew rare, then ceased entirely. My heart no longer felt welcome there.

We didn't entirely lose touch over the years, God and I: a cordial visit at Christmastime, maybe Easter. I never resisted going to Mass when I was with my father, a small hypocrisy I excused as a token of love. Why hurt him by spurning the faith he cherished? Faith, I told myself, was a paltry thing compared with charity, a far more useful gift for life in the here and now. Give me good works any day. Forget about faith.

Lord knows I tried to. Still, every once in a while I'd catch a glimpse of it: my father's face upturned to the light as he awaited the Host . . . my beloved mother-in-law making each small moment of her daily existence a kind of sacrament. Grace Dodd had the bluest eyes. My father's eyes were the color of root beer. How, then, could I remember their eyes as so alike? It was the trust I saw in them, God's thin disguise. It filled me with an envy I did not understand.

I was never utterly bereft of faith. I held fast to a faith in faith itself. To be frank, I coveted faith. But I no longer asked for it. *Lord, I am not worthy.*

There came a night in Chicago, though, when my father appeared to be dying. I was in my late twenties, unhappily married but not admitting it, lost in my own life. Dad was almost seventy—if not a ripe old age, a respectable one. To lose my father then would not have been unheard of. It simply was unthinkable.

Routine surgery, then twelve hours, fourteen . . . the bleeding would not stop. "He's still in recovery . . . we're going to take you in to see him." I was ushered into an area just outside the operating theater, a sanctuary usually forbidden to laity.

My father, swathed in linen, lay on a gurney. His face, gone gray, was bathed in a merciless light.

"We're losing him," the surgeon said. Said it right there in front of him, as if my father were already past hearing or caring, had shed all interest in his own life.

My father did not die that particular night, but he remembered how close he came. "I heard what that doctor said," he told me later. " *'We're losing him.'* " The mild voice went edgy with scorn. "Oh, I heard exactly what he said. It made me so damn mad. And I told God, 'I'm not ready yet. Don't You know my kids still need me?' "

I did. I needed my father's breath to keep blowing on the small spark of faith that remained in me, my faith in the faith of my father.

That was, I believe, in 1973. My father lived nearly twenty years past that night when he pushed God around. I wonder whether the surgeon who performed the second operation that everyone said was a miracle believed in God. Perhaps he simply believed in himself. Even that can be something of a miracle.

I had no such gift. When all the odds and every sign and portent pointed to my father's dying, I called his friend Joe.

It was close to midnight. "What can I do?" Joe said.

"You can pray," I said.

Joe was one of my father's racetrack buddies. The two had coffee together every morning in the cafeteria of the office building where they both had law offices they were always trying to sneak out of to get to Arlington Park.

Joe, Dad had told me, had recently backed into a charismatic version of Catholicism and got himself all caught up in it. My father was amused and fascinated, skeptical and entranced. "He holds forth on the Bible, you should hear it." Dad shrugged. "He's a new man, he says, and maybe he is." He smiled. "But he's still Joe, thank God."

Thank God. Less than an hour after I called him, Joe walked into my father's hospital room. Down in the Loop in the middle of the night, with his stubby hands that smelled of cigar smoke stretched across an empty hospital bed, holding his pal's kid's icy fingers . . . the same old Joe, made new with some age-old raucous faith.

"I thought you might want me to pray with you," he said.

It may have been the surgeon who saved my father's life. It seemed to me it was Joe saving mine. Joe who, knowing how to pray, could make it clear to God that I needed my old man to stay put for the time being, to stick around long enough for his kid to get the hang of believing again.

✛

Kansas City, 1991. This time I can tell he means to go through with it. He's really going to leave.

"It's all right, Daddy," I tell him. "We'll be all right." The claim has more to do with love, of course, than with belief. I suspect charity will always come to me more easily than faith.

Again my father, now eighty-six, beats the odds, but this time for only a couple of weeks. He will die in early November and I will not be there, as I somehow always knew I would not be. This October afternoon, though, I am with him. Much of the time he doesn't know me. His kidneys have shut down. Jimmy the Greek, even Joe, would give him lousy odds.

"You're such a wonderful woman," my father says to me. "I wish I had met you sooner." Then his brown eyes look past my shoulder. For a moment I feel as if I can see how far beyond me he already sees. *Don't think I don't need you still.* It's only the truth. Only love keeps me from saying it.

"Daddy," I whisper, "are you afraid?"

He is my father. His is my faith. I depend on him to deny it.

"Yes," he says.

Something steadies in me. "Why?" I say. "What are you afraid of?"

He looks bewildered, as if he has forgotten the subject.

I lean down, bring my face close to his. "Do you remember back when I didn't go to church all those years, except I used to pretend I did when you were around?"

He isn't following me. He doesn't need to.

"I used to tell myself you had enough faith for both of us." I try to smile. His eyes have moved far, so far beyond me. "Daddy, listen," I say. "*I* have enough now," I tell him. "Enough for both of us."

If I exaggerate, he doesn't notice. "That's good," he says. There is perfect trust in his gaze.

✝

Faith a *gift* . . . how can it be? Are we really expected to sit around cooling our heels while we wait for something so essential to this life? (There are, of course, those who manage to live without faith . . . how, I cannot imagine.) Is faith some crushing force, like an avalanche, maybe, that can fall only when we don't expect it? Will it take no less than a cataclysm to pound us into fit receptacles for the Lord's capricious grace?

Faith. As I grew into myself, as life exacted its toll, faith came to be a gift I wanted so desperately I couldn't wait around anymore for the giving. I just went ahead and helped myself. After twenty years of exile I made it my business to barge back into the Catholic Church and make myself at home. And that is what I discovered: that the Church is, has always been, my soul's true home.

Do I, in my eagerness for God, stumble into sacrilege? This is makeshift dogma, jerry-built to fit my soul and my life. Faith is a decision. Faith is *my* decision. God helps those who help themselves.

✝

A member of the Catholic faith . . . what does it mean? What does it mean to someone like me, someone who sometimes finds herself cringing at papal pronouncements, unwilling to rise to the defense of certain positions and activities undertaken in the name of her Church, disappointed at that Church's failings? As a woman, can I overlook the various messages my Church has sent me that I, that all women, have been endowed by the Creator with a somewhat lesser status, potential, and worth than Adam and his sons? The leader of my Church—the direct descendant of Saint Peter, I am told—reaffirms his determination that women shall never be ordained to the priesthood. On the radio I hear a liberal nun telling of a child in catechism class who, when asked how many Sacraments there are, answers, "Seven . . . unless you are a girl. Then there are six." It is not a joke. The punch line makes me weep.

I am a member of the Catholic faith, but perhaps not in good standing. I am divorced. I am a member of a faith that for centuries implied I am by my very nature inferior and unsavory. I am a woman. I am a member of a faith whose most revered female archetypes earned their stripes through maternity or virginity, and/or martyrdom. I am childless, but no celibate. For some years I tried to practice martyrdom. I showed little aptitude for it.

Why I am still a Catholic. . . .

Why I am a Catholic *again* is more to the point. Twenty years away . . . but then I always was, wasn't I? A member of the Catholic faith. . . .

Because when you come right down to it, I didn't know how *not* to be.

I am a member of the Catholic faith the way I am a member of my family: often uncomfortably, occasionally resentfully, always helplessly. Irrevocably. Who says you have to like it? You just have to love it. *Helplessly*. Seems like something that just can't be helped. Who you are. *Still a Catholic*. And what. And why, mostly isn't even a question.

In a peculiar way I don't fully understand, I believe I came to be a Catholic again because I came to be a writer . . . a writer, specifically, of fiction.

Saint Paul, something of a gadabout in his day, found faith in a fall on the road to Damascus. I happened to be sitting at a typewriter when I was knocked off my high horse, not nearly so shapely a narrative or dramatic a denouement as Paul's. There was no single moment, just a slow erosion over time of a built-up resistence to my own yearning for God. It wasn't me, you see, but *my characters* who were seeking faith, then finding it—Lo!—in themselves. You might say they kind of backed me into it.

I was writing a novel, my first, about a rather plain young woman named Murana Bill, who lives in a small Kentucky town and looks after her brother. Lyman Gene Bill has come back from the Vietnam War emotionally damaged and unable to speak. Murana and Lyman Gene's parents have been dead for years. Murana's brother is her whole life.

The situation sounds awfully bleak, I suppose, but I never really saw it that way. What had drawn me to Murana's story and held me captive there was her simple goodness, a goodness rooted in belief and love and pure devotion. Having been raised on *The Lives of the Saints*, I am, of course, partial to such stories.

In her first version, Murana was, by virtue of geography, a Baptist—what else would she be in Kentucky, I thought, with that woeful sort of oversimplification of Protestantism so many Catholics of my generation were prone to. While my would-be novel was hardly more than an infant, I dragged it along to a writers' conference (also my first) and placed it in the hands of the teacher and writer Doris Betts, a woman of no small faith herself. ("I am kissing cousin to Abraham's tribe, southern WASP branch-head division . . . Associate Reformed Presbyterian, A.R.P.'s—the All Right People, my mother said.")

Doris, like all good teachers, managed to dig out of my work something to praise and encourage. But something about Murana stymied and stopped her cold. Where in the world, Doris wanted to know, had this pitiful girl got the idea of turning herself into a lump of pure self-sacrifice? That just didn't make a lick of sense. Sorry.

It was Doris, I'm afraid, who didn't make much sense to me. Since when did self-sacrifice require justification?

I had trouble sleeping that night. The July air lay thick and still over the Connecticut River valley. Smothering. *Don't make a lick of sense . . . a lick of sense to me.* I sat up suddenly in the darkness. Of course it made sense, all the sense in the world. Murana Bill was no Baptist, that was all.

And so Murana became what at heart she had always been, a good Catholic girl, and eventually I followed in her footsteps without (as has often been the case with the most important life choices I've made) quite knowing what I was doing.

The novel, called *No Earthly Notion*, was finally finished, Murana's faith a greater weight in it than its author had grasped. What strikes me as amazing now is only that I failed to be amazed at the time . . . I had written a "religious novel" without ever quite catching on to what I was up to. It was, I told myself, Murana's doing.

One day when the novel seemed about as done as it was liable to get, it did occur to me that maybe I ought to stop by church. I'd kept away during the very years when the liturgy was being transformed. At the rare Masses I'd attended with my father, I'd betrayed my "lapsed" state by having to follow the words in the missalette. I no longer knew the proper responses by heart. Even the prayers that sounded mostly the same concealed little traps: the Holy Ghost, for instance, had metamorphosed into the Holy Spirit. My rendering through Murana's faithful eyes of Mass in the former feed and grain store in Mount Vadalia, Kentucky, was likely rife with error . . . even, for all I knew, heresy. I'd best catch up with the new liturgy.

✠

How, I wonder, did he feel when he fell? *"Saul, Saul . . . Why dost thou persecute me?"* Did he tumble to stony ground? Were there cuts on his palms from sharp gravel, and was the robe, immaculate just that morning, suddenly filthy and torn? Did he think, *I am not presentable?*

Persecute You . . . *You*, Lord?

I walked like a tourist into the church . . . curious and a little jaded, tired, prepared to be bored. Five o'clock on a Saturday afternoon. The pews were largely filled, but I don't recall that I had any trouble finding myself a place.

Then there I was. Nothing much happened. I didn't fall or hear voices.

No clouds parted. Of course not. An epiphany, any writer worth her salt could tell you, has got to be earned. So what did you expect?

It was the last thing in the world I expected in this homely church squatting on the border between Rhode Island and Connecticut: finding myself at home.

☩

Murana Bill, these long years later, is as real to me, as fully loved and essential to my life and well-being, as my friend Rosanne, my dog Elliot, my own two legs. I don't think of Murana as a fictional character, and certainly not as *my creation*. Like all those I love, Murana crosses my mind every day, visiting gratitude upon me. And surprisingly often, these words echo in her wake: *"And a little child shall lead them. . . ."*

I did not begin to measure Murana's gift to me until I wandered into St. Michael's Church in Pawcatuck, Connecticut. And even then it took some time for me to see that gift for treasure. What Murana offered me was one last chance to love my faith with a child's simple heart. I had, for one God-given moment in that church that day, no history, no questions, no bone to pick. . . . I had no expectations.

Maybe faith *is* a gift, after all.

II.

The question of what effect the church has on the fiction writer who is a Catholic cannot always be answered by pointing to the presence of Graham Greene among us.

—FLANNERY O'CONNOR,
"The Church and the Fiction Writer"

THAT FLANNERY, though I don't understand more than half what she says, is a caution. I would surely have some questions, were she still around to ask. How, for instance, did a nice Catholic girl (not to mention *Southern* girl, Miss Regina's well-brought-up child) get by with such peppery opinions? And right many of them, too.

I celebrate Mr. Greene's "presence" among us, indeed I do. Still, I tend to turn bashful when "the Catholic Writer" is discussed. I expect that's because I'm neither a good enough writer nor a good enough Catholic to feel entitled to open my mouth.

The talk I can't keep to myself, though, is the rich, mysterious babble about these two tongues of mine, writing and worship—how alike they can be, how sometimes they'll both start talking at once until it's hard to tell the difference between a story and a prayer. *Glossolalia*: I speak in tongues I do not understand. I love the all of it, the noise and the mystery and the idiocy.

I sometimes think that the writer is engaged in the sacred work of learning the names of God, discovering His aliases. We do not utter the secret names aloud. We whisper them into the world. The right whisper can bring rain and part rivers, can hold despair at bay.

Flannery, keener than I and less fanciful, said, "The Lord doesn't speak to the novelist as he did to his servant, Moses, mouth to mouth. He speaks to him as he did to those two complainers, Aaron and Aaron's sister, Mary: through dreams and visions, in fits and starts, by all the lesser and limited ways and then some of the imagination."

That is, I suspect, about as close as words will ever come to explaining how the novelist's ridiculous, impossible, holy work is accomplished. And Miss Flannery shows herself for a pretty good psychologist, too. Look how she eggs you on with a promise of dreams and visions, reassures you that fits and starts come with the territory, before she slips in that hard truth about limitations. The great artists, I think, are those able both to acknowledge the limits of the imagination and to disregard them. Simultaneously. True art, like true love, is a commitment to the impossible, which may be why we tend to call it a vocation.

The artist, like the person of faith, is sometimes pressed into service as a vessel of prophecy, it seems. Flannery suggests the prophetic vision should characterize the fiction writer's way of seeing the world: "Prophecy, which is dependent on the imaginative and not the moral faculty, need not be a matter of predicting the future. The prophet is a realist of distances . . . the realism which does not hesitate to distort appearances in order to show a hidden truth."

A fairly tall order, that, even without the onus of soothsaying. Thinking hard about it could probably put a body down with a fair case of writer's block. But have artists ever really hesitated to distort reality in truth's service? Madonnas' complexions have luminesced for five centuries thanks largely to algae-colored pigments. Did ever a human heart possess the purity of Felicite's, a living face with Helen of Troy's beauty? Are we to call Flaubert and Homer liars, then? The point Miss Flannery, no small-time operator herself in the exaggeration-for-truth's-sake racket, wants taken to heart, I believe, is the part about retiring the pompous moral faculty, letting the lively imagination get on about art's business.

And part of art's business is, like religion's, belief in the yet-unseen. Indeed, what is writing if not an act of faith? Writers, like those who pray, wrest words from their very souls with an implicit belief that somehow those words will be received. And we betray ourselves with the words we call forth, giving away our deepest secrets. All we believe and fear, all we desire and love, is laid bare. Praise bursts out of us, our alleluias dead giveaways of what we cherish and even covet. We discriminate. What is set down on paper, committed to language, attests to the soul's selection of its own society. We beg and choose and gild lilies. We have, if we're worth an ounce of writer's salt, not a thing in the world left to hide by the time we get through.

I believe there is authentic holiness at the heart of the artist's striving, a kind of purity that holds a special place in the Creator's heart. Rilke sensed this purity in Cezanne's paintings and expressed it in a series of letters, gorgeous and profound in their simplicity: "whatever is present [in Cezanne's work] is utterly and urgently present, as if prostrate on its knees and praying for you." Later Rilke notes how Cezanne sees everything "as a poor man . . . and his love for all these things is directed at the nameless. . . . He does not show it, he has it. And quickly takes it out of himself and puts it . . . into the innermost and incessant part of the work."

That, of course, is Cezanne, an authentic genius, with Rilke, another genius, making a case for him. Still, I believe with all my heart (probably because my life depends on it) that there is holiness in the struggle itself, even when our efforts fall far short of the sublime. Perhaps especially then. For isn't the creative process at heart the enactment of our endless reaching for God? How else to explain the boundless *love* in it, after all, love that may seem for whole lifetimes to go unrequited, yet carries within itself a fiery and self-fulfilling hope? The striving to make a work of art can lure us toward the deepest levels of self. What we may find there, if we do not blink or flinch or fib, is God, God dwelling within us to whisper intimations of such wisdom and grace that we cannot in good conscience claim them entirely as our own.

Needless to say, not everyone will grant this inner force the name of God. Often it is referred to as *talent* or *genius*, with implications that it's to be found in the possession of only a deserving few. *Gift* seems to me closer to the truth, but its distribution remains a mystery. I am certain only that its source is God, the God who, at certain moments in the act of creation, seems so tantalizingly *close*, so palpable.

The writer Isaac Bashevis Singer derived from his labors a marvelous sense of kinship with the Creator:

> God was for me an eternal belletrist. His main attribute was creativity and what he created was made of the same stuff as He and shared His desire: to create again. I quoted to myself that passage from the Midrash which says God created and destroyed many worlds before he created this one. Like my brother [I. J. Singer, also a novelist] and myself God also threw His unsuccessful works into the wastebasket. The Flood, the destruction of Sodom, the wanderings of the Jews in the desert, the wars of Joshua—these were all episodes in a divine novel, full of suspense and adventure. Yes, God was a creator, and that which He created had a passion to create. Each atom, each molecule had creative needs and possibilities. The sun, the planets, the fixed stars, the whole cosmos seethed with creativity and creative fantasies. I could feel this turmoil within myself.

I read these words from Singer, blessed be his memory, and feel less alone both with my work and with my faith. I also find comfort in the Jewish proverb suggesting God created humankind because He loves stories. Does He listen to our stories, read them? Both owning up to and snubbing imagination's limits, I embrace and dance with the whimsical notion that maybe the Lord made writers to give Himself a bit of company. Does not our very loneliness reflect His image and likeness? Might we, in the blackness that falls upon so many of us between the visions and the dreams, be those who best understand why His first recorded words had to be *"Let there be light"?*

Like the person of faith, the novelist, that aspiring "realist of distances," must love this world as its Creator does, with a love that neither flinches nor fails. Many religions, my own among them, teach ways of enlightenment that steer us from worldly attachment. Yet the faith we nurture in the long-term hope that it will lead to kingdom come heightens the attraction of the here and now.

Does that sound like a paradox? I don't think it is. For millions of souls throughout time, the intricate beauty and mystery of the physical world have provided the most compelling proof of God's existence. We stare at the ocean's turbulence and for an instant imagine we can conceive of His power. The perfection of a newborn baby hints at the eternity of love we hope to be in for. We get wind in this world of the Creator's sense of humor—how else account for the giraffe, the coincidence, the muddle the smartest person can make of the simplest thing? The more we seek God in His Heaven, the more we find Him in all that is right in His world . . . in all that's beautiful, all that astonishes and confounds.

The writer lavishes upon the physical world the same sort of loving attention the child of God accords it, embracing both the mystery and the mundane. Such wonders as He hath wrought justify the very senses He saddled us with. Poke your nose into the background of any saint and you'll likely as not find a sensualist on a spiritual journey, with a tangle of roots sunk in the physical world: Francis might renounce food and fine clothing, but give up the feel of a creature's tongue or beak or muzzle feeding from his palm? And surely no accident for Jesus to have chosen bread and wine as accoutrements to our most precious Sacrament, acknowledging not only our hunger and thirst but the earth's cordial provision for them.

A dozen years ago, when I thought I had rid myself of all need and desire for the sacramental, I read a passage in my friend Andre Dubus's novel *Voices from the Moon*. Describing the response of his young protagonist to receiving the Eucharist, Andre wrote:

> Father Oberti placed the Host on his palm. [Richie] looked at it as he turned to go down the aisle. Then with his right thumb and forefinger he put it in his mouth, let it rest on his tongue, then softly chewed as he walked to the pew. He felt that he embraced the universe, and was in the arms of God.

My tears caught me off guard. Whatever made me cry like that? I was hungry, starving for bread, the bread that, if only I could admit to the appetite, would return me to the arms of God. The safest of neighborhoods . . . I remember living there as a child. Child of privilege . . . child of God, in Whose arms I was thoroughly at home. But then I managed to get myself lost, all turned around in the vast dark that lay between what I am and what I thought I was expected to be: virgin, martyr, bride of Christ, saint, little Sister. . . .

All that promise. All that hope. Then I go and turn out to be just . . . you know, *me*. Nothing special. Not even a spectacular disappointment, really . . . just your average, run-of-the-mill, falling-short life, the mea-culpa failed marriage and the pride and white lies and the sorry human rest of it. Me. Living in the arms of God—imagine. We really do manage to make a muddle of the simplest things, don't we? It should have been obvious all along: I lived in God's arms as a child because He *wanted* me there. Just as He does right now, and always did.

Now and forever, amen.

✠

It was my vocation, writing, that retrieved and returned me to my original faith, to the practice and privilege and *home* of it. The Catholicism to which I was born is ingrained in me, to be sure. The creative process made it impossible to deny, overlook, disown that faith. To find and accept my faith again has restored to my soul a kind of wholeness. I am no less imperfect than I ever was, but a large missing piece of me has been set back in place. I can stand on my own two feet now as these weak hands and puny arms strain toward God.

The Catholic I am now, a writer, accepts that I am God's work in progress, far less than I need or hope to be, but not without promise. I even, as my characters sometimes do with me, argue with God, nag Him. For on my sorry sabbatical from my own faith, I did learn a thing or two from the great rabbis. The Jews have a tradition not only of arguing with the Lord, but bossing Him around, calling Him to account. The God I love can take a lot of guff.

I don't mean to make it sound too simple. I have a lot to answer for. God, as many of the great Jewish spiritual leaders have suggested, may have some explaining to do Himself. This world created in His likeness, in infinite wisdom and compassion and love, can show itself for a sorry and brutal place. Evil and injustice seem to flourish. What are we to make of an omnipotent God Who not only permits suffering but appears to have created it?

Centuries of learned argument, premises, and proofs address such questions. *Theodicy*, theologians call it, the attempt to reconcile the seemingly contradictory existence of divinity and evil in the world. I confess such fine-tuned hypotheses are way beyond me. I can't always bring the long view into focus, not when the world in front of my face is tempting me to despair. It is then I turn my eyes to my God and pray He'll see no misgiving there.

Jesus came to us to tell us to hang on, I think . . . to reassure us that loving purpose lies behind all the terrible suffering that appears to constitute an unconscionable portion of this life. That loving purpose we fail to grasp has always been God's promise to us, as our promise to Him is a love that does not hinge on proof.

As a writer, I am obligated to look at the world without blinking and to say what I see.

As my father's daughter, I turn upon the Lord eyes filled with all the trust I can muster.

As a member of the Catholic faith, I embrace those beliefs I cannot live without.

I, you see, get to choose.

Anchored in the Church
Maria Shriver

Forty years after being baptized, I remain a committed Catholic. Why? Because it works. It works for me in my personal life and its teachings are my moral compass in my professional life as a television correspondent. I am a woman, a mother, a wife, a daughter, a sister, and a friend, but equally important, I am an Irish Catholic and proud of it.

There is no doubt in my mind that I received the gift of faith from my parents and my maternal grandmother. They were and are my major examples of lived faith and my inspiration for what being a Roman Catholic means. My parents and grandmother are and were daily communicants. Whenever we would visit my grandmother, and we did a lot, we could set our clocks by her schedule of going to Mass. Her amazing faith enabled her to withstand a lifetime of tragedies and to continue to look out at the world with hope. I marveled at her peace of mind, her Christian example, and the way she lived her life. I admired the way she talked about people, the way she treated everyone. All of this came from her faith in God. All of this was sustained by her daily participation in the Roman Catholic Church and its traditions—the Mass, Eucharist, confession, the rosary. I will always be grateful to her for the elegant memories she left me of what it means to be a practicing and believing Catholic.

My parents' faith continues to sustain the gift of faith in me. Their unending work on behalf of those less fortunate, their amazing kindness, their personal joy, and their deep spirituality all come from their faith and their commitment to Catholicism. Their sense of Catholic mission has led them to be involved in efforts such as the Special Olympics, the Joseph P. Kennedy, Jr., Fund, and work on behalf of the mentally retarded. They were founders of Community and Caring, Inc., in 1986. It is my parents' firm adherence to the Roman Catholic Church's teachings that has enabled them to live meaningful and full lives in this crazy world. Like my grandmother, they treat people with respect. They are selfless. They continue to walk the walk. They do all this not by sight, but by faith in God.

When my four brothers and I were growing up, our parents sought to pass on the example of faith to us in some wonderful ways of devotion. Every morning of Lent, my father would rouse us from bed to attend the 6:45 A.M. celebration of the Eucharist. I cannot say that I always enjoyed going to Mass, especially at that hour. But we saw him do it and, needless to say, we had no choice but to follow. During the month of May, my mother had us make a May Altar to the Blessed Mother Mary in our home. We would say the rosary as a family at night in front of that altar.

The gift of faith is still being given to me by my parents. I was recently talking to my eighty-year-old father about Heaven. He launched into a fifteen-minute discourse about what an incredible place Heaven is. He spoke with confidence of how he was looking forward to being there someday. He was not and is not the least bit afraid of death, because his faith gives him hope and peace.

As a child I liked being a Catholic, in spite of the fact that for more years than I care to admit, I lived in fear that I would be eternally damned if I were to miss Mass on Sunday, and that I grumbled about not being allowed to be an altar boy. I attended the Convent School of the Sacred Heart in Washington, DC, from first grade on. While I know many people who have horror stories about their education by nuns, I flourished with Religious Sisters of the Sacred Heart. Although I never wanted to be one of them (well . . . maybe for a minute, just so I could see what they did with their hair under those wild habits), I was always impressed with their dedication, their belief, and their faith. I also enjoyed reading the biographies of the saints, especially women saints of the Church. Along with my grandmother, my parents, and the nuns, the saints impressed me with their enviable inner strength made possible by their faith in God. Sharing in the Catholic faith gave me a sense of belonging, and I feel that belonging now more than ever.

Like so many others, during my college years at Georgetown, my Catholicism and my Sunday Mass attendance were not as high a priority as my party schedule. As I entered the highly competitive world of television, making time for Mass and reflection fell by the wayside. Then came the realization that more and more in my work I was having to make moral and ethical decisions. I was having to decide what was right and what was wrong. I was having to decide how I would treat people. I found myself turning back to the Church's teachings to help me in my everyday life. Could I keep my word? Would I lie to people to get a story? Would I back-stab in order to get ahead? Could I really practice the difficult task of forgiveness in life? I went back to the Church for support and guidance to get me through life and work.

Although I have made an adult commitment to the Roman Catholic Church, and to the Christian faith, I must be honest and say that I do not always do everything that the official Church instructs its members to do. In fact, I do have some very strong disagreements with the Church and with some of the perspectives of Pope John Paul II. I wish to be a loyal and faithful Catholic; however, Jesus came to take away our sins and not our brains. So I do have some questions about certain policies of the Church in this changing world.

It troubles me that so many divorced Catholics feel alienated from the community. I grieve over the fact that many gay and lesbian people feel that the Church shuts them out. I am angered that so many women feel that there is no future for them as ordained ministers of the Church, when in fact they have the gifts and the call to serve in such a capacity. Why is papal teaching so intransigent on the issue of birth control?

In the midst of these question and struggles, I nonetheless remain a committed Catholic. I feel at peace and at home when I take my children to Sunday Mass. I feel good about raising our children with faith, a set of values and a set of beliefs. I would not want to raise children without the help the Church has given us for this purpose. It is important to me that our children will have a sense of obligation to give something to those less fortunate than they are. It has always been a tenet of the Kennedy family to be concerned with the poor in spirit and the poor in gifts and talent. I feel confident that my children's Catholicism will help them become better people. It will surround them with positive role models and give them an inner moral compass that I hope they will use as they head out into a complicated and fast-paced world. My hope for them is that the Church will be a place where they can find refuge and where they can be constantly reminded that good does overpower evil; that faith, real, true faith, will help them face life's difficult challenges. My hope is that they will always be as proud of their Catholicism as I have always been of mine.

Now, They Were Really Tough!
Mark Bavaro

M Y LIFE has always revolved around the Catholic Church. My strongest and fondest memories as a child are glorious Sunday feasts that were always preceded by the Sunday Mass. To me they were inseparable. Never did we attend Mass without being rewarded with the family banquet, and never did we celebrate food and family without first giving thanks to God and showing our respect and devotion in His house of worship.

I grew up in a traditional Italian-American family on the verge of becoming more American than Italian. Both my grandfathers immigrated to this country from their native Italy, and both settled in the same Italian neighborhood of East Boston.

East Boston always has been and always will be dear to me because it represents all that is good in life. The neighborhood itself is not much to look at; in fact, if viewed from above, it looks like no more than an outline of houses around Logan Airport. Indeed, it seems as though the airport is pushing the tiny, congested community into the murky waters of Boston Harbor. If it is viewed from eye level, one sees a jumbled mess of three-story apartment buildings in crooked rows, shoulder to shoulder, with an occasional brick tenement thrown in to break up the monotony. Throughout the neighborhood, the smell of jet fuel permeates the already polluted air of the city. On a good day, though, if the wind is blowing in off the ocean, the salty air of Boston Harbor at low tide is enough to make you forget there is a major airport in your backyard.

But even on these days, that illusion is quickly dispelled every ten minutes or so when a 747 or another jumbo jet suddenly appears overhead, struggling to gain altitude in order to avoid toppling the rows of triple-deckers like so many dominoes. The phenomenon of a giant steel aircraft loaded with tons of highly flammable jet fuel and highly valuable human beings executing the most dangerous phase of its flight, the take-off, over a highly compact and densely populated neighborhood, amazes me to this day. When those planes would seemingly use the rooftops of those triple-deckers as an extension of the runway, the ground would shake and rumble, and the thrust of those mighty engines would drown out all the noises a busy city like Boston could produce. This racket goes a long way toward explaining why East Boston residents talk at least four times louder than the average human being.

When I was two years old, the noise, the jet fuel, and the very cramped quarters of East Boston convinced my young parents to seek a quieter and more peaceful environment. They wanted a place on the desirable North Shore of Boston, home of exclusive communities like Marblehead, Manchester-by-the-Sea, and Beverly Farms. The North Shore has long conjured up images of white church steeples set on quaint New England village greens, sailboats and yacht clubs, polo fields and golf courses, seaside mansions and country estates. After surveying the wide-open new world of the North Shore and counting the contents of their nearly empty pocketbook, my parents settled in Danvers, a small town cut off from the treasured shore by the stately cities of Beverly and Salem.

The town of Danvers was established in 1752 when it seceded from the city of Salem and changed its name from Salem Village to its present title. The origin of the name is not fully known, the best guess being that it took its name from the mysterious Earl d'Anvers. If this is true, you would be hard pressed to find any evidence of the man in the town memorabilia. I have always suspected that it was an attempt by the town fathers to give an air of nobility to the town in keeping with its more prestigious neighbors. But no matter how hard they tried to dress up the lowly farming community, Danvers was destined to be known forever in the history books as Salem Village, the home of the infamous Salem witch trials. According to the history books, in 1692 hundreds of men, women, and children were accused of practicing witchcraft. When the hysteria subsided, nineteen people had been put to death by hanging. Their graves are still marked and taken care of by their descendants, many of whom live in the town.

The town's most valuable natural resource back then was the tidal flats that neither Beverly nor Salem cared to claim. The Danvers River oozes inland like an excretion from the bowels of Beverly Harbor. While the harbor is home to magnificent sailing and fishing, the Danvers River becomes three distinct valleys of briny mud at low tide. Although the townspeople would have gladly given up the odor, they were grateful for the fertile farming soil it produced. And, indeed, Danvers became renowned for its outstanding produce, most notably the famous Danvers onion. That onion was so exceptional that for a long period of time the town identified itself as, and intimidated its opponents with, the fearsome sports moniker, Danvers Oniontowners. Sadly, I never knew the pride that one felt being an Oniontowner, for industrial parks and shopping malls had, by the time I entered the local sports scene, replaced the family farms and made the Danvers onion little more than a memory. I did, however, have the honor of participating in the Danvers Youth Football Championship game, known as the Onion Bowl. We won that bowl, and our victory party was held at the local YMCA, where we were allowed to swim all day and eat as many McDonald's hamburgers as we could stuff in our bellies. When the celebration was over, all that remained on the floor were soggy French fries and about 1,000 little cubes of onion that we boys had picked off every burger. We were all very proud of capturing the coveted Onion Bowl Trophy, but none of us actually wanted to savor the fruit of our victory.

And so when I was two years old, my mother, father, sisters, and I left the noisy cramped smell of low tide at Boston Harbor and resettled seventeen miles to the north, finding security and familiarity amid the smell of low tide along the Danvers River. I am the product of these two communities. For although we were physically residing in Danvers, socially we were still rooted in East Boston. My mother and father were devoted parents and also dutiful children, and in my family that meant frequent visits to our grandparents. On Sundays we would gather for church and dinner.

My mother's father had come from Italy when he was seventeen years old, in search of better opportunities in the New World and to escape service in the Italian Army. Ironically, he never was more than a manual laborer and ended up fighting for his new country in the First World War. He lived to the age of ninety-six, and went out every day of his life in a shirt and tie and top hat. He roamed the streets of Boston, holding court and sharing his views on life with anyone who would listen. I truly believe that had he been able to the conquer the English language, he would have been mayor. My Grandpa Lalli always thought very highly of himself because in Italy he was an apprentice barrelmaker. He had a trade, and in Italy having a trade separated you from the peasants. He brought this view of himself to America, and even though the closest he ever came to a trade here was painting firehouses, he carried himself with an air of dignity uncommon among his fellow immigrants. But like most expatriates, he had an inherent toughness. He was small in stature, but a lifetime of digging ditches with a pick and a shovel made him hard as steel.

He was always proud to tell the story of how he fell off a wall fifty feet high, then got up and walked home. Whenever I began to doubt his recollection of the altitude and his ability to survive a fall from such a height, I would recall the story of how, when he was eighty-five years old, he was attacked by a group of young punks who encircled him, stole his precious hat, and began to taunt and abuse him. My grandfather gathered his strength and courage, and with his pocketknife in one hand and his cane in the other, he began to beat his assailants, sending them running for safety. As it turned out, the only thing that ever stopped my grandfather was an automobile that plowed into him when he was ninety-four. He was on one of his daily walks when he was struck by the car. He flew through the air, landed on his side, and broke his hip. Even though he recovered and was back on his feet rather quickly, enough damage was done that he needed constant care in a nursing home. And I believe the confinement and inactivity of the nursing home was what did him in. He became lethargic. The zip was gone from his step and, worst of all, they wouldn't allow him to go on his daily jaunts around the city. After a year or two, he seemed to tire of life as he appreciated it, and he began to fade. On his deathbed he turned to my mother, who was keeping vigil, and said calmly: "Go home, it's okay, I'm going to leave now." He took one more breath and closed his eyes. He was one of the two toughest guys I ever knew.

The other tough guy was my Grandpa Bavaro. My father's father came from Italy when he was a young boy. Just before he and his parents left on their arduous journey across the sea, little Dominic became gravely ill. My great-grandmother did the best thing she thought she could possibly do for her son. She prayed to St. Francis to intercede for her on Dominic's behalf. As a result of her faith, little Dom was miraculously cured, and in return for St. Francis prayers, my great-grandma honored the loving saint by dressing her son in the habit of Saint Francis. As the overcrowded steamer entered New York Harbor, there was at least one little boy among the wretched masses waving joyously at the Statue of Liberty who was dressed as a Franciscan monk! And true to her word, my great-grandmother put that brown sackcloth robe on her son and tied it with a rope around his waist every day of his life for the next two years. But I think the real payback, and what pleased Saint Francis more than anything, was the day that Dominic's first son, my Uncle John, became a true member of the Order of St. Francis by being ordained a Franciscan priest.

Like my Grandpa Lalli, my Grandpa Bavaro never quite captured the American dream. Being the oldest of eleven children, he was encouraged to leave the family's small apartment at an early age, and spent most of his life on the streets and in the factories of East Boston. Here he filled his lungs with deadly asbestos. Lungs have always been weak in the Bavaro family and at the age of sixty-nine, he died of lung cancer. He didn't go as peacefully as my Grandpa Lalli. He suffered for a few years first, and it was during this time that I realized how tough he really was.

I knew that around the neighborhood it was said that in his youth he was "the toughest guy in East Boston." The story was often repeated that in order to win the title, he defeated the reigning champ in a street fight that lasted thirteen blocks. I was always a little nervous around him. Unlike my Grandpa Lalli, my Grandpa Bavaro came from the peasant class and had no desire to ascend any social ladder. I never saw him in a coat and tie. He wore white sleeveless T-shirts that revealed his musculature and exposed myriad intimidating and provocative tattoos all up and down his bulging arms. His great passion for making his own wine was exceeded only by his great passion for drinking it. He spent as much time down at the corner bar and social club as he did betting on dogs and horses at the track. I still remember the night my father got a phone call informing him that Dominic was in the hospital, being treated for stab wounds. It seemed that my grandfather, who had to have been in his early sixties, was coming off the subway, on his way home from the track, when he was mugged while crossing through a vacant lot. But rather than give up his wallet, he instinctively attacked. Despite being stabbed, he succeeded in fighting off a man half his age and, bleeding profusely, he walked the rest of the way home. Then he called for an ambulance to take him to the hospital because he didn't own a car. He was a hard man who lived a hard life, but although he had that hard edge to him, underneath he was a very loving man. They say he cried every night for a year when his youngest son, Donald, was fighting in Vietnam. The pride he felt when he would see his oldest son, John, say Mass at the altar was plain for everyone to see. The satisfaction of seeing his middle son, my father, graduate from college cannot be overstated.

When I was a junior in high school, we lost a football game that would have won us the league championship. It was our Thanksgiving Day game against our traditional rival, the rough-and-tumble Fishermen of Gloucester. When the game was over, I tried to shake it off and be upbeat because we were going to visit my grandfather, who was in the hospital dying of cancer. When we arrived in his room, he looked like a skeleton; his tattoos were shriveled into incomprehensible doodlings. I went over to kiss him, and he looked at me and growled: "What's the matter? You can't win one game? You could have won it all, but now you're just losers." I wasn't offended. That's just the way he was, and I knew that. But I was shocked that amid all his pain and suffering, and the multitude of family members for whom he was the patriarch, he cared enough about me to follow my life so closely. I never realized that I meant that much to him. I was overcome with sorrow and disappointment that I wasn't able to provide him with that championship. It would have made him so happy during his last hours of suffering. It pains me to this day that he wasn't around to see me play professional football, and especially to see me play on a Super Bowl championship team. He would have enjoyed that more than anyone.

Shortly after that Thanksgiving Day, my grandfather died. Prior to his death, my father had been with him one day while he was still in his right mind. In the midst of a rational conversation with my father, my grandfather turned his head quickly to the opposite corner of the room and exclaimed: "Hey, what are you doing here?" My father looked in that direction, but saw no one. Then my grandfather turned back to my father and said, "Excuse us, Anthony, let me and my friend here have some privacy. Come back in a few minutes." My father left the room warily, and when he was finally called back, my grandfather explained how his old friend had come to see him. My father didn't know what to say, for he knew the old friend had been dead for several years. Yet, there was my grandfather, with all his faculties, seemingly communing with a deceased loved one right in front of his living ones. And it wasn't the only time that happened. Other family members were witnesses to similar incidents.

Short of my parents, my grandparents were, and still are, the most influential people in my life. These men and women taught me the virtues of faith, hope, and charity, along with the toughness that is needed in this world.

When I began my career as a professional football player with the New York Giants, I found myself in the company of men like Lawrence Taylor, Harry Carsons, and Phil Simms. These players are Hall of Fame caliber, and during their playing days they were regarded as the toughest players in the game. I must admit that when I arrived at my first training camp as a rookie, I was terrified. These guys were big and mean and had little compassion. I had had a good career at Notre Dame and I came to camp with a good reputation, but when I got to camp, I realized that the pros were different from college players. These guys were making their living at this game of football. In college everyone made the team. You played hard and tried to break into the lineup; if you didn't do it as a freshman, you waited patiently for the guy in front of you to graduate. And that is what happened to me. I didn't get to play at Notre Dame until I was a junior. For two years I sat on the bench, eagerly waiting for my turn on the field. In the pros there is no waiting. You are either good enough now or you are gone tomorrow. In college there were over 100 players on the roster. In the pros there are only forty-five. In the pros the team is already complete, and no one can stay in the shadow of another player. In order to break into these ranks, you have to do something special or show something extraordinary in order to take someone's job. The hardest part of doing that is the competition. After all, the veterans are proven, experienced professional athletes and rookies are not. Physically, it was an enormous challenge.

Training camp lasted for eight weeks. We practiced three times a day, six days a week, in the hot sun. The practice day started at 6 A.M. and ended at 11 P.M., when we were allowed to collapse into bed. It was a long, painful day. There was little comfort to be found anywhere. One day I lost eighteen pounds between the time I woke up and the time I dragged my aching body to bed. Almost every day I contemplated quitting, and almost every day something kept me hanging in there. That extra something was the thought of my grandfathers. When I was at the end of my strength and didn't think I could go any farther, I remembered how my Grandpa Lalli sweated in the sun, swinging that pick and shovel, working in the rocky landscape of New England, building roads and dams until he didn't think he could go on. But somehow he found the strength to continue, and if he could do it, so could I. When I was confronted with a maniacal linebacker out to break my neck and send me home with my tail between my legs, I thought of my Grandpa Bavaro and all the times he was forced to defend himself in the factories and on the streets of East Boston. He never backed down from anyone, and even though he didn't always win, he never ran away. And if he did it, I sure wasn't going to let anyone whip me without a fight. Every time I wanted to quit and every time I had to fight, I drew strength from the two toughest guys I knew, and when the dust had finally settled and my first training camp was over, I had become a New York Giant. I had earned the respect of my teammates not only for my talent on the field but also for my toughness.

My grandparents, although they are no longer in this world, are still with me, and have always been there for me in my time of need. As much as they were an example of toughness, they were also an example of devotion of God. Their lives revolved around the Church. Their apartments were littered with religious objects, everything from rosary beads to crucifixes. The greatest day of the week was Sunday, when we would attend Mass at their parish church, Our Lady of Mt. Carmel. We would walk into one of their apartments, and the smell of the Sunday feast would almost knock you over. On the stove there would be the big vat of tomato sauce simmering, and in the oven would be a roast and potatoes next to a pan of lasagna. Rice cakes would be frying in a skillet, and my grandmother would be breading the cutlets and stuffing the artichokes. In the den, homemade macaroni was drying on a folding clothes rack, and my grandfather would appear at the top of the cellar steps with a gallon of his homemade wine, fresh from the barrel. The smell of garlic was so strong it made my eyes water, and the tears dripped down my cheeks to mingle with the saliva that was drooling out of the corner of my mouth. In those days you weren't supposed to eat anything from midnight of the previous night until Communion the next day. I've always had a healthy appetite, and for me to skip a meal requires a lot of willpower. Usually, in order to do something like that, I have to remove myself from any evidence of food. Walking into that apartment on a Sunday morning, when I was already starving, was pure torture. If I had seen anyone even pick up a pistachio and put it in his mouth, I would have joined in despite my guilt, but never once did I see anything like that happen. The food was strictly off limits until after church. Keeping a watchful eye over everyone, especially us kids, was my grandfather. He never had any moral dilemma with the rules of the Church. He simply and faithfully obeyed them as best he could. I saw that obedience, and I wanted to do the same.

After saying hello with kisses and hugs, we headed down the block to the magnificent parish church that was built by the Italian immigrants as a manifestation of their enormous faith. These people, who came to this country with little in their pockets and who filled them with little more after they had arrived, nonetheless gave inordinate amounts of the little they had to ensure a proper and fitting dwelling place for their Lord and Savior.

All along the way to church, the air was filled with the smells of Sunday feasts being prepared in all the other apartments of the neighborhood. For one day a week, the smell of food actually overpowered the nauseating jet fuel and dank low tide so familiar to this corner of the city. As I walked down the street, my nose was inundated with new culinary delights, and with every step I took, my mouth watered more and more. Finally I reached the sanctuary of the church, where the fog of incense enveloped the congregation and momentarily took my mind off of food. But as the fog cleared, the smell of meatballs and sausages poured out of the rectory kitchen, just to the side of the altar, where the Italian priests were preparing their own Sunday feast. As the Mass proceeded, I agonized through the readings and then the homily until at long last Communion appeared on the horizon, lifting my spirits, as the sight of land must do for sailors lost at sea. I would walk up the aisle, staring intently at that little wafer the priest was holding in his hand. In my mind, I knew it was the Body and Blood but, more important to me at that time, it was food—and I was starving. I longed for that tiny morsel of bread with all my heart. I knew that once I had tasted that sacred Eucharist, Mass would be nearly over and I would finally be allowed to eat the fabulous banquet that awaited me at my grandmother's.

When the priest laid the wafer on my tongue, a spasm of joy went through my body. It was the first food I had tasted in over twelve hours, and it was good. It was the first of many things I would consume that day. The joy I felt at Communion carried over to the family dinner, where brothers and sisters, aunts and uncles, nieces and nephews and cousins all caught up with each other and renewed their family ties over food, wine, and conversation. The day was filled with happiness as I experienced all that is good in life, sitting there with my family in the small confines of that East Boston apartment.

When I got older and better understood the meaning of Communion, I began to realize how special those family get-togethers were. They were an early version of Paradise. Mass was the equivalent of the Beatific Vision, the closest we will ever get to God in this world. The Sunday dinner was the equivalent of the heavenly banquet that Jesus invites us all to attend. And the family, coming together as one, was reminiscent of the saints coming together to form the Mystical Body of Christ. The one precept of church teaching that is most dear to me is the Communion of Saints. The idea that the saints in heaven, the Church Triumphant; the saints in purgatory, the Church Suffering; and the saints on earth, the Church Militant, can all communicate with one another is powerful. Although we are a world apart, the door is open between us, and God encourages our contact with each other through prayer. This is a great source of comfort and security for me: to know that those family members who were so dear to me and are gone from this world still exist as themselves in another. Although I cannot seem them, I know they are only a breath away, praying for us to reunite with them. And as was the case with my grandfather's deceased friend in the hospital, I believe that on occasion the dear departed are sometimes allowed to come back to help us on our way.

When people ask me why I am Catholic, I try to explain that the reason I am Catholic is because I was raised Catholic. But the reason I remain Catholic is because the Church keeps me close to my loved ones, living and dead. When I was a kid, my life revolved around the Church because I knew I had to endure the Mass before I could partake of the feast that awaited me and loved ones at my grandparents' house. Today, as an adult, my life revolves around the Church because I know that it is the Mass that prepares me to partake of the heavenly feast, reunited with all my loved ones, especially my grandparents, in the presence of God.

I am very fortunate that my grandparents imparted to me their faith and toughness. Both of these attributes have helped me immensely in my life. I know that they are now united with the people who handed these qualities down to them. And I pray and hope that I can provide the same example to my children, instilling in them the lessons that my grandparents taught me: that the Catholic Church is nothing more and nothing less than the vessel that will carry us all home to our ancestors and our Creator.

A Twitch Upon the Thread
Kathleen Howley

I WAS a bit of a dreamer when I was a child. Today, people find this hard to believe, but when I was young, I was painfully shy. I found it difficult to make friends, so I opted, instead, to spend my after-school hours in my bedroom, reading.

In fact, I think I was the only kid on the block who was ordered by her parents not to read so much. My favorite books were about girl detectives who managed to solve mysteries and make friends, seemingly without effort.

I attended a parochial School in Norwood, a suburb of Boston. The only time I can remember getting in trouble was in a fifth-grade religion class, when I was caught reading during a lecture. As the nun droned on about the attributes of God, I kept a detective book partially hidden under my catechism text. When the ploy was discovered, Sister reprimanded me, but I think I saw a trace of a smile on her face. I was getting an A in the class. I learned my prayers and I memorized my catechism. I provided all the right answers. It was only skin deep, though; religion just didn't interest me.

The only time I remember feeling even vaguely spiritual was around my grandmother, Nora. She died when I was young, but she is the one who taught me how to pray the "Hail Mary." She was a sweet and gentle soul. I have faint memories of her holding me in her lap while she prayed the rosary. In fact, whenever I think of her, I picture her fingering the rosary beads, her lips moving in whispered prayer. Her faith was simple—she believed that sanctification could be gained, for her, through attending Mass, praying every day, taking good care of her family, and washing her kitchen floor.

She was born a Larkin, and lived the first part of her life on a dairy and sheep farm near Craughwell, a tiny village in County Galway. In late September 1914, she eloped with Michael Joseph Howley, the handsome boy from the farm next door, and ran away to America. It was romantic, but I don't think it was impulsive. They waited until the crops were in and the hay was cut. They didn't tell their families. There was no chance for their parents to say good-bye, no time for an "American wake," as the Irish called the parties on the eve of departure. She was twenty years old, and he was twenty-four.

They traveled to the south of Ireland, to the docks of Queenstown (the British name for Cobh), in County Cork. When World War I was barely two months old, they boarded a Cunard steamship, the *Laconia*. My grandfather had the equivalent of fifty dollars in his pocket. My grandmother had her rosary beads in her pocket.

It was a calculated risk. They knew there was a chance that the ship could be sunk by German submarines. In fact, seven months later, another Cunard liner, the *Lusitania*, was torpedoed off the coast of Queenstown, with the loss of almost 1200 lives. What gave them the courage, at such a young age, to dare such a dangerous crossing? I suspect it was their deep faith. Before they boarded the ship, I'm sure they walked to the nearest church, St. Colman's Cathedral, on the hill overlooking the wharves. No doubt they went to confession and attended Mass.

The second part of Nora's life was spent in the shadow of St. Peter's, an old stone church in Dorchester, a working-class section of Boston that was filled with Irish immigrants. Her children and many of her grandchildren, myself included, were baptized there. Her husband's requiem Mass, and then her own, were offered there.

I have dim childhood memories of St. Peter's—my parents kneeling at the altar rail, the smell of incense, jam-packed pews, and the red tinge of sun streaming through the stained glass windows. It gave me a feeling of awe. That era, though, disappeared before I really knew it.

My earliest, clearest memory of Mass is traumatically different: a Sunday Mass in an overly bright school cafeteria. There was lots of guitar music, the altar was a folding table, and the priest began the Holy Sacrifice of Mass with "Good morning. How is everybody?" The Mass seemed like a meeting of the "Do-Gooders Club." The prayers evoked no sense of the sacred, and the ritual demanded no acknowledgment of the majesty of God or the existence of the supernatural. The point of it all seemed to be "Try to be a good person." To me, it was the liturgical equivalent of "Have a nice day."

Frankly, I wasn't interested. One Sunday morning, in my mid-teens, I simply locked myself in my room and refused to go to Mass. My parents objected, but to no avail. Later, we reached a truce: I didn't have to go to Mass, but I did have to attend a religious education class taught by my father, a former seminarian and longtime CCD instructor.

That year, he tried a new approach. He said to his students, "Let's pretend that you don't believe in God. I'm going to show you, over the next few months, how His existence can be proven, using the human intellect."

I doubt that my father will suffer a moment in Purgatory, given the opportunities for sanctification he received in that class. His own daughter was the most vocal student, arguing against the existence of God.

I supported the Big Bang theory—that our world is the result of the collision of two universes. He used phrases like "uncaused cause," arguing that nothing comes from a vacuum. He asked me how these two theoretical universes were created. My reply was that science hadn't explained everything to us—yet. But someday it would.

Lucky for me, my father is an easygoing man who, unlike most Irish people, never holds a grudge. Years later, after my conversion, I related to him how worried I was about someone else who was away from the Catholic Church.

He replied, simply, "Well, I'll do what I did with you."

Intrigued, I asked, "And what was that?"

"I'll spend some time in front of the Blessed Sacrament," he said with a grin.

✝

Today, people tend to assume that I was always a practicing Catholic. In fact, sometimes, when I mention that I attended the University of Massachusetts at Amherst, I'm asked, "How did you ever get through it with your faith intact?" My answer is, "My faith was untouched. I went in with none, and I left with none."

At a school with almost 20,000 students, I wasn't alone in my unbelief. About half of the residents of Massachusetts are Roman Catholic. The people in my dormitory seemed to be a fair cross section of the state's population. Yet I didn't know anyone who went to Mass. No one.

My friends and I attended keg parties any day of the week. We had the energy to pull "all nighters" to catch up on our schoolwork on the eve of big exams. But we had neither the time nor the inclination to attend Mass on Sundays. That was for nerds.

I worked for the student-run daily newspaper. A few months after I started, my editor assigned me a feature on the Newman Center, a Catholic organization. I tried to pawn the story off on other reporters. I begged my roommate, who also worked at the paper, to do it. She was a lapsed Catholic, too, so she wasn't interested. I went back to my editor, and told him to find someone else. Nothing worked. I had to write it.

At that point, I had been in Amherst for more than a year, yet I needed to ask directions to the Newman Center. I knew the exact location of every pub within a ten-mile radius, but I didn't know the location of the nearest Catholic Mass.

While I was at the Newman Center, it didn't occur to me to visit the chapel. But I talked to several students who were sitting in the small cafeteria in the basement, and I interviewed the director.

The story ranks as the worst I've ever done. The lead was "The Newman Center is not just for Catholics. . . ." I wrote the entire article about nonreligious activities at the center. I didn't address any aspect of the Catholic faith.

My Catholic past intruded upon my four-year stay in Amherst on just one other occasion. In 1981, on my way to the newspaper office, I noticed a crowd gathered around a television set in the student union. "Someone shot the Pope," a friend told me.

When I heard those words, I felt a jolt in the pit of my stomach. Then it occurred to me: "I'm not really a Catholic. Why should it bother me so much?"

I went into the newsroom and followed the story there. Of course, I didn't think to pray, because I didn't believe in prayer. Other reporters gathered around the TV, too, some of them with furrowed brows. Many had Irish, Italian, or Polish surnames. I suppose they were baptized Catholics. They had never mentioned religion to me. They didn't go to Mass.

Without realizing it, I was seeing on their faces, and feeling in my own stomach, an example of the "indelible mark of the Sacraments," a phrase I memorized in my long-ago religion class. We could reject our faith, but deep inside, we could never stop being Catholic. Our souls were branded.

Twelve years later, after the Holy Spirit pulled me back into the Church, I went to World Youth Day in Denver. Because I had a press pass, I happened to be standing in a secure area when John Paul II passed by.

He stopped. I felt in my soul that I was in the presence of the Vicar of Christ.

"Papa, I pray for you every day," I said, addressing him with the name the Italians use.

"Good, good, good," the Pope said as he smiled, squeezed my hand gently, and continued on his way.

✠

G. K. Chesterton aptly described the conversion process in one of his Father Brown mysteries. His main character says, of a recent convert, "I caught him with an unseen hook and an invisible line which is long enough to let him wander to the ends of the world, and still to bring him back with a twitch upon the thread."

In my case, I wandered as far as Liberia, a country in West Africa. After graduating from college in 1982, I took a volunteer position in

Monrovia, the capital city. My job was to coordinate the establishment of a newspaper, and in my spare time, I taught writing to anyone who was interested.

Nothing could have prepared me for the conditions I encountered. Families lived in shacks that Americans wouldn't use for animals. Hungry children were everywhere, begging for food. Stray dogs and cats didn't last long; they were caught and eaten. There were no public works facilities, so residents emptied their garbage into neighborhood piles. When the heaps grew too large, they were set on fire and smoldered for days, filling the air with a rancid haze. "If I did believe in Hell, maybe it would be something like this," I said to myself as I walked down a smoke-filled city street.

Years earlier, the United States had built a modern hospital for the residents of Monrovia and named it after John Fitzgerald Kennedy. Officially it was known as JFK. But, the Liberians had another name for it—"Just For Killing." They brought people there to die. It was a fine building. But the medical equipment didn't work because there were no spare parts. The shelves of the dispensary were empty—even simple antimalarial tablets were impossible to get. There were no sheets for the beds. There were no bandages nor sutures.

If God did exist, surely He wouldn't let people live like this, I thought. It never occurred to me that the Almighty has given us ample opportunities to address such ills. We simply lack the will to do it.

I had always mixed liberal amounts of alcohol with writing, but in Africa, my alcoholism took a more serious turn. I drank every day. Usually I met English friends at noon for "sundowning drinks"; we told each other that was when the sun began to go down. Once we started, we kept going. As the months went by, I started drinking in the mornings, to relieve my hangovers.

I caught malaria. An Irish friend came to my aid with a bottle of Johnny Walker Red—widely believed, by the expatriates living in Liberia, to be an effective cure for anything that ailed us. A mix of alcoholism and tropical illness was effective in opening a crack in my defenses. As I lay in my bed, shivering in the heat and listening to the sounds of the African night, I grew a bit less sure that atheism was a good idea. I was feeling the "twitch upon the thread."

One morning, after a full night of drinking, I had a moment of truth. I said to a friend, "I think I'm an alcoholic." It seemed an absurd statement because, I thought, surely I was too young. But my friend didn't argue. She just nodded her head.

Within a few weeks, I returned to America, joined a Twelve Step program, and stopped drinking. I was twenty-four years old.

Eventually, I got a job at a newspaper. But I couldn't shake a feeling of depression. A cousin suggested I try praying for a few minutes each morning.

"I don't believe in God," I reminded her. She was not deterred.

"It doesn't matter," she said. "Prayer works, whether you believe in it or not."

She seemed to have a happy and peaceful life. She was also an alcoholic who had managed to stop drinking. So, after some prodding, I tried it.

Every morning, I got on my knees and asked God for help. I said, almost by rote, "God help me, an alcoholic, to stay sober just for today." That wasn't too hard. Then I spent a few minutes trying to converse with God. It seemed a bit odd to speak to Someone I felt sure didn't exist.

For a while, nothing happened. But after seven months, I had life-changing experience. As it turned out, I didn't have to worry about getting in touch with God. Once I made a sincere effort to till the soil and make myself open to Him, He got in touch with me.

I didn't see anything. I just felt the presence of God inside of me. To my empty and thirsting soul, it felt quite dramatic. But when I described it to my cousin, she was unsurprised.

"That's what God feels like," she said.

One second, you could not have convinced me that God exists. The next, you could not have convinced me otherwise. If no one else on earth believed in Him, I still couldn't have denied His reality. For a few moments I had experienced God as plainly as I experienced the presence of a friend.

I had mistakenly thought that deeply spiritual people based their faith purely on intellect or, in some cases, mere habit. It never occurred to me that God's love could actually be felt inside, or that I could have a personal relationship with Him.

But, now that I knew God existed, I wasn't sure what to do next. I continued to pray. I read spiritual literature—but never anything Catholic.

I asked God each morning for the knowledge of His Will, and the ability to carry it out. I was doing the best I could, but I wasn't getting the full picture. I didn't go to Mass. Believing in God and searching for Him was the best I could do.

My cousin urged me to go to confession, but I resisted stubbornly. I didn't think I could ever say the words "Bless me, Father, for I have sinned. It has been ten years since my last Confession. . . . "

She twisted my arm, and twisted, and twisted, until I finally did it. I made the long walk into the confessional with fear and trepidation. I was absolved of everything, and the priest made no demands on me to change my life. "God loves you. You're doing fine," I remember him saying.

So I continued living in the same way, praying every day and basing my life on the principle that I should be "nice," whatever that meant to me.

It was a long time before I returned to Confession or attended Mass.

A series of three events caused me to return to the Catholic Church. First, I visited my family in Galway. There my cousin Father Ray confronted me, privately, about not going to Mass. He tended to have a happy-go-lucky personality, and I was surprised to see him looking so serious. When I visited Ireland at the age of eighteen, I had announced that I was an atheist. Now I was a lapsed Catholic who believed in God. It was a vast improvement, as I pointed out to him. But he wouldn't budge an inch. I tried to explain to him that although I now believed in God, I just wasn't the type to belong to an "organized religion," as I then referred to Holy Mother Church.

"But this is the faith that your ancestors died for!" he said, with obvious distress.

"That was fine for them. But it's just not for me."

We talked for almost an hour. Eventually, he gave up.

I'm sure Father Ray thought his efforts had been wasted. Unfortunately, he died of cancer before I had a chance to return.

Later, back in America, I was channel-surfing one night and came across an elderly nun reading from the Bible. She turned out to be Mother Angelica, head of EWTN, the national Catholic television network. She didn't pull any punches. She wagged a finger at the screen. "It doesn't matter whether you believe in Hell or not. There IS a Hell, and you ARE going there, if you don't change the way you're living," she said.

It was a startling possibility: Could Hell really exist, even though I didn't believe in it?

A few days later, I was walking in downtown Boston and decided, on the spur of the moment, to pop into the Arch Street Chapel for confession. I got a priest who was more concerned with saving my immortal soul than with being nice.

I didn't list my sins, because at the time I didn't believe in the concept of sin. But I told him everything else that was on my mind.

"Do you go to Mass on Sunday?" he asked, when I was finished. I thought that perhaps he had missed the point.

"No, Father, but I don't really think that's important."

"You have got to go to Mass on Sunday," he said, firmly but charitably. "First, because that is the starting point for your spiritual life, and second, because it's a mortal sin to miss it."

I was polite, of course, but I was irked. As I left the confessional, I remember muttering something about "those Catholics and their stupid rules."

But soon after, I started going to Mass. Because that courageous priest dared to speak the truth, the sheep finally was able to hear the Shepherd's voice.

Someone once said that alcoholics are deeply spiritual people, even if they claim to be atheists. If you look in the dictionary, under the heading "spirit" you'll find these definitions: (1) a supernatural being, (2) a soul, (3) a ghost, and (4) a liquid containing ethyl alcohol.

"When you were drinking, you were trying to fill up that empty space inside with God. You were just knocking at the wrong door," said a friend who is also a recovering alcoholic.

I was sober for about six years before my spiritual journey placed me, ready to knock, in front of the right door—that of the 2000-year-old Roman Catholic Church.

✢

In the late 1980s, I was writing for a neighborhood newspaper in Boston, primarily covering zoning meetings and real estate stories. An editor for the *Boston Herald* called me, and asked me if I wanted to do a weekly column titled "Charlie on the MBTA," about Boston's public transportation system. I wouldn't get a byline, he explained. I would simply be known as "Charlie."

My father's repertoire of funny stories included the one about Charlie, who got stuck on the subway because he didn't have the fare to get off. As the folk song he derived it from explained, "He will ride forever 'neath the streets of Boston. He's the man who never returned."

I accepted the assignment and found I loved writing under the persona of "Charlie." Little old ladies and frustrated commuters would send in complaints or questions, and Charlie would get answers. Later, my editor asked me to do two other weekly columns, one about real estate and the other about interior design.

I was living in South Boston and writing in my home office. Around the corner loomed the spires of Gate of Heaven Church, built during the Civil War.

That's where I went when I started going back to Mass. I was pushed by the priest in confession, but I also was pulled. I felt a vague beckoning emanating from the interior of the massive church. So, I went.

I'm told that the reason Saint Mary Magdalene witnessed the Resurrection is that after her conversion, she went to everything. I didn't quite go to everything, but I started attending a Monday night Scripture class and a Tuesday night young adult group, both at the Gate of Heaven rectory. I even joined the choir.

During the six months I sang in the choir, my father often drove to south Boston to attend Sunday Mass. "I just have to see this," he'd tell me with a chuckle.

I felt a sense of healing at Mass, especially at the beginning. It seemed like my soul was being restored. But after ten years in the wilderness, I also discovered a lot had changed. In place of the strong Catholic Church that once commanded the respect of almost all—members and nonmembers alike—it now seemed like a battlefield where so-called liberals fought so-called conservatives. What I used to call "organized religion" turned out, after all, not to be so organized.

The fact that I was a journalist helped me to sort it all out. I learned not to believe what I heard about Catholic teaching or history until I had researched it for myself, using credible sources. I started with Holy Scripture. I read the Gospel beginning with the first words of Matthew, and ended with the last words of Revelation. The Savior I discovered there was different than I expected. He wasn't vengeful and angry, but neither was he a teddy bear, as some today seem to suggest.

After that, I read autobiographies written by some of the greatest saints of the Church. First, I tackled Saint Augustine's *Confessions*, the story of his life before and after his conversion. One paragraph, in particular, made my eyes fill with tears: "Too late have I loved You, a Love so ancient and yet so new. You were within me, but I was outside. . . . You called and cried aloud, and broke upon my deafness. I tasted, and I did hunger and thirst. You touched me, and I did burn for Your peace."

By reading *The Story of a Soul*, by Saint Therese of Lisieux, I learned how simple the act of faith can be. Later, I finished the autobiography of Saint Margaret Mary Alacoque, an intimate story of her relationship with Our Lord.

As a nonbeliever, I had scoffed at much of Catholic doctrine without bothering to read any supporting documents—not even a papal encyclical. Now, I read it all—encyclicals, catechisms, canon law—and I discovered that the Apostolic Faith made sense.

But when it came to a belief in the Real Presence in the Eucharist, I didn't attain it by research. I developed a habit of stopping for a moment of prayer at Boston's Arch Street Chapel, where there was daily exposition of the Blessed Sacrament. One day, as I was on my knees, it struck me out of the clear blue. There He is, Jesus. It looks like a simple Host. But in reality, it is God. By spending time in the presence of the Blessed Sacrament, I was given the gift of faith.

Eventually, I jumped from the *Herald* to the *Boston Globe*, where I spent most of my time writing about real estate, still as a freelancer.

I moved to a town south of Boston, into a carriage house on the ocean. In my spare time, I started writing a weekly opinion column for the Catholic press that was eventually syndicated in a dozen newspapers.

Still, I didn't feel I had found my right place in the Church. At my local parishes I attended Masses that were completely one-dimensional, with the emphasis on the tangible—the world I had lived in for too long, when I was a nonbeliever. One Sunday morning, I ended up at the traditional Latin Mass at Holy Trinity in Boston. I sat near the back of the church, letting the supernatural wash over me. I was astounded. At other Masses, I had to remind myself of what was really happening. I had to work at communion with God. Here, it was effortless.

The Prayers at the foot of the altar were beautiful: "I will go up to the altar of God, to God Who gives joy to my youth." I had never heard them before. They are missing in the newer form of Mass. As the priest ascended the high altar, it hit me, at a gut level, that he was offering a holy sacrifice. I didn't need a catechism to tell me that—it looked like it.

The Canon was "in secret"—whispered, emphasizing the priest's role before God and the intimacy of that crucial part of the Mass. At Communion, we knelt at the altar rail and received on the tongue. The priest blessed each person with the Eucharist, saying, "May the Body of Our Lord Jesus Christ preserve your soul to life everlasting. Amen."

A second Gospel was read at the end of the Mass, the Last Gospel, always the same: "In the beginning was the Word. . . ." It was like a review of everything that had just happened.

This wasn't a liturgy brought down to my level. It wasn't "relevant." It was something far above. It infused me with a desire to try to reach up toward it.

Not everyone has such a reaction to the older form of Mass. I understand that. But my soul felt as if I was finally hearing my native language after years of being around people who were speaking to me in a foreign tongue.

It wasn't just the use of Latin. It was much more. The form of Mass I was witnessing was one that would be instantly recognizable by Catholics throughout the ages, from the fourth century, when the Mass was first codified by Pope Damasus I, up to the dramatic changes thirty years ago. It was a link to all who had gone before me.

In 1988, John Paul II issued "Ecclesia Dei," an apostolic letter mandating that the traditional Latin Mass, specifically the Roman Missal of 1962, be "widely and generously" available to any Catholic who prefers it. He called it a "rightful aspiration" to desire the older form of Mass.

I have met many young people who have had their lives changed by discovering the traditional Latin Mass. In some cases, it has brought them back to the Church. But I often think of the many post–Vatican II Catholics have never had a chance to experience their patrimony—the rich liturgical tradition of the Roman Rite. The Catholics who thrive with the modern form of Mass are evident in the pews of local parishes, but in most cases, those who don't thrive aren't around to be counted.

In 1996, I made a pilgrimage to Chartres Cathedral, in France, as Catholics have done since the Middle Ages. I was one of 16,000 people from around the world to take part in the annual Pentecost pilgrimage sponsored by the Priestly Fraternity of St. Peter, an order of priests established by John Paul II to serve Catholics who prefer the traditional Latin Mass. Since the early 1980s, young Catholics have made the arduous seventy-mile trek to show their love for Holy Mother Church.

They begin in front of Notre Dame Cathedral in Paris. At night, they sleep in the fields. The first day, they walk about twenty-five miles. The second day, more than thirty. The third day, fifteen. When the distant spires of Chartres Cathedral became visible, they fall to their knees and sing "Salve Regina," as pilgrims to Charters have done for centuries.

The three days of walking seemed like a metaphor for my own spiritual journey, filled with moments of joy and peace, suffering and pain.

At the end of the march, after we fill the vast interior of Chartres Cathedral, a message is read from the Holy Father, imparting his Apostolic blessing upon the young pilgrims. Then, a three-hour Solemn High Mass begins. It is an unforgettable experience.

Each year, as I kneel in the cathedral, listening to the sublime Gregorian chant, witnessing a form of Mass almost identical to that offered during the time of the Black Plague, the veil between Heaven and earth feels very thin.

Like my immigrant grandmother, who spent her life pining away for the land of her birth, the solemn High Mass at Chartres Cathedral infused me with an enduring desire for home—the eternal life that awaits.

A Diplomat's Journey
Nicholas Burns

I AM typical of many Catholics who grew up in middle-class America after the Second World War. My grandparents left western Ireland for Boston during the great, second wave of immigration to the United States in the last decade of the nineteenth century. Like millions of others, they arrived with little education and no money. But they did have hope for a better life, and they brought with them their religious faith, which they passed down to their children and grandchildren. Like most of my Catholic friends, my brothers and sister and I were raised strictly, to observe the Church's teachings and to attend Mass without fail on Sundays and Holy Days of Obligation.

I don't think I ever doubted my faith from the time I made my First Communion until my graduation from college. My early religious education was entirely positive; I had wonderful role models in the Church. Our parish priest, Father Turner, taught my brothers and me Latin when we were altar boys and cheered on our CYO basketball team. Two of my cousins were nuns, and a distant relative had worked with Sister Elizabeth Seton, caring for Union soldiers during the Civil War. As a teenager, one of my closest friends was a young Stigmatine priest with whom I played golf and baseball. And when I attended Boston College, several of my favorite professors were Jesuits. I admired their lives of simplicity. They donated their salaries to the college, they taught us with great dedication and spirit, and they spent enormous amounts of time with us outside of the classroom.

Maybe that is why I find it difficult to identify with some of the lapsed Catholics of my own generation who are fond of saying that the Church somehow "ruined their youth." In the politically correct 1990s, some yuppies conveniently blame the "Catholic guilt" syndrome for their problems. They see the church as too strict in its adherence to the ancient traditions and overly harsh in demanding that its followers acknowledge their imperfections. Many people I know left the Church to escape its restrictions and to live without the burden of expectations that come with it. I left for a time, too, but have now returned to the Church as I seek to have my three daughters raised in the way I was, and as many generations of my family experienced it before us.

From an early age, I was a part of the life of my church—St. James in Wellesley, Massachusetts. I remember the pride and excitement of making my First Communion on a beautiful May Day and the feeling of purity that enveloped my seven-year-old friends and me as we sat in white suits and dresses. I also recall feeling utterly bewildered as I battled to learn the Latin verses that altar boys must know before they can serve their first Mass. Father Turner worked patiently with us after school to help us memorize long Latin passages. After many months and many tears, I passed my Latin test and was allowed to join my older brothers on the altar. When Vatican II did away with the Latin Mass just one year later, I joined the traditionalists who objected, not because I was attached to its beauty and mystery, but because it had taken me an enormous effort to learn the Latin, and now we had to learn the English!

We were proud altar boys as we performed our sacred duties in the hushed atmosphere of a packed church. Great care was given as we put on the surplice and gown, the priests inspecting us for the final adjustments that must be made before we marched to the altar. It felt much like being on stage; all eyes in the congregation followed our every move, or so we imagined. We had important duties to perform: ringing the bells at crucial moments of the Mass, assisting the priest as he delivered the Host to our friends and neighbors. I sometimes wondered why the Church dared to entrust such crucial tasks to young boys, and not to adults.

It was as an altar boy that I first learned of the sometimes bitter and cruel world beyond our comfortable suburban town. In 1967, when I was eleven, I served at two funeral Masses for young men from my parish who had died in Vietnam. I can recall vividly a young, dark-haired widow wearing a black veil. She sat in the front pew, a picture of utter devastation. The shattered look on her face expressed a sense of grief I had not encountered until that day. As Father Turner drove me home, I was in shock that violence and death could strike so close to our lives. A few years earlier, on a cold and clear Friday afternoon, the principal had sent us home early from school without explaining why. As I walked across the baseball field, one of the school's pranksters yelled that someone had shot President Kennedy. I didn't really believe him. I ran home and found my mother and sister staring at the television, in tears. President Kennedy had indeed been shot, and Walter Cronkite was announcing his death in Dallas. I was too young, at age seven, to understand with clarity the impact of his death on our country or to appreciate the collective grief in our parish. But I knew there had been a great tragedy. The next morning we went to a packed church where a Mass was said for him. He was one of us, an Irish Catholic from Boston, and church seemed to be the right place to be as we said good-bye to him.

Beyond these special memories of great and significant events in my young life was the daily order and ceremony of the Catholic way, which was such a familiar part of my family's routine. Like most Catholics of that time, we adhered to a strict regime: no meat on Friday, church every Sunday, no eating one hour before taking Communion. I remember my mother requiring my brothers and me to stay quietly inside our bedrooms every Good Friday from noon until 3 P.M. while the neighborhood kids played basketball outside. I can see now the value of that kind of spiritual reflection, although I certainly did not appreciate it at the time. My parents insisted on observing all of the rules and conventions of Catholic life without exception. I did not rebel against this regime when I was young, and it does not give me any pause to remember it.

In fact, I can see now that the discipline of my parents' faith sent a strong message to us that religion should be at the center of our concerns.

What stood out in my young mind was a feeling of absolute clarity about who we were and where we had come from. We were Catholics. My father's mother reminded us from time to time that Cromwell had stabled his horses in the Catholic church back where she came from in Galway. My mother's family business was clerical garments for priests and uniforms for the Catholic schools that dotted eastern Massachusetts in those years. It seemed to me as a kid that all Catholics observed without questioning and without bending the rules. I remember feeling that Catholics were different from the Protestants I knew, many of whom went to church irregularly or when they felt like it. We were jealous of Protestant kids who could play baseball on Sunday instead of getting dressed in a suit and tie and spending the morning at church. Most of all, church was a time to be together. I admired my father very much and liked the chance to be in his company. He and my mother set stiff rules, but they were loving and they cared about us more than we may ever know. The picture of our family that stands forth most clearly many decades later is our sitting, all in a row, in church.

My mother set the religious tone in our house. She had attended Catholic boarding school and seemed to know everything there was to know about the Church. She could recite the names of obscure saints. She never failed to remember the Holy Days of Obligation. She had a strong and positive belief in the Church. She also didn't fool around when it came to imparting all of that knowledge to her children. When I was seventeen, I went to a Congregational service one spring morning with a girlfriend and her family. Upon returning home, I threw off my jacket and began to loosen my tie. My mother, who had not been enthusiastic in the first place about my attending a Protestant service, asked which Mass I planned to attend. I sensed this was not merely an idle question, and so decided to play it cool. I said calmly that I had already gone to church and wanted to meet the guys for a game of basketball. She stood up, pointed her finger at me, and said I knew very well that the Protestant service hadn't "counted" and that I must attend Mass. We argued. I remember demanding why a Protestant service did not equal a Catholic Mass. But my mother was then, and still is, a determined defender of the faith. She won the argument. I trudged off, angry that I had to sit in church for another hour on a beautiful day. I pledged then and there that I wouldn't demand such discipline from my own children. Looking back on that episode now, I feel no anger nor resentment. While it is true that I might not ask the same of my own kids, I continue to admire my mother's strong discipline and faith.

Our religious roots were also a big part of my family's heritage. My father and mother came from very large families. Together, my siblings and I had over sixty first cousins. Since we all lived in eastern Massachusetts, we would assemble regularly at family events that often revolved around the Church—a wedding or funeral or wake. The central story that I remember hearing on those occasions was the extraordinary drama of my mother's upbringing. The eleventh of twelve children, she lost her parents when she was four. Rather than split up the family, my mother's older brothers and sisters banded together to bring up the younger ones. Some of the older ones became the breadwinners by quitting college to go to work. Others delayed marriage for years to be at home. All of them pitched in to create a loving family home for the younger ones from 1925 until the end of the Second World War! I never tire of listening to that story. Politicians talk incessantly now about family values. I don't know a better example of what that really means than my mother's family. Their extraordinary bond and unity gave me another lesson from my mother that she believes fervently—family loyalty is important above all else.

Many years later, when my mother had just delivered my oldest brother, Stan, she contracted a crippling case of polio that nearly killed her. Locked in an iron lung and told that she might not live, much less walk, she prayed. My father and aunts and uncles went into action. They organized special Masses and prayed to the Infant of Prague. After many weeks, her condition improved against heavy odds. She recovered sufficiently to learn to walk again, although she would never again enjoy the normal activities of a young adult—running, swimming, or riding a bike. My mother believes she survived because of her faith and prayers, the support of my father and of her amazing family. She lived to have my two other older brothers and me. When I heard that story as a young boy, I marveled that the three of us might never have been born had it not been for my mother's strong and active faith. And to this day, I have the greatest admiration for her courage and eternal optimism that anything is possible if you believe in God and in yourself.

Like most people, my understanding of religion took a quantum leap in my teenage years. We learned about the great moral foundations of Catholicism from our eighth grade religion teacher, Tony Penna, a Stigmatine priest. He taught us a critical lesson that I have never forgotten: "the condition of man is fallen." Tony told us this was one of the central tenets of Christianity. We are imperfect. But we must strive, he said, to overcome it by seeking moral improvement, by being a better person, someone who made a positive difference in the world. This message had real significance for me amid the moral confusion of the Vietnam War and the sordid corruption of Watergate. Tony asked us to write our epitaphs and to think about how we wanted to be remembered when we died. Until that day, I don't believe I ever thought I would really die one day. Tony was a terrific teacher. He made religion relevant to my friends and me by linking it to what was changing inside us and in the wider world. Tony hasn't lost his touch; he ministers now as chaplain to a new generation of students at Boston College.

As I began high school, Tony influenced me to seek the "man" who would emerge one day from my teenage frame. He loved history and introduced me to the Bible as one of its great books. Jesus became for me that year one of history's most compelling figures. I became a lector at church and joined a Bible study group at my high school that met before classes began. I remember being impressed that my Protestant friends knew the Bible inside and out, and I felt uncomfortable that I did not. We Catholics had never been encouraged actually to read the Bible and to learn by heart the many biblical epics that my Protestant friends could recite at will. As I read through the New Testament for the first time, I was surprised at how much I liked it. Here was a person,

Jesus Christ, who prized moral truths above all others, who preached peace and forgiveness, who believed that rich people would never enter the gates of Heaven. That message was tailor-made for a young teenager like me who was trying to sort out the confusing moral complexity of the early 1970s.

I thought Jesus had something to teach us about America's political struggles. Teenagers tend to read life in black and white, and Jesus seemed to me to be one of the few people I had ever read about who had not compromised his values. I also saw Jesus as a pure and idealistic figure who contrasted starkly with our own national leaders of the late 1960s and 1970s. From then on, I gravitated toward people who shared Jesus' mission of peace and whom I believed were doing the Lord's work in our time. I was captivated by César Chávez, who struggled for the rights of migrant workers. I read everything I could find about the late Robert Kennedy. But it was Martin Luther King, Jr., who became my great idol. I listened over and over again to his "I Have a Dream" speech in my room until I had it memorized. His blend of religion and politics made him in my eyes, then and now, the greatest American of his time and the person who best embodied Christ's message on earth. This was a significant time for my life in the Church. While the ritual of the Mass and the traditions had attracted me when I was a very young boy, it was the teachings of Jesus that held me as a teenager—nonviolence, dedication to peace, forgiveness, redemption.

I thus became in high school and college a more complete Catholic. I respected all of the outer obligations of the Church in attending Mass and going to confession, but I felt then, as now, that it was more important to try to apply Jesus' teaching to my own life. Religion helped to direct me and shaped my core beliefs about what the world should be like. I even considered the priesthood, only to admit finally that I liked girls too much to live a celibate life! As I look back, there isn't any question that my Catholic faith was the single most important element in my education and life until my graduation from Boston College. When I left home and Boston for Washington, DC, and graduate school, I did not know that I was to begin a long process of losing the faith I have only recently regained. As I rented my first apartment and lived apart from my parents and friends for the first time, I certainly did not expect to cease being Catholic. I had no intellectual or emotional urge to rebel in any way against the Church. But I slowly drifted away from it for many years.

How could a devout young man lose his faith so easily? I can cite several experiences that led me to doubt the divinity of Christ and the relevance of Catholicism to my life. I spent a good part of my twenties in France, Mauritania, Egypt, and Israel. For the first time in my life, I saw horrible poverty in African refugee camps and in the cities of the Middle East. The bitter misery and desperation of so much of the Third World did not square with my previous and rather naive belief that there was a God who protected us all on earth. I wondered why a benevolent God would permit so many of the earth's inhabitants to live in such cruel conditions.

I studied Islam and Judaism as I served as an American diplomat in Egypt and then Israel. As I learned Arabic, I read parts of the Koran and attended both Muslim and Jewish feasts and religious observances. In discovering the two other monotheistic religions, I began to compare their strengths with Christianity. The Muslims seemed to have few of the social problems that afflicted the West. They were God-fearing, family-oriented, and peaceful. Cairo was a city of fifteen million people and a homicide rate the equal of a much smaller city in our own country. In Jerusalem, I felt the great internal strength and unity of the Jewish people. I now had a basis to compare my own religion against the others that shared with us Abraham, Isaac, Rebecca, and Sarah, and most of the biblical epics. Gradually, I began to conclude that adherence to one particular faith might be less important than pursuing the central religious truths and values that run through the Torah, Koran, and New Testament. I became less confident of my prior and absolute Catholic faith, and more inclined to see the Bible as history rather than as a divine story.

Living in Jerusalem, ironically, made me grow even more distant from my religious roots. I had extraordinary opportunities to observe the different religions in the Old City. What is most striking about the Christian community in Jerusalem is its remarkable disunity. The six Christian sects that together administer and pray in the Church of the Holy Sepulchre, built by Constantine's mother, Helena, on the spot of the Crucifixion, compete for control and influence. Jealousy and competition are the rule among these sects. Some are not on speaking terms with others. The Ethiopian Copts occupied the rooftop perch of the Egyptian Copts over twenty years ago and have refused to give it back. During one pre-Easter cleaning of the church while I lived in Jerusalem, Greek and Armenian Orthodox priests actually had a fistfight over the right to wash a certain wall that lay on the cusp of their respective domains within the church. Because the six sects distrust each other so completely, only the Muslim Dajani family of Jerusalem has been entrusted with the keys to the church for several hundred years. Witnessing the daily battles among these Christian holy men was often comical, but also a bit dispiriting. It weakened my belief in the special mission of the Christian faith, much less the Catholic Church.

But the most convincing experience that chipped away at my prior, certain belief in Jesus as a divine figure was the studies my wife and I made of Jesus' past in the Holy Land. We spent much of our free time visiting Crusader castles, old churches, and biblical sites. We hiked from time to time with an Irish priest, Father Gerry O'Connor, who was and still is a noted biblical archaeologist. For the very first time, I became aware of the deep controversies surrounding the New Testament accounts of the life of Jesus. I learned that nearly all modern scholars place Jesus' birth in or near his native Nazareth in the Galilee, and not in Bethlehem in far-away Judea. The Gospel writers had him born there, we learned, to link him to the royal line of David. The Gospel writers never knew Jesus and wrote, in some cases, decades after he had died. Even the modern route that marks Christ's path to his crucifixion—the Via Dolorosa—is now believed to be in the wrong part of Jerusalem. Comparing the major stories of the four Gospels was a revelation because it showed that they do not agree on some of the most basic aspects of His life story. And the recently revealed Gnostic Gospels portray a Jesus less divine than human. I began to wonder about some of the pillars of the Christian story I had learned as a child. How did we really know that these stories about Jesus were true?

In Jerusalem, I came slowly to see Jesus as more of a historical than a divine figure. The clashing images produced from visits to different Christian churches—Lutheran, Episcopal, Catholic, Syrian Orthodox— led me to believe that the life of Jesus was more of a mystery than a certainty that one could build a faith on. Catholicism became for me in these years a version of history among many competitors. I still adhered to Catholic and Christian values. But I seriously doubted that the many odd twists of historical fate that kept Christianity alive in the early centuries and that led Emperor Constantine to convert the Byzantine Empire to Christianity in the fourth century, were much more than coincidences. Without Constantine's conversion, there was no reason to think that Christianity would have survived the many empires that rolled over one another in succeeding centuries. What some believed to be God's plan, I concluded, was mere happenstance. Without Constantine, we might not even remember Jesus' name in the twentieth century.

Despite these theological uncertainties and wanderings, our Jerusalem experience was spiritually uplifting in many ways. We walked one day along the old Roman road carved into the Judean hills, descending from Jerusalem down to Jericho in the Jordan valley. Father Jerry told us that Jesus had taken it on his way up to the Holy City from the Galilee. To think that Jesus and Roman legions had actually walked on those stones two millennia before was a powerful idea indeed! On other days, we drove up to the surpassingly beautiful hills above the Sea of Galilee to visit Capernaum, where He lived and worked before His years in Jerusalem. That Jesus had lived in that region was indisputable. But who, exactly, was He? God or man?

Jerusalem is a city built on the faith of true believers, not doubters like me. A random walk in the twisting alleys of the old city's Muslim and Christian quarters revealed a certainty and depth of faith that I could not disregard. Our years in Jerusalem left a profound spiritual mark on my wife and me. I will never forget the memories of Crusader crosses etched in the stone walls of an old church; the stark beauty of Gethsemane at dusk; brilliant blue rays of light on the pink Jerusalem stone; my daughter Elizabeth's baptism in Bethlehem as church bells rang and as we laid her on the very spot where Jesus was said to have been born. While my years in Jerusalem rattled my Catholic faith, instilling in me deep doubts about the basic story of the New Testament, they were also the most meaningful of my life. They convinced me that however many doubts we may have, the intellectual and spiritual pursuit of these questions makes our lives richer.

After my spiritual wanderings in Jerusalem, I never expected to return to the Church completely. But a few years later, I drifted back to what I had slowly drifted away from ten years earlier. As our oldest daughter, Sarah, went off to grammar school, we decided that she had to be given some religious structure. So we went back to the place we knew, our local Catholic church. At first, we took Sarah to religion class but did not attend Mass regularly ourselves. She objected that if she had to go to religion class, we should have to go to church, too. And she was right.

Thus began our return to the Catholic Church. We began to attend Mass regularly as a family. I found that I enjoyed the familiarity of our parish and the beautiful choral music on Sunday mornings. And I appreciated the link to my childhood and my parent's home. As the years went by and our two other daughters, Elizabeth and Caroline, entered religious education, I became convinced that we had made the right decision. My return to the Church did not resolve some of my doubts about the whole story of Jesus and of the Catholic faith, a few of which remain. But I found that it was important for me to tend to my spiritual needs even if my religious faith was imperfect. Resuming a religious life made me a more whole and happy person.

I think now that I came back to the Catholic Church because it was what I knew best. It was my parent's religion, and their parents', too. I have not yet resolved in my mind all of the theological questions that developed during my years in Jerusalem. Unlike many Catholics, I am troubled intellectually by papal infallibility. I am opposed to the Church's position on contraception. And I certainly wish the Archdiocese of Arlington, Virginia, would join the rest of Catholic America to permit my daughters to serve on the altar. I also think members of the clergy ought to be permitted to marry; it would bring them closer to average Catholics in a confusing age and would serve the utilitarian purpose of expanding the ranks of a rapidly depleted corps.

I am still far from being a complete Catholic, and I may never enjoy the orthodox beliefs held by millions of churchgoers. But I do find personal and spiritual satisfaction in the Sunday Mass at our parish church, in listening to lovely choral music, and in reading Scripture. I retain enormous respect for the clergy. In fact, I can't think of a more useful and worthy profession than what nuns and priests do for our communities and for all of us individually. Recently, I spent time with my cousins Maureen and Cathleen, sisters who entered religious life as nuns more than forty years ago. I marveled at their goodness, their concern for the poorest in our societies, and their vitality. When I think of all they and others, like Tony Penna and the late Cardinal Bernadin, have contributed to our society, I am convinced that our world would be vastly poorer without them.

I have returned to the Church because I find in it an institution, rituals, beliefs, and people that give me hope for the future. The Catholic Church is the only truly universal and global Christian faith. I have visited Catholic churches not only throughout the United States but also in Hanoi, Paris, São Paulo, Dakar, and many other cities of the world. I have seen how important the Church was in sustaining the hopes of the people of eastern Europe under communism, and how its rapid growth in Africa and Latin America represents a new age for its global mission. The Catholic Church links us more directly to our past—to the Holy Land of Jesus' time, to the simplicity and courage of the early Christians in the Judean desert, to the Crusaders, to the Jesuits who founded many of our great universities—than any other institution. It links us to a great tradition and shows us the way forward to live a good and moral life in our own time.

Most of all, I find Catholicism to be a demanding religion that asks much of its believers. In essence, it challenges us to be good. Catholics understand a central truth: that our own lives are not first about ourselves. We can find true meaning in our lives only if we extend ourselves toward others. This stark but powerful core of the Catholic faith stands in absolute and welcome contrast to many of the popular, evangelical churches that place the individual squarely at the center of their faith, some even promising a "personal relationship" with Jesus Christ. This misses the fundamentally important point about religion that the Catholic Church understands—religion must challenge us to live lives that extend beyond a narrow material and spiritual focus on ourselves. We can find greater meaning in living beyond ourselves as we negotiate our way in a complex age.

I will continue to attend Mass on Sunday and I will remain part of the Church. My daughters will learn the Catholic faith as I did, and as generations in our family did before us. But I expect many Catholics who have had the patience and fortitude to read this far may look askance at my casual and incomplete faith. I apologize if my interpretation of the Church is too flexible for more traditional Catholics. But my faith is a personal journey, one that has revealed to me inner truths and strengths. These, in turn, have made my life not only more meaningful but also understandable. But I am a traveler and, yes, I still have a way to go on my journey.

Sacraments

Andre Dubus

A SACRAMENT is physical, and within it is God's love; as a sandwich is physical, and nutritious and pleasurable, and within it is love, if someone makes it for you and gives it to you with love; even harried or tired or impatient love, but with love's direction and concern, love's again and again wavering and distorted focus on goodness; then God's love, too, is in the sandwich. A sacrament is an outward sign of God's love, they taught me when I was a boy, and in the Catholic Church there are seven. But, no, I say, for the Church is catholic, the world is catholic, and there are seven times seventy sacraments, to infinity. Today I sit at my desk in June in Massachusetts; a breeze from the southeast comes through the window behind me, touches me, and goes through the open glass door in front of me. The sky is blue, and cumulus clouds are motionless above green trees lit brightly by the sun shining in dry air. In humid air the leaves would be darker, but now they are bright, and you can see lighted space between them, so that each leaf is distinct; and each leaf is receiving sacraments of light and air and water and earth. So am I, in the breeze on my skin, the air I breathe, the sky and earth and trees I look at.

Sacraments are myriad. It is good to be baptized, to confess and be reconciled, to receive Communion, to be confirmed, to be ordained a priest, to marry, or to be anointed with the sacrament of healing. But it is limiting to believe that sacraments occur only in churches, or when someone comes to us in a hospital or at home and anoints our brows and eyes and ears, our noses and lips, hearts and hands and feet.

I try to receive Communion daily, although I never go to Mass day after day after day, because I cannot sleep when I want to; I take pills, and if the pills allow me to sleep before midnight, I usually can wake up at 7:30 and do what I must to get to Mass. But I know that when I do not go to Mass, I am still receiving Communion, because I desire it; and because God is in me, as He is in the light, the earth, the leaf. I only have to lie on my bed, waking after Mass has already ended, and I am receiving sacraments with each breath, as I did while I slept; with each movement of my body as I exercise my lower abdomen to ease the pain in my back caused by sitting for fifteen hours: in my wheelchair, in my car, and on my couch, before going to bed for the night; receiving sacraments as I perform crunches and leg lifts, then dress and make the bed while sitting on it. Being at Mass and receiving Communion give me joy and strength. Receiving Communion of desire on my bed does not, for I cannot feel joy with my brain alone. I need sacraments I can receive through my senses. I need God manifested as Christ, Who ate and drank and shat and suffered; and laughed. So I can dance with Him as the leaf dances in the breeze under the sun.

Not remembering that we are always receiving sacraments is an isolation the leaves do not have to endure: they receive and give, and they are green. Not remembering this is an isolation only the human soul has to endure. But the isolation of a human soul may be the cause of not remembering this. Between isolation and harmony, there is not always a vast distance. Sometimes it is a distance that can be traversed in a moment, by choosing to focus on the essence of what is occurring rather than on its exterior: its difficulty or beauty, its demands or joy, peace or grief, passion or humor. This is not a matter of courage or discipline or will; it is a receptive condition.

I am divorced. On Tuesdays I drive to my daughters' school, where they are in the seventh and second grades. I have them with me on other days, and some nights, but Tuesday is the school day. They do not like the food at their school, and the school does not allow them to bring food, so after classes they are hungry, and I bring them sandwiches, potato chips, Cokes, Reese's peanut butter cups. My kitchen is very small; if one person is standing in it, I cannot make a 360 degree turn. When I roll into the kitchen to make the girls' sandwiches, if I remember to stop at the first set of drawers on my right, just inside the door, and get plastic bags and write *Cadence* on one and *Madeleine* on the other; then stop at the second set of drawers and get three knives for spreading mayonnaise and mustard and cutting the sandwiches in half; then turn sharply left and reach over the sink for the cutting board leaning upright behind the faucet; then put all these things on the counter to my right, beside the refrigerator, and bend forward and reach into the refrigerator for the meat and cheese and mustard and mayonnaise, and reach up into the freezer for bread, I can do all of this with one turn of the chair. This is a First World problem; I ought to be only grateful. Sometimes I remember this, and then I believe that most biped fathers in the world would exchange their legs for my wheelchair and house and food, my medical insurance and my daughters' school.

Making sandwiches while sitting in a wheelchair is not physically difficult. But it can be a spiritual trial; the chair always makes me remember my legs, and how I lived with them. I am beginning my ninth year as a cripple, and have learned to try to move slowly, with concentration, with precision, with peace. Forgetting plastic bags in the first set of drawers and having to turn the chair around to get them is nothing. The memory of having legs that held me upright at this counter, and the image of simply turning from the counter and stepping to the drawer, are the demons I must keep at bay, or I will rage and grieve because of space, and time, and this wheeled thing that has replaced my legs. So I must try to know the spiritual essence of what I am doing.

On Tuesdays when I make lunches for my girls, I focus on this: the sandwiches are sacraments. Not the miracle of transubstantiation, but certainly parallel with it, moving in the same direction. If I could give my children my body to eat, again and again without losing it, my body like the loaves and fishes going endlessly into mouths and stomachs, I would do it. And each motion is a sacrament, this holding of plastic bags, of knives, of bread, of cutting board, this pushing of the chair, this spreading of mustard on bread, this trimming of liverwurst, of ham. All sacraments, as putting the lunches into a zippered book bag is, and going down my six ramps to my car is. I drive on the highway to the girls' town, to their school, and this is not simply a transition; it is my love moving by car from a place where my girls are not to a place where they are; even if I do not feel or acknowledge it, this is a sacrament. If I remember it, then I feel it, too. Feeling it does not always mean that I am a happy man driving in traffic; it simply means that I know what I am doing in the presence of God.

If I were much wiser, and much more patient, and had much greater concentration, I could sit in silence in my chair, look out my windows at a green tree and the blue sky, and know that breathing is a gift; that a breath is sufficient for the moment; and that breathing air is breathing God.

You can receive and give sacraments with a telephone. In a very lonely time, two years after my crippling, I met a woman with dark skin and black hair and wit and verbal grace. We were together for an autumn afternoon, and I liked her, and that evening I sat on my couch with her, and held and kissed her. Then she drove three and a half hours north to her home in Vermont. I had a car then, with hand controls, but I had not learned to drive it; my soul was not ready for the tension and fear. I did not see the woman again until five weeks later. I courted her by telephone, daily or nightly or both. She agreed to visit me and my family at Thanksgiving. On Halloween I had a heart attack, and courted her via the bedside telephone in the hospital. Once after midnight, while I was talking to her, a nurse came into the room, smiled at me, and took the clipboard from the foot of the bed and wrote what she saw. Next morning, in my wheelchair, I read: *Twelve-fifteen. Patient alert and cheerful, talking on the phone.*

In the five weeks since that sunlit October day when I first saw her, I knew this woman through her voice. Then on Thanksgiving she drove to a motel in the town where I live, and in early afternoon came to my house for dinner with my family: my first wife and our four grown children, and one daughter's boyfriend and one son's girlfriend, and my two young daughters. That night, after the family left, she stayed and made love to my crippled body, which did not feel crippled with her, save for some pain in my leg. Making love can be a sacrament, if our souls are as naked as our bodies, if our souls are in harmony with our bodies, and through our bodies are embracing one another in love and fear and trembling, knowing that this act could be the beginning of a third human being, if we are a man and a woman; knowing that the roots and trunk of death are within each of us, and that one of its branches may block or rupture an artery as we kiss. Surely this is a sacrament, as it may not be if we are with someone whose arms we would not want holding us as, suddenly, in passion, we died; someone whose death in our arms would pierce us not with grief but regret, fear, shame; someone who would not want to give life to that third person who is always present in lovemaking between fertile men and women. On the day after Thanksgiving she checked out of the motel and stayed with me until Monday and I loved her; then she went home.

She came to me on other weekends, four to six weeks apart, and we loved each other daily by telephone. That winter she moved to New York City. I still did not drive, and her apartment was not a place I could enter and be in with my wheelchair; it was very small, and so was the shared bathroom down the hall. I could not fly to her, because my right knee does not bend, so I have to sit on the first seat of an airplane, and that means a first-class ticket. Trains are inaccessible horrors for someone in a wheelchair: the aisles are too narrow. A weekend in New York, if I flew there and stayed in a hotel, would have cost over a thousand dollars, before we bought a drink or a meal. So she flew to Boston or rode on the train, and a friend drove me to meet her. I was a virtual shut-in who was in love. One day a week my oldest son drove me to horseback riding lessons; in the barn he pushed me up a ramp to a platform level with the horse's back, and I mounted and rode, guarded from falling by my son and volunteer women who walked and jogged beside me. A driver of a wheelchair van came for me two mornings a week and took me to Mass and left, then came back and took me to physical therapy, then came back and took me home, where I lay on my bed and held the telephone and talked to the woman, sometimes more than once a day. Via the telephone she gave me sacraments I needed during that fall and winter when my body seemed to be my enemy. We were lovers for a year, and then we were not, and now our love remains and sharing our flesh is no longer essential.

On Christmas Eve, in that year when we were lovers, I was very sad and I called her. The Christmas tree was in the living room, tall and full, and from the kitchen doorway, where I held the telephone, I could see in the front windows the reflection of the tree and its ornaments and lights. My young daughters' stockings were hanging at the windows, but my girls were at their mother's house, and would wake there Christmas morning, and would come to me in the afternoon. I was a crippled father in an empty house. In my life I have been too much a father in an empty house; and since the vocation of fatherhood includes living with the mother, this is the deepest shame of my life, and its abiding regret. I sat in my chair and spoke into the phone of the pain in my soul, and she listened, and talked to me, and finally said, "You're supposed to be happy. It's your hero's birthday."

I laughed with my whole heart at the humor of it, at the truth of it, and now my pain was bearable, my sorrow not a well but drops of water drying in the winter room.

In March I decided one day that I must stop talking to her on the telephone because, while I did, I was amused, interested, passionate, joyful; then I said good-bye and I was a cripple who had been sitting in his wheelchair or lying on his bed, holding plastic to his ear. I told her that if I were whole, and could hang up the telephone and walk out of the house, I would not stop calling her; but I knew that living this way, receiving her by telephone, was not a good crippled way to live; and I knew there was a better crippled way to live, but I did not know yet what it was. She understood; she always does, whether or not she agrees.

I did not call her for days, and on the first day of April I woke crying, and on the second; and on the third I could not stop, and I phoned my doctor's receptionist and, still crying, I told her to tell him to give me a shot or put me away someplace, because I could not bear it anymore. At noon he brought me spinach pie and chili dogs, and I said, "That's cholesterol."

"Depression will kill you sooner," he said, and I ate with him and still did not understand that the food and his presence at my table were sacraments. He made an appointment for me with a psychologist, and two days later my youngest son drove me to the office of this paternal and compassionate man, who said, "This is not depression; it's sorrow, and it'll always be with you, because you can't replace your legs."

As my son drove me home, I told him that I wanted a swimming pool, but I did not want to be a man who needed a swimming pool to be happy. He said, "You're not asking the world for a swimming pool. You're asking it for motion."

At home I called a paraplegic friend and asked him to teach me to drive my car, and two days later he did. I phoned a swimming pool contractor, a durably merry and kind man, and his cost for building me a forty-by-fifteen-by-three-foot lap pool was so generous that I attribute it to gimpathy. Sacraments abounded. I paid for some, and the money itself was sacramental: my being alive to receive it and give it for good work. On that first day, after calling the paraplegic and the contractor, I called the woman, and I continued to call her, and to receive that grace.

On the last day of my father's life, he was thirsty and he asked me to crush some ice and feed it to him. I was a Marine captain, stationed at Whidbey Island, Washington, and I had flown home to Lake Charles, Louisiana, to be with my father before he died, and when he died, and to bury him. I did not know then that the night flight from Seattle was more than a movement in air from my wife and four young children to my dying father, that every moment of it, even as I slept, was a sacrament I gave my father; and they were sacraments he gave me, his siring and his love drawing me to him through the night; and sacraments between my mother and two sisters and me, and all the relatives and friends I was flying home to; and my wife and children and me, for their love was with me on the plane and I loved them and I would return to them after burying my father; and from Time itself, God's mystery we often do not clearly see—there was time now to be with my father. Sacraments came from those who flew the plane and worked aboard it and maintained it and controlled its comings and goings; and from the major who gave me emergency leave, and the gunnery sergeant who did my work while I was gone. I did not know any of this. I thought I was a son flying alone.

My father's cancer had begun in his colon, and on the Saturday before the early Sunday morning when he died, it was consuming him, and he was thin and weak on his bed, and he asked for ice. In the kitchen I emptied a tray of ice cubes onto a dish towel and held its four corners and twisted it, then held it on the counter and with a rolling pin pounded the ice till it was crushed. This is how my father crushed ice, and how my sisters and I, when we were children, crushed it and put it in a glass and spooned sugar on it, to eat on a hot summer day. I put my father's ice into a tall glass and brought it with an iced tea spoon to the bedroom and fed him the ice, one small piece at a time, until his mouth and throat were no longer dry.

As a boy I was shy with my father. Perhaps he was shy with me, too. When we were alone in a car, we were mostly silent. On some nights, when a championship boxing match was broadcast on the radio, we listened to it in the living room. He took me to professional wrestling matches because I wanted to go, and he told me they were fake, and I refused to believe it. He took me to minor league baseball games. While we listened to boxing matches and watched wrestling and baseball, we talked about what we were hearing and seeing. He took me fishing and dove-hunting with his friends, before I was old enough to shoot; but I could fish from the bank of a bayou, and he taught me to shoot my air rifle—taught me so well that, years later, my instructors in the Marine Corps simply polished his work. When I was still too young to use a shotgun, he learned to play golf and stopped fishing and hunting, and on Saturdays and Sundays he brought me to the golf course as his caddy. I did not want to caddy, but I had no choice, and I earned a dollar and a quarter; all my adult life I have been grateful that I watched him and listened to him with his friends, and talked with him about his game. My shyness with him was a burden I did not like carrying, and I could not put down. Then I was twenty-one and a husband and a Marine, and on the morning my pregnant wife and I left home, to drive to the Officers' Basic School in Quantico, Virginia, my father and I tightly embraced, then looked in one another's damp eyes. I wanted to say *I love you*, but I could not.

I wanted to say it to him before he died. In the afternoon of his last day, he wanted bourbon and water. A lot of ice, he told me, and a lot of water. I made drinks for my sister and me, too, and brought his in a tall glass. I did not hold it for him. I do not remember whether he lifted it to his mouth, or rested it on his chest and drank from an angled hospital straw. My sister and I sat in chairs at the foot of the bed, my mother talked with relatives and friends in the living room and brought them in to speak to my father, and I told him stories of my year of sea duty on an aircraft carrier, of my work at Whidbey Island. Once he asked me to light him a cigarette. I went to his bedside table, put one of his cigarettes between my lips, lit his Zippo, then looked beyond the cigarette and flame at my father's eyes: they were watching me. All my life at home before I left for the Marine Corps, I had felt him watching me, a glance during a meal or in the living room or on the lawn, had felt he was trying to see my soul, to see if I were strong and honorable, to see if I could go out into the world, and live in it without him. His eyes watching me light his cigarette were tender, and they were saying good-bye.

That night my father's sisters slept in the beds that had been mine and my sister's, and she and I went to the house of a neighbor across the street. We did not sleep. We sat in the kitchen and drank and cried, and I told her that tomorrow I would tell my father I loved him. Before dawn he died, and for years I regretted not saying the words. But I did not understand love then, and the sacraments that make it tactile. I had not lived enough and lost enough to enable me to know the holiness of working with meat and mustard and bread; of moving on wheels or wings or by foot from one place to another; of holding a telephone and speaking into it and listening to a voice; of pounding ice with wood and spooning the shards onto a dry tongue; of lighting a cigarette and placing it between the fingers of a man trying to enjoy tobacco and bourbon and his family as he dies.

The Rock-Solid Nuns

Kathleen Kennedy Townsend

"WHY AM I still a Catholic?" is the most un-Catholic of questions. I am a Catholic, period. I could no more change my religion than my history. Being Catholic is less a question of reason and choice and more of birth, identity, and culture—like being an American or a Democrat.

I grew up Catholic at the most marvelous moment in our country's history for Catholics. The old stereotype of Catholics as ignorant and superstitious had all but evaporated, and there was little, if any, discrimination. My uncle John F. Kennedy became the first Catholic President, and Pope John XXIII was reaching out to a welcoming world.

Religion was very alive to us. My mother went to daily Mass, and during the summer, when most children played ball or at least slept in, my mother took us to eight o'clock Mass. My parents insisted that we say morning prayers, and prayers before and after every meal. Every night, our family gathered for evening prayers, asking that John Kennedy would be the best President ever and our daddy the best Attorney General. We also prayed the rosary and listened to the stories of the saints or a chapter from the Bible—always the Old Testament.

When I told my grandmother Rose Kennedy that my father, her son, read from the Bible, she was surprised. "Catholics don't read the Bible," she told me. She was right, of course. The tradition of having priests read and interpret had grown deep roots over the centuries. I don't know where my father developed his love for the Old Testament, but he did, and he imparted it to his children. In fact, he used to be so disappointed in the priests' sermons that seemed to have but a single theme for all those years—the building fund—that he would often bring the Bible to Mass and read it rather than listen to pleas for money. Like a broken record, after every Mass my parents complained that the priest talked only of money—why couldn't he say something more spiritual? (When I finally moved away from Washington, I was very pleasantly surprised to discover that many sermons actually referred to the day's Gospel.)

I attended Catholic schools from kindergarten through tenth grade (1956 through 1967). At that time, nuns taught all the classes, and I was pleased to discover that they loved my family. My father once said that nuns were Democrats and priests were Republicans. Little in my experience has disproved his assessment.

I went to parochial school at Our Lady of Victory in Washington, DC—forty to forty-five kids in a single classroom led by one nun, who taught reading, writing, arithmetic, and, of course, religion. She read stories about Jesus, Mary, and the saints, and made us memorize the answers from our Baltimore Catechism.

I didn't want to go to school. The first few days, I cried terribly at having to leave home. My best friend, Anne Coffey (now godmother to my oldest child), recalls that her first impression of me was of a screaming child. Sometimes I did more than simply yell. A few mornings I kicked and punched. Once, when I was particularly vigorous, I counted six nuns trying to hold me down. They dragged me down a flight of stairs, collecting worried nuns on the way. By the spring of first grade, I had become a delightful child.

For all my resistance, the nuns provided one of the most important role models in my life. I am sure that the nuns were very pleased to have the President's nieces and nephews in their school. But they were not overawed. At Christmas one year, my family went to the convent for special prayers and to sing carols. On the way home, my father told how he'd overheard the nuns, having just heard us sing, whisper, "Well, those Kennedys, I guess they can't have *everything*."

As much as was possible, the nuns tried to treat my sisters and me the same as any other children. Sometimes it was simply not possible. There was a time when Teamsters President Jimmy Hoffa had threatened us because of my father's determination to rid the unions of their mob influence. Unlike other children, who were dismissed freely, we waited in the principal's office for our ride.

That episode notwithstanding, the nuns effectively delivered the message that we were no different from the other children just because our family was in political life. The measuring stick the nuns were using was not power or wealth or physical beauty, but goodness. God didn't care whether or not you belonged to a country club, and neither did the nuns. In many ways, the culture of the school was very much like what our country always aspired to be: a true meritocracy, where virtue, intelligence, and hard work were rewarded, and where birth or class was no protection if you did something wrong. Every person is self-made: we were judged by actions and actions alone. You could never get more democratic than that.

The nuns also had a way of cutting to the heart of a debate. Their positions offered them a security that allowed them to dismiss any pretensions. At the same time, the moral glasses through which they looked at everything gave them a unique perspective on the world, especially politics.

To this day, I am still extremely impressed with their answers to the question of why Communism was so bad. Senator Joe McCarthy had just been discredited and the country's witch-hunting fever had just broken. Communism, however, was no more in vogue than it ever was. The House Un-American Activities Committee was still active, if not hyperactive.

As good American, Catholic children, we prayed for the souls in Russia and the end of Communism after every Mass. The anti-religious nature of the Soviet Union and the persecution of Christians there horrified us. But when it came to the economic and social principles of Communism, the nuns were not shocked. How different was it from the lives that they themselves were living, the lives that Christ had asked them to live? After all, they pointed out, they, too, shared property.

Their lives in a way subverted the pure capitalist instinct to make as much money as you can, at any cost. Unlike much of the country, they lived lives that revolved around justice and truth, rather than money. Considering the depths of the country's distrust and hatred of Communism, such an outlook took remarkable courage and personal conviction.

In fourth grade I decided that I wanted to change schools. Anne Coffey's sister attended the Convent of the Sacred Heart, which boasted smaller classes and French. How exotic, I thought. But I was quickly disabused of the notion. I was terrible at French. However, I did like the smaller class size and the cosmopolitan children. The Mothers of the Sacré Coeur, as these nuns were called, served the more fortunate Catholics. For instance, in my class we had the daughters of the British, Spanish, Mexican, and Nicaraguan ambassadors. The Mothers had convents all over the world—Dublin, Paris, Rome, New York, Tokyo. My mother and aunts had gone to a Sacred Heart high school and college. In fact, my mother had roomed with my Aunt Jean at Manhattanville, which is where she met my father.

Being at a Sacred Heart school made the Catholicism of the Roman Catholic Church come alive. I felt connected to a much broader world. We were told solemnly that we could take our "très bien" card to any convent in the world, and we would be let in. Since one convent was at the top of the Spanish Steps in Rome, I was always eager to cash in on this benefit. (Incidentally, when Anne Coffey and I knocked at the front door many years later, the nun simply gave us the name of a nearby youth hostel and sent us on our way.)

If our pride at being members of a secret, international club was short-lived, the sense of responsibility for those less fortunate than ourselves was not. We learned over and over again Saint Luke's admonition that from those to whom much is given, much is expected. Each class adopted a missionary. Anne Coffey's uncle was a missionary priest in Chol-Chol, Chile, so naturally we adopted Father Jurg Mundell. We prayed for him and sent money that we collected. In turn, he sent pictures and wrote letters describing life in a small village. We felt connected to this faraway missionary and to the idea that each of us, too, should take risks to do good.

We also were encouraged to visit senior centers, volunteer in my Aunt Eunice's camp for the retarded (which eventually developed into the Special Olympics), and bring in cans of food for the hungry.

Works of charity do not always come easily to young children. But the nuns' examples, and the expectation that we, too, would make giving a regular part of our lives, washed away many of the second thoughts and rationalizations. And always, the focus was less on what giving did for us, as givers, and more on what it did for those who needed our help.

When I was twelve years old, a friend and I delivered a Christmas dinner to a family in a tenement building in inner-city Washington. We walked up three flights of narrow, poorly lit stairs to deliver turkey, stuffing, vegetables, and a bag of toys. After a little boy greeted us at the door, his mother quickly came, thanked us, took the packages—and then we left.

The entire exchange took less than five minutes. I still recall the vaguely embarrassed feeling I had as I walked down the stairs. Were they resentful of our good fortune? Had we made the mother feel inadequate because she had NOT provided for her children? And what about us? Were our motives for volunteering pure, or were we trying to soothe our guilty consciences?

Good questions, but ones that could easily be enlisted to rationalize not making further trips into the ghetto. While it is easy to dismiss the trip as just another manifestation of Lady Bountiful, the bottom line is that there was a good result. The family had a real Christmas dinner. Our guilt was irrelevant.

My husband often complains that I did not learn much science at Stone Ridge. My classmate Maggie Morton's husband agrees. "Most people who get a flat tire learn to fix it. You learned to pray for a guardian angel." While this must be a slight exaggeration (a number of our classmates have become successful doctors), we certainly were imbued with a sense of the miraculous. My favorite story was about the nun who created a fresco of the Annunciation. Like the tales of Mother Barre, this one was repeated often. One young novice dreamed that Our Lady had asked her to paint a picture of the Annunciation. After much hardship, she finally convinced the doubting elderly nuns at least to let her try. When she was finished, they were horrified by the result. The painting was bright and garish—totally inappropriate for the convent. The nuns ordered her to cover it up. She did. But when she uncovered it a few days later, the painting had become a thing of great peace and beauty. We were always left to wonder whether Our Lady had intervened on the novice's behalf or whether the natural course of the fresco had done its work. In either case, the moral of the story was "Believe in God and His Mother. They won't let you down."

But my husband is for the most part correct. Scientific know-how was not as important as our spiritual growth, which the nuns took great care in nurturing. We went to Mass on every First Friday and had daily religious instruction. In grades five through eight, we had a one-day retreat during Lent, and three days when we entered high school. This meant one day, and then three days, of enforced silence.

We were taught to value self-discipline and self-sacrifice. Our lives and talents were gifts, not to be wasted on self-indulgence or laziness. Each Lent was preceded with endless discussions regarding what we had chosen to give up; who was to be the toughest. Children's natural competitiveness for once left the playground and moved into the realm of the spiritual. One Lent I gave up TV. Difficult, but not impossible, I thought. And I was right, until I came down with chicken pox. I was home from school for two weeks and didn't watch any shows.

While Lent was the epitome of sacrifice and abnegation, the importance of duty and discipline was instilled in us year round. One of the most widely used teaching methods was to require us to be silent. I often wondered who reaped more of a benefit, ourselves or the exasperated nuns. We were supposed to walk to class in silence, sit silently before class began, and stand silently in the lunch line. I found this very difficult. I loved speaking in class—either to my friends or shouting out the answers before waiting patiently to be called on. My fifth grade teacher was so frustrated with me that she took Scotch tape and put it over my mouth.

While we learned catechism and studied religion, I think that being good was less an intellectual endeavor and more a question of right habits. Moral character is not programmed in our genes. Children need to *learn* to be good, and we learned to be good the same way we learn anything: by hearing, by seeing, and by doing. That is, by being told what qualities are productive, by witnessing examples of such behavior, and by practicing these virtues themselves. We spent much less time deciphering the mysteries of the Virgin Birth, and much more hearing how we should be honest, caring, polite, and orderly.

Each week we would have Prêmes, our school assembly. The principal would read the names of the students who had done best in the academic subjects—and the names of all those who were polite and orderly. I was never a serious contender for the latter. However, once I received the *most improved* for orderly, most likely because I started so far behind the other children. It was such an achievement that the entire student body burst into laughter.

Our report card had as many areas of behavior as it did of academic subjects, including posture, effort, seriousness of purpose, and "intercourse with companions." It was only in eighth grade that somebody whispered what other meaning that might have. I have heard that the category is no longer included.

Many of my peers who attended other Catholic schools reminisce about the nuns' obsessions with sins—the admonition not to wear patent leather shoes because boys could see the reflection of underpants. But I don't remember this as a major source of concern. Sure, we were told to "avoid the occasion of sins," but stories of hellfire took a backseat to the admonitions to be good and noble people.

The one exception to this general rule involved my mother—and, once again, my friend Anne Coffey. In our religion class, the nun had taught us that since our bodies were the "receptacles of the Holy Spirit," we should treat them with respect and consider them beautiful. Anne Coffey was telling my brother Bobby how beautiful her body was—and my mother overheard. Imagining that something untoward was afoot, she marched Bobby and Anne to the bathroom, where she washed their mouths out with soap.

In tenth grade, I decided to leave Stone Ridge for two reasons. First, it was 1966, a time of unrest and rebellion. Wearing uniforms and white gloves lacked the romance and intrigue of the outside world. And second, the major topic of conversation was, typically for teenage girls, who was invited to what dance by whom, and what we should wear. The point of a girls' school, of course, was to remove an obvious distraction so that we could concentrate on our studies. But if we were to be obsessed with boys anyway, I'd rather see them every day and have a more natural relationship with them, rather than first meet at dances and parties.

My brother Bobby had visited a coed boarding school, Putney, in Vermont. It seemed perfect: coed, no uniform, a decidedly more relaxed attitude toward discipline; students called teachers by their first names. I left a school where we were judged on how well polished our shoes were, for one in which, during the spring and fall, at least, the students didn't bother to wear shoes at all.

And so, for the first time in my life, I became a Catholic in a non-Catholic world. My mother did not like my going to Putney. She feared the bad influences of "Potney," as my father referred to it, and looking back, I can understand. Only three of the students at the school went to church, and I was the only Catholic who did.

I still went to church while at Putney. Rather than making me feel uncomfortably different, it gave me a sense of comfort and made me feel special. Once, when a group of students went on a three-day camp-out, I insisted that I be driven an hour away so that I could go to church—and admittedly this churchgoing had its temporal advantages. During senior year, when I was grounded (along with the student body president) for taking off for the weekend without permission, I argued persuasively that the curfew could not apply to my churchgoing—and so I still was able to make a weekly trip to town.

I don't want to make this churchgoing appear too frivolous. As I said, Catholicism grounded me. This is who I am. On a very basic level, it meant that I would "examine my conscience," avoid some (if not all) occasions of sin, and consider on at least a weekly basis what I had done and what I had failed to do. In short, it served as a baseline for all my behavior, as it has throughout my life.

That's not to say there were not priests with whom I felt frustrated and with whom I disagreed. One sermon that strongly advocated the war in Vietnam made me quite angry. After Mass, I got into a heated argument with the priest about the importance of separation between church and state.

But despite these occasional disagreements, the Church was always a source of strength, especially in times of adversity. The Church teaches that life is tough. The central image, after all, is Christ crucified. The stories of the saints tell of men and women who have been tortured and killed for their beliefs. Suffering is part of life. In fact, the nuns and my mother often said that we should offer up our suffering for the souls in Purgatory or those behind the Iron Curtain. Pain had its purpose.

Personal happiness and satisfaction were not to be expected in this life. Just the opposite. Life was a series of tests: temptations by the Devil, confrontations with evil. Even in the midst of tremendous sadness or horrors, despair was not an option. The worst sin committed by Judas was not that he betrayed Jesus but that he despaired of God's forgiveness and mercy. One source of comfort was that God would not test beyond our capacity to endure hardship. Another was that ultimately we could look forward to a better life after death.

These teachings may seem harsh, but they reflect experience. Death has always been near. I was named for my Aunt Kathleen, who died in a plane crash before I was born, and my brother Joe was named for our uncle who had died in World War II. My earliest memories include praying for them.

My mother's parents' names were added when I was about five years old, after they had been killed in a plane crash. We always believed that they were looking down on us and watching out for our best interests. When I was about twelve, my mother's brother, George Skakel, was killed in another plane accident, along with one of my father's best friends, Dean Markham. Nine months later my Aunt Pat, George's wife, choked to death on a chicken bone. I remember going to wakes, attending funerals, and comforting cousins and friends.

Throughout this time, and especially after John Kennedy died, my family was stoic. We did not indulge in speculation. There was little second-guessing of how things could have been different. My father quoted Aeschylus: "Pain which we cannot forget falls drop by drop upon our heart until in our own despair, against our will, comes wisdom through the awful grace of God." Aeschylus wrote before Christ's birth, of course, but this sentiment seemed consistent with what I had learned at Our Lady of Victory.

My father's dedication to family after his brother died provided an example to me once he, too, had gone. That summer I worked on an Indian reservation because he said that we should give something to our country. In college, one of my best friends committed suicide. It would have been understandable if I had simply given up, perhaps gotten involved with drugs. But I believe the habits of churchgoing and praying were so ingrained, I had a foundation that would not allow me to collapse. Life was difficult, but it had been difficult for Job, for the saints, and, of course, for Jesus. They had not given up. Nor should I.

It's easy to poke fun with stories of autocratic nuns and patent leather shoes. It's easy to look askance at the pageantry and ritual. But underlying the lighthearted stories is a rock-solid appreciation of the truths the Church taught, and teaches to this day. To my mind, no one better exemplified this than the nuns who taught me.

What my peers and I learned from the nuns was the sense of living for something greater than yourself. When the Mother Superior at my grammar school asserted that each of us must develop our talents for the greater glory of God, we believed her. Whispered rumors that she had once been a Mardi Gras queen gave credence to her sermon that whatever our vocation would be—lawyer, doctor, teacher, or housewife— we had a responsibility to strive for excellence and to work hard for the well-being of the community. Her decision to give up wealth and beauty for the convent evidenced the power of belief and inspired our own quest for a life well lived. Even if we ourselves were unwilling to take the vow of poverty, we could not be entirely satisfied in finding the good in accumulated possessions. Moral courage was not something asked only of heroes. The stories of the saints were not mere stories; they were a standard that all of us should, at the very least, try to live up to. I remember Mother Mouton saying, "Silence is golden, but sometimes it's just plain yellow."

If I haven't always been honest and morally courageous, at least I— and the others in my class—learned what those words meant. Religious conviction—in all faiths—gives us the ability to reject the easy and safe road, or at least to speak truthfully and act responsibly. It teaches us— rightly, I think—that personal happiness and comfort are hollow and ephemeral compared with the satisfactions of a life spent in service to a greater cause. It is a lesson I am still learning, and a principle that will guide me for the rest of my life.

His Way, Truth, and Life
Mary Cunningham Agee

WHY I AM A CATHOLIC

Why am I still a Catholic? My first reaction is to answer, perhaps a little too glibly, that given the extreme ups and downs, the unexpected twists and turns of almost epic proportions that my life has taken, why would I ever consider being *anything but* a Catholic? Where else could I possibly have found such a compassionate, understanding, and inspirational mother than in the Catholic Church? How else but through the raw materials and sacred tools of my Catholic faith—prayer, the sacraments, holy scripture, the rich heritage of the saints, the inspired papal documents—could I have survived in this world of ours? Where else could I have turned for spiritual sustenance, nonjudgmental support, and an interpretation of human suffering that would become more meaningful with each new challenge that fate tossed my way?

My Catholicism is both my home and my way of life. In a very real sense, it *is* my life. The Church baptized me as an infant into the only Life that truly matters, and it continues to "deliver me from my evil" by nurturing this Life at each defining moment of my earthly existence with its unique treasury of sacramental gifts.

MY ARTICLES OF FAITH

In sharing even these preliminary words of appreciation for all that the Church has come to mean in my life, it occurs to me that it may be helpful to identify at the outset any articles of faith upon which my religious commitment may rest. We can assume that by their very nature, I will need to return to these fundamental tenets again and again in order to support my reasoning and illustrate my life experience. In a very real sense, these basic truths are also an essential part of the spiritual bounty that the Church has bestowed upon me. Each is recited daily at Mass in The Creed and each has been supported beyond any reasonable doubt by the Church's vast treasury of inspired writers including the saints, bishops, cardinals, popes, and doctors of the Church.

Surprisingly enough, I find that there are only four bedrock beliefs that form the cornerstones of my Catholic faith; all other issues no matter how provocative or profound, inevitably seem to return as footnotes to one of these underlying principles:

First, I believe in the reality of an all-loving and powerful God Who created me and every other human being in "His image and likeness" and entrusted each of us with an eternal soul and the gift of free will so that we might choose to live as children of God and be united with Him forever.

Second, I believe in the divinity of God's only Son, Jesus Christ, Who was sent by the Father and born of the Virgin Mary in order to redeem all of mankind from sin. I believe that Jesus Christ, as the Son of God, was "like us in all ways except sin" and, therefore, was absolutely honest and utterly accurate when He described Himself as "the Son of the living God."

Third, I believe in the authenticity of the Sacred Scripture as the Word of God as set forth by Christ's apostles under the inspiration of the third person of the Blessed Trinity, the Holy Spirit. As such, it is the single richest and truest source of wisdom about the person and the teachings of Jesus Christ.

Fourth, I believe in the absolute authority of the Catholic Church as founded by Christ Himself and as revealed in Sacred Scripture when Jesus said, "You are Peter, and upon this rock I will build my church" and "As the Father has sent Me, I also send you." I believe that this divinely ordained power to teach and guide on all matters of faith and morality has been passed down through the ages by means of papal succession and lives on today in the person of the Holy Father and the body of knowledge called Sacred Tradition.

I cannot consider a reasonable part of this essay to be an effort to explain or defend these four underlying principles of faith. Many of the greatest theological minds throughout history have tackled this project with dedication and vigor and have still concluded their exhaustive studies and writings with the most humble of admissions about the limitations of reason and language. Nonetheless, I cannot think of a more noble pursuit or more worthwhile expenditure of intellectual energy than probing the depths of these fundamental keystones of Catholic faith.

MY RESPONSE: THE CHURCH AS HIS WAY, TRUTH AND LIFE

I have often thought that the most unambiguous and comprehensive words Jesus Christ ever said about Himself were, "I am the *Way*, the *Truth*, and the *Life*." I find that these three words provide the most meaningful structure for me to shape my response to the question: Why am I still a Catholic.

First, I choose to still be Catholic because I *love the Truth*. Jesus Christ *is* the Truth. We know this because He said so. As the Truth, He is incapable of deceit in anything He says or does. One of His greatest deeds was the creation of His Church. He understood that we would need His ongoing, living Presence in our lives, and so, He gave His first priests, the apostles, the Holy Eucharist and asked us to recognize Him in the breaking of the bread and the drinking of the wine. Just as I love the Truth, I love His Presence in His Church and would never knowingly choose to be separated from Him.

Second, I choose to still be Catholic because I *need to follow the Way*. Jesus told us that He *is* the Way. His Way is the way to salvation. This is the true purpose for which I was created. My task is to grow in love for His Truth and work diligently to obey His commands which light and guide the Way to eternal Life. When Jesus said, "If you love me, obey my commandments," He linked love to obedience. And when He said, "If anyone keep my word, he will never see death," He linked obedience to eternal Life. Since the grace needed to overcome my many weaknesses and to be obedient is given through the sacraments of His Church, I choose to participate as fully as possible in the Life of the Church.

Third, I choose to still be Catholic because, in the words of the Mosaic Law, I *choose Life*. Jesus said that He *is* Life. He was sent by our Creator, His Father, so that "we might have new Life and have it more abundantly." He gave us Himself in the ultimate act of sacrifice on the Cross in order to "free us from sin and death." He anticipated our need for forgiveness, communion and spiritual fortification and so He asked us to partake of His instruments of grace, the sacraments of His Church. He connected a Life of holiness with salvation and salvation with participation in the sacraments: "Whoever eats my flesh and drinks my blood will have eternal life and I will raise him up on the last day." Therefore, I would not deliberately choose to separate myself from the Source of all Life by denying my soul the vital nourishment of the Church's grace-filled sacraments.

Frankly, as I review these thoughts about the reasons for my religious commitment as a Catholic, it all seems much more reasonable than I would have expected, but there is a far greater part of me than these three logical explanations would suggest. I practice my faith in much the same way as I practice the art of loving—without the need for words of rational support.

MY FIRST RESPONSIBILITY: LOVE OF GOD

It could be accurately said that the entirety of Christian ethics can be captured in the "Great Commandment" given by Jesus Christ Himself. "You shall love the Lord your God with all your heart, with all your soul and all your mind. You shall love your neighbor as yourself." He made it clear that these were not mere suggestions but commands with dire consequences if not followed.

I believe that Christ's command demands a concrete and practical expression. I can think of no more authentic or effective manifestation of this genuine love than through humble and courageous service to His beloved Church. This deep, abiding love that Jesus is calling for in the first part of His Great Commandment is, I believe, the kind that will safely guide His Church through this challenging period of history.

CRITERIA FOR PERSONAL RESPONSIBILITY

Social scientists have determined that three conditions need to be met in order for a person to feel a strong sense of personal responsibility. First, the person must feel a sense of *importance* about the need to perform this task; second, the individual must believe that the task is *doable*; and third, a person must feel *uniquely qualified* to perform the task at hand. As I reflect upon the Catholic Church's pressing need for renewal, I must confess to reluctantly answering "yes" to all three.

It should be obvious why I consider the task helping and healing the Church to be "important." And given any number of scriptural passages that remind us that "in God all things are possible," it should come as no surprise that I believe the task is "doable."

But it is the third criteria for assuming personal responsibility that almost caused me to stumble. Most of us would be hard-pressed to describe ourselves as "uniquely qualified" to assist in the ongoing formation of the Life of the Church. And yet, the scriptural passages that refer to *each of us* as being "called by name" and putting to good use the many varieties of gifts of the Spirit cannot be ignored. So I have come to believe that there are three unique gifts that have, in particular, shaped my willingness to "stand up and be counted" whenever the Church or any of Her members is in need of support. I can discern their catalyzing influence at the very heart of all that I do.

Each of these "gifts" initially came wrapped in the riveting anguish of human tragedy. Each would demand that I learn an invaluable lesson: to convert a life-altering loss into a Life-saving gain. Each would require me to put into full practice the spiritual survival skills of faith, hope and love if I were to overcome the temptations that await anyone who has known profound grief: despair, self-pity, and anger. Upon reflection, only a most loving God intimately in tune with the precise needs of my individual soul could have pinpointed the perfect time and circumstances for each of these "gifts" to be presented. At age five, I lost my father; at age thirty I lost my privacy; at age thirty-three, I lost my first child.

I believe that it was in these moments of extreme brokenness that I managed to discover the singularity of purpose and clarity of mission that might otherwise have eluded me for longer than I care to speculate.

And that each of these life-altering events have, by the grace of God, been converted into the "leaven" in the bread of my life. Through the invitation to let go of my human father, I received the gift of compassionate love for any child who feels abandoned. I was also given a far more intimate relationship with my Heavenly Father Who kept His promise not "to leave me orphaned" and never seemed to tire of reminding me of my "belovedness" as a "child of God." Through relinquishing safety of my privacy, I received the gift of compassionate love for those brave souls throughout history who have been "persecuted for the sake of righteousness." Through the invitation to release the life of my first child, Angela Grace, I received the gift of compassionate love for every mother who has ever lost a child in any manner.

MY SECOND RESPONSIBILITY: LOVE OF NEIGHBOR

The Catholic faith was not designed by its Founder to be a tidy set of doctrines that could be neatly practiced alone. It is a generous religion that demands authentic expression in practical and loving service to others. Its Founder was not mincing words when He warned, "Anyone who says that he loves God and hates his neighbor is a liar." This is why we find included in the same Great Commandment that demands an absolute love of God, an equally stringent requirement of an unconditional love of one's neighbor. Christ left no room for confusion.

For me, this call to loving action has taken a very specific and concrete form. It is my small but determined attempt to "light a candle rather than to curse the darkness" of the "culture of death" in which we find ourselves living. My response to the second part of Jesus' Great Commandment is called The Nurturing Network.

MY RESPONSE TO HIS CALL TO ACTION: THE NURTURING NETWORK

The idea of The Nurturing Network did not come to me in a dream, but in the nightmare of a mid-trimester miscarriage, when the emptiness makes you want to cry out, "Why me, God, why me?" I was initiated into a sorority of loss, listening for the cry of a child whom I would never be able to hold or comfort. As I put away the empty crib and folded the handmade baby blanket, I began to comprehend the vivid truth in what Bishop Fulton Sheen had said so often, "There could never have been an Easter Sunday without there first being a Good Friday."

I'd like to believe that it was the Holy Spirit who whispered to my broken heart the possibility that *the life of many could be born out of the death of one*. If I could feel that much pain and loss over a child I wanted, how must other women feel when they are coerced by circumstances or family members to surrender the life of their child to abortion? How deep must be their grief, anger, and guilt. How cruel it must seem to those who feel they have *no other* choice. I knew I was being given a rare glimpse into the injured hearts of so many women whose babies are aborted: "I felt alone, violated. My child was taken from me. My little child, not a 'fetus,' not 'tissue,' not 'membrane,' but a baby. My baby!" The personal "call by name" to be my sisters' keeper came over a decade ago and with it was born an organization that to date has saved over eight thousand children's lives and provided a hope-filled solution to each of their mothers. I structured this grassroots organization with the hope that one day we would live in a society that no longer required our services. My prayer was that we would someday literally "be put out of business" by compassion and love: Love of a parent so strong that it might withstand the onslaught of a thing called shame; love of a mate or boyfriend so binding in fidelity that it would not instantly check out; love of a community so Christ-like that it would not cast the first stone of judgment but transform that stone into the bread of Life. For there are literally hundreds of thousands of women in our midst who are in immediate, desperate need of our practical life-saving compassion.

I know, because I hear their mothers' broken voices on our telephone lifeline. I listen to their stories of abandonment and betrayal and discover not only the father of the baby at the heart of their struggle, but you and I. I believe that we are accomplices in these desperate decisions every time we turn a deaf ear to Our Lord's command to "love one another as I have loved you."

I believe that if we are "for life," we have a moral obligation to provide the means to support and sustain it. The underlying weakness in the pro-life movement in America at this time may be the Christian community's lukewarm and inconsistent response to this vital issue. Despite almost two million abortions each year, Christ's call to action is still too often met with a series of lame excuses, conditional promises and allegedly higher priorities.

Our practical research at The Nurturing Network has debunked the false assumption that the majority of those experiencing abortion are uneducated young teens from disadvantaged backgrounds. Rather, we have found that the most likely candidate for this procedure is an unmarried, middle-class woman in her twenties, who has earned at least a high-school diploma. You know this woman. She is your next-door neighbor, your waitress, your colleague at work, the cashier at your favorite restaurant. She could even be your own daughter. These are women you encounter everyday and yet, their scars are hidden—some with Band-aids called denial, others with armored rhetoric called "reproductive freedom."

During the twelve years that I have worked face-to-face and heart-to-heart with these living "profiles in courage," I have learned that most abortions do *not* occur as a result of "free choice" but because women in crisis feel they have *no other* choice. My informal research with hundreds of women who have experienced prior abortions reveals that over 90 percent of these mothers would have chosen a positive, life-saving alternative *if only it had been made available to them.*

The facts are that there are four basic influences that weigh heavily in all abortion decisions: the threats that having the baby will cause the mother to lose her relationship with the baby's father or her own family, or will damage her social standing or her career.

None of these threats has anything to do with freedom of choice. All have to do with unfair, seemingly impossible tradeoffs. This is why The Nurturing Network was formed—to give a woman a positive alternative, one which recognizes her unique values, needs and circumstances. Our Network of twenty-two thousand volunteer members is made up of doctors, counselors, educators, employers and nurturing families from every state in this nation and from fourteen foreign countries. They empower a mother to nurture her baby's life—while making the most of hers as well. Our volunteers devote their time, talent, and treasure to creating an option, making sure that no woman feels she has been left without the choice to give birth.

And, as if the moral absolute to protect and nurture all life were not enough, our clients have shown us time and time again that an unwanted pregnancy does not have to mean an unwanted baby. There is an obvious correlation between how much practical compassionate support we are willing to give women with crisis pregnancies and how many healthy infants will be available for the hundreds of thousands of potential parents wishing to adopt. But unless we are willing to offer the emotional, social, and financial support needed by women facing this kind of pregnancy, we cannot legitimately express either condemnation or surprise when we discover that they have chosen a less hopeful solution.

You could say that The Nurturing Network was my "Field of Dreams" with that recurring and haunting voice that said, "Build it, and they will come." Indeed they have. And they continue to come. For our Network is no longer a dream but a powerful reality to the women and children of this country, a reality that is only a toll-free phone call away: 1-800-TNN-4MOM. This compassionate outreach is my living testimony to the daily miracles that can occur when each of us takes to heart the Divine Carpenter of Nazareth's plea to "Feed My lambs."

CONCLUSION

I hope that I have been able to convey why the notion of choosing to walk away from the banquet table of the Catholic Church's grace-filled gifts bordered on the absurd. Not only do I value these gifts beyond all others, but I take seriously the words set forth so clearly in Article 14 of the Constitution of the Church: "Anyone knowing that the Catholic Church was made necessary by God (for salvation) through Jesus Christ, (who) would refuse to enter Her or remain in Her *could not be saved*."

It is crystal clear to me that the Catholic Church with Her abundant gifts of grace is the only hope I have of approaching my day of judgment with any confidence. And maybe, just maybe, as I lay my earthly burdens down, a few familiar faces will be there waiting in the wings. As I turn to hear the Almighty's verdict, I might catch a grateful wink here or a knowing nod there for having played some small part that helped to nudge them on their way. I pray that with the help of my Holy Mother Church, I will hear the words from the Father Himself, "Well done, my good and faithful servant."

A God-Given Talent for a Child's Game
Bob Cousy

THE COUSY story begins in France, in a region called Alsace. I was conceived in France and born in the United States three months after my parents left Europe in 1928. After the boat docked in New York, we immigrants landed on 46th Street and East End Avenue, a rough Manhattan neighborhood. I have no specific memories of my early years except of living in the streets. I ran with the pack. We were street rats just getting by, in and out of minor trouble continuously. After recently reading the book *Sleepers*, which is set in Hell's Kitchen, twelve blocks west of where I was raised, a few things have come back to me. *Sleepers* is about four kids who are sent to a brutal reform school. Thank God we didn't end up in reform school. Until I read the book and realized it, I had blocked out the first twelve years of my life. There isn't much I wanted to remember from my childhood. I lived the ghetto life with a dysfunctional family. Of course I didn't know this at the time. I remember the fourth floor tenement apartment where we lived: the rats, the cockroaches, the terrible summer heat. In the summer my body was covered with bedbug bites. So I spent my days in the street. When my mother wanted me home, she hung a white rag on the fire escape railing. But for all the squalor and crime, neighbors took care of each other: word passed from block to block, communicating news or orders. "Hey, Flenchy, time to go home. The flag is up." I was called "Flenchy," rather than "Frenchy," in the usual ghetto use of ethnicity to dictate nicknames, due to my inability to pronounce the letter "r," which I have to this day.

I remember two other events from those early days: I saw two people gunned down. One was shot across the street from me, and another time someone was shot quite close to me. But all the rest of the events of those first twelve years are buried deep in some inaccessible part of my memory. I seem to have cut off most recollection of my early life in the streets of New York.

From my earliest days I went to church, although neither of my parents was religious at the time. I can never recall being anywhere but at Mass on Sundays, and that was because of my grandmother. She was the liaison between me and the Church. She dressed me and literally took me by the hand to Mass. Thank God she did, or I would have been on the streets on Sundays, too. I don't recall any priest like the character in *Sleepers* taking me in tow, but I attended a Catholic school kindergarten, and became close to my teacher, Sister Mary Patricia. I've kept in touch with her since. At eighty-eight, she is still lively and full of energy.

In 1966, at the age of thirty-eight, I began to appreciate the move my parents made in leaving France and coming to America during the Depression. It was such a difficult childhood that I had never thought about what they left behind in France. On a promotional tour for the Gillette Company in 1966, I was able to visit the small farm in Alsace where they had lived, and met my uncles, who still worked their farm in the old ways, living without electricity. They had earthen floors, and they milked goats to give us something to drink. Rather ironically they asked about my father: "Comment est le bon vivant?" (How is the high life?) They assumed he was living the good life in America. Little did they know that my father died penniless. He drove a cab in New York when we first arrived. Then he worked for the WPA (Works Progress Administration). He was good with his hands (maybe I got that from him) and a good mechanic. He had saved $500 after twelve years, and with that money we moved to St. Albans on Long Island.

It was in this small town, then, on the edge of New York City, that I became acquainted with a child's game, basketball, which has taken up so much of my life. St. Albans was a hotbed of basketball fever. I had played all sorts of ball games in New York; I played stoopball, boxball, stickball, all the ghetto games—and, of course, the occasional hubcap and hotdog. In St. Albans I learned about "hoop," as it was known, because all the kids were playing basketball.

Basketball became my life. I was an only child and eager for a focus. I was socially retarded; that is, I was not one to reach out to others. My high school had won the city championship once or twice, and I was thrown into this milieu. I had good hand-eye coordination, inherited from my father, but also a God-given talent. I must have been looking for something to fulfill my needs.

Religion didn't always provide a constant force for good in my life. I was a street kid, after all. But I suppose religion gave me a backup conscience. Somewhere along the way I developed a keen sense of right and wrong, a sort of moral compass that guides me. I've never really leaned on my Catholic faith or bargained with God to do me a favor. Given my loner background, I've used God as Someone to communicate with. I would talk to God, but not necessarily about problems. That isn't my way of operating. A loner has a way of expecting to solve his own problems. But I have relied on having Someone for a little tête-à-tête now and then. I never had that kind of close, dependent relationship with my parents, so God was important in filling a void.

Today young people have their role models: some good influences, some not so great. We never had role models in sports or anywhere else. I do recall when I was a kid, we used to listen to Joe Louis fights on the radio, and we snuck into a few games at Yankee Stadium. In college we went to Madison Square Garden with the team. But when I went to Andrew Jackson High School on Long Island, I had no sports heroes to look to for guidance. My basketball beginnings should encourage young athletes. I tried out for but didn't make the team until my junior year. I wasn't a standout ball handler. I didn't distinguish myself until my senior year. Then the team did well, and I made the All-City team.

No one had paid me any attention until the All-City Championships. Then someone—I've forgotten who—grabbed me and said, "You are going to do well in basketball, and this could be your ticket out. Basketball will allow you to choose a college." Basketball was my ticket upward and onward, but I hadn't known it. I was far behind scholastically, and had to pass the Regents exams and a college prep course. So I began to focus on school. I was motivated enough to become a B-plus student my last year. I could see where I was going, and I worked hard.

Only two colleges recruited me for their teams: Holy Cross and Boston College, both Jesuit schools. College recruiting was very unorganized at that time, and there was neither major scouting nor big scholarship offers. B.C. invited me to come up. The coach was very nice and showed me around the campus. I put aside my shyness and asked, "Where am I going to live?" and "Where is the gym?" In those days Boston College had no dormitories, and I was told that I would have to live with a family off campus. Most of the students commuted by public transportation from various parts of the city. Being so painfully shy, I didn't like the idea of fitting into another family's life. The fact that they had no gym frightened me as well.

Holy Cross was easier. I never got to visit, but I heard there were dormitories there, so I enrolled. I took the train to Worcester, Massachusetts, that fall. Although Holy Cross had dormitories, it did not have a regulation-size gym in which to play home games. Instead, the team played most of its games fifty miles away, at the Boston Garden and the Boston Arena, and some at South High School in Worcester. Practices were held in a wooden barn that had once housed cows that produced milk for the dining halls. But that didn't bother us. It was 1946, the war was over, and we were happy to play basketball.

In those days, Holy Cross was considered the second strictest college in America, after West Point. There were 2500 students in the Jesuit school in 1946. We had to be in our rooms at 7 P.M. during the week and at 10:30 on weekends. Learning a new discipline was easy for a teenager like me, but many of the students were veterans just back from World War II, taking advantage of the GI Bill and looking for new training. They had come back from fighting in Europe and the Pacific, and now they were subject to strict hours. Some of those guys couldn't live with this new discipline. Mass was required each morning. We are all creatures of habit, and I've been a Sunday communicant ever since. I also learned to be part of a team.

It was a memorable team to be a part of. In that first season, we won the N.C.A.A. Tournament at Madison Square Garden, beating Navy, City College, and then Oklahoma. When we got back to Worcester on the train, there were 20,000 people waiting to greet us. There was a parade and later a reception for the team, then it was back to class. After all, Holy Cross was a strict Jesuit school.

In the summers a bunch of the college team members worked in the Catskill Mountains and played basketball in a hotel league. We worked in the kitchens and on grounds crews, and we waited tables. That first year I came home with $1500 in dollar bills, since most of the pay for waiters was in tips. My suitcase was stuffed full of small bills. My mom took one look at this pile of money and ran for the phone to call the police—she had never seen so much money before. In the Catskills, we played basketball twice a week.

In 1950 I joined the Boston Celtics. Having attained a regional fame after college, my teammate Frank Oftring and I had started a couple of small businesses. We opened a gas station and a driving school. If it hadn't been for the Celtics' offer that summer, we would still have been teaching old ladies how to drive.

After graduation I married my wife, Marie. We were married on a Saturday morning, I played that night at the Garden, and left on an extended road trip right after that game. In those days no one got the time off from the Celtics to go on a honeymoon.

We all need structure and discipline. I learned both from being a Celtic and a Catholic. With my chaotic background, the structures of both sport and the Church were stabilizing influences in my life. I believe we live a more satisfying existence with discipline than if we are free-flowing through life. I have seen people try it both ways, and I prefer the structure. On the team we were subject to the discipline of Arnold "Red" Auerbach. With Red it was "Find the talent, get them in shape, keep them motivated and 'don't get fancy.'" That's basically what he did. A simple formula for winning. Years later, when I started coaching at Boston College, I tried the same strategy. After all, it worked. Red was tough. He didn't like us to fraternize with players from other teams. He didn't want any distractions. He screamed at us endlessly about our outside distractions. He needed our attention and our commitment. There was a code, and we were all forced to live by it. He didn't want us to make money on the side by endorsing jerseys or sneakers. There was none of this business of making commercials with players from other teams, even if we really could have used the money.

My Catholic faith has never really cost me. If I have ever been discriminated against, I am not aware of it. When I applied for membership in the Worcester Golf Club in 1963, it was said that Catholics were eaten for breakfast there, but I was accepted. I suppose they wondered if I would bring my black team friends, and I did. I brought my young black friend Kevin Murphy, whom I met through the Big Brother and Big Sister program, to dinner at the club often. No one said a thing, at least within my hearing.

My Catholic upbringing taught me all people are created equal in the eyes of God. This background makes me keenly aware of discrimination. When I saw segregated churches in the 1950s, my sense of right and wrong was violated. I almost left the Church in that decade because of the discrimination I saw. I became involved in the Big Brother and Big Sister program in the 1950s on the local level, and in later decades on the national level. This is a program for fatherless boys, and we Big Brothers get a chance to coach these kids as parents. Two of my three Little Brothers were black. Some of my strong feelings about equality of all people come from knowing and playing with Bill Russell and Chuck Cooper. Because of my friendship with them, I understand how race plays a role in American sports. Coming from the ghetto myself, I've always understood how motivated you can be when you see a game as your way out and to the top.

My quirky personality demands a great deal of privacy. Maybe my Catholic upbringing contributes to my need to be alone. During play-offs on the road, I had my meals sent to my room. I barricaded myself in the room, shut off the phone, thinking of little except the opponents. Even as a broadcaster, I need to get focused on the day of the game. I get my rest and I study my notes. I minimize distractions and prepare to analyze the game. As a player, how many things can you concentrate on and function to maximum capacity?

Motivation and emotion are top components in our sport, and in any sport. Certainly the ghetto experience motivated me to do well. Today's ghetto jock will fight hard to get to the top of the hill, but he won't fight as hard to stay there. We all came from the ghetto: Red Auerbach, Frank Otting. Survival and self-interest are basic instincts in the ghetto, and these persist. After all, the basketball world requires animal instincts. But they must be complemented by God-given skills.

Player, coach, broadcaster—each role required different talents. Much of what worked in the ghetto helped me to be a team player who could look after himself. As a coach I still had to be myself. No artificial temperament works with players. The locker room stories about coaches crying and players saying, "Gosh, Coach, if we had known you wanted to win so much, we would have played harder," are true only if the coach is honest.

I have an acute sense of what I think is right and wrong. This may have to do with the dictates of conscience, but surely it was deepened and extended by the Holy Cross courses in philosophy, theology, and my major, sociology. I don't think it is accidental that I wrote my senior thesis on social justice and the persecution of minorities; I have always been interested in fair play. At times I am troubled by the lack of public conscience. I don't see the Ten Commandments applied often enough in this society, whether in government, politics, sports, business, or even the Church. We live in such a competitive society—and

I am a competitive person—in which motivation comes from the strong need for survival and self-interest. People have been killing each other from the beginning of recorded history to this day. But I still don't understand it. It is the need for security that causes discrimination. Feeling discriminated against is behind much of the violence we see every day. Street life is hostile and aggressive. Competitiveness is part of the democratic system, but it has taken over when it leads to insecurity and bigotry.

What keeps me in the Church: I believe in a few people, a discipline, and a God. Fr. John Driscoll was a scholastic when I was at Holy Cross. He always had a strong sense of social justice, and I think he influenced my sense of justice. I choose to maintain an ordered discipline in my life. I don't follow a free-flow life, making it up as I go along. Religion has given me an anchor and a discipline. I follow the ritual. The Church's teaching maintains another sense of discipline, a need to give back something to the community. I also believe in a cosmic order. I don't need the Pope to tell me there is intelligent reason to explain why we are here. I believe in God, and I can't believe we were put here by accident. Every life form is fascinating. It's the human animal that is the problem for me. I have lost confidence in our leaders, and now too many people fail to take responsibility for their actions. I believe individuals should do good simply for the sake of doing good things. We cannot survive as a society in this competitive world by following only the dictates of self-interest, the way I learned to survive in the ghetto. Good must be done for its own sake.

As a broadcaster, my sense of fair play and right and wrong gives me focus. Fairness comes into the game often. I could feel sorry that I wasn't a player when the big money came along in sports. It has been said that I was twenty years too early. But I don't think of my career as any less because there weren't millions of dollars in contracts for basketball players in my time. In fact, money has changed the sport, and I am just as happy to have been a Celtic in the years of the legends who had their shirts retired to the rafters of the old Boston Garden. I could have ended up a derelict, but instead I was able to play and remain involved with a sport I love. I feel that God has looked after me.

Bowie Kuhn's Confessions
Bowie Kuhn

THIS IS my confession.

I am a Catholic, the faith into which I was born. I am not in any sense "still" a Catholic, as the title of this book might suggest. I am a Catholic—period. I am madly in love with Jesus Christ. Though I have crucified Him anew and broken my filial relation with God, I have always come home like the prodigal I am. I have never thought of myself as anything but a Catholic. It is my personal bedrock.

Some may think that confession comes easily to Catholics. It is, after all, a Sacrament of the Church. But confession does not come easily to me, nor do I think it does to most Catholics. Nor do I think it should. The story that follows is not easy to tell. I am shy about discussing my faith, but I feel compelled to tell this story straight from my heart. Faith is not monkey business, and I think we are held to a high standard of truth when we discuss it. I would not want to stand before Our Lord on the awesome day and admit that I had written this with my fingers crossed.

Why write it at all? I earnestly hope that somewhere a single pilgrim may be helped by my story, as I have been helped by others.

I was not born into or raised in a Catholic culture. The world around me was firmly Protestant, save my parents and a handful of dedicated Catholics in my mother's family. Born (and raised) in the District of Columbia and Maryland the year before Lindbergh flew the Atlantic and Ruth hit sixty home runs, I might as well have been in Mississippi as far as customs and religion were concerned. The Civil War was only sixty years behind us, and Manassas, Antietam, and Chancellorsville were more vivid to me than World War I, which had only recently ended and in which my father had proudly served. Among my kin there were mixed reactions about the results at Gettysburg, and pictures of Robert E. Lee outnumbered any of General Grant in their homes. Blacks were generally treated with condescending affection, including the black woman who worked in our house and who played a large role in my upbringing.

Catholicism was generally seen as a curiosity and its observances as idolatrous. If there was hostility, it was well concealed behind the good manners of my people, an aspect of the Old South that I have always admired. We were just eccentrics in their eyes. I was rather proud to be part of this minority. I sensed a feeling that Bowie was a nice child, with a markedly un-Catholic name, who would surely, when he was sensible, come around to the Episcopal Church of his grandfather. And though I spent a good deal of time in Episcopal churches and admired their beauty and style, as well as the genteel people, I never came to stay. I was always drawn back to that mysterious place where the red sanctuary light burned next to the tabernacle—and the Irish priests dared to be eloquent about sin.

My Mother was a strong Catholic. My loyalty to the Church was her gift. There was strength in that loyalty, which she gave me by example. Long before I had any grasp of Catholic theology or history, I believed that the Church was my team and that I should stick by my team, no matter what.

It was the same loyalty with my baseball team. By 1933, I had become a fan of the Washington Senators, as was my mother. That year they won the American League pennant, then lost the World Series to the Giants, one of those hated teams from New York. The next year the Senators took an unprecedented plunge into the second division, where they stayed throughout my childhood. I did not abandon them. Like the Church, they were my team and got my fidelity, no matter what.

After the 1971 season, the Senators moved to Texas and were called the Rangers. That was not my team. The Senators have vanished from public view for over twenty-five years, but not from mine. They are as vivid to me today as they were in 1933, and my loyalty survives, together with my faith that they will be resurrected in my native town.

My mother might have been an Episcopalian, as was her father, Joseph Kent Roberts, from whom I got my middle name. He was a country lawyer of some skill and reputation. He developed a drinking problem, separated from my grandmother, and was institutionalized until his death. My strong-minded grandmother moved to Washington with her three daughters, ran a rooming house, grew her own vegetables and fruit, made her own wine, raised her own chickens, and survived to the age of ninety-three. She was a Catholic with a particular devotion to the Holy Mother and the rosary. She made her daughters Church loyalists. For her, there was no other church. For my mother, and indeed for me, she was a model of triumphalism. She was a powerful influence in my life because of her toughness, resilience, and faith.

I should say that neither woman's Catholicism was based on formation in any formal sense. I think it came from a lineage going back to Tudor and Stuart England; the Catholic persecutions by those royal houses led in time to my English ancestors' coming to Maryland in the seventeenth century. They had fought and (I imagine) been martyred for their faith. Their heirs were not about to give it up. It was that kind of loyalty that was in my blood.

I recall with some embarrassment the boneheaded fierceness of my early faith. Let a friend suggest that there had been immoral Popes, and I'd be on him, like a leopard, with irate denials. Or let it be suggested that Methodists knew more about the Bible than Catholics, and I would fire back angry assertions about how the Catholics had invented the Bible. There was no bottom to my youthful ignorance.

Neither at my parents' knees nor in school did I learn much about the Church. Except for Sunday school, where I faithfully but mindlessly learned the Baltimore Catechism, I never attended a Catholic school. While I was introduced to the Sacraments in normal course, I did not learn much about their true meaning or efficacy. The Bible was certainly available in our house, but there was little encouragement to read it. The

Real Presence of Jesus in the Eucharist was a subject of which I had no real grasp until much later in my life. At the time of my First Communion, I distinctly recall believing that Our Lord was somehow kept inside the altar, and that if I could only get the lid off, I'd find him there. On the other hand, we did learn about the reality of sin in the form of lying, cheating, stealing, and failing to carry out assigned tasks, although not in the context of offending God so much as our parents.

We attended Sunday Mass, kept the Holy Days of Obligation, and abstained from meat on Fridays, even though my father thought abstinence was silly because he liked lobster, oysters, and soft-shelled crabs better than most other food. It was all good, solid, surface Catholicism but not much more.

In my father's case, there was not much to impart. His Catholicism was simply a label. He ignored the Sacraments and rarely attended Mass, although he drove us there when we were children. No Mass seemed complete unless we heard him rail against the priests for the lack of traffic control around the church. He also had biases against almost all ethnic groups. He was pretty much anti-Catholic, but did not actively discourage the rest of us from practicing the faith. These biases had an adverse effect on me. My best friends in grade school were Jews and Greeks. My very best friend, aside from my sister Alice, was Virginia Mixon, the black woman who worked for us. Virginia and I talked about Joe Louis in hushed tones.

My father did not have an easy childhood. Born near Munich in 1893, he lost his mother at his birth. The next year he was brought as a babe in arms by his mother's sister Anna to his grandparents in Pittsburgh. Anna was a saint, but by all family accounts my grandfather was a Teutonic terror. Partly to escape him (and possibly to spite him), my father enlisted in the Army and spent two years in France during World War I. The enemy included his German cousins. My grandfather died in the great flu epidemic of 1919. I cannot recall my father ever mentioning his name.

Since the Kuhn side of my family lives in Pittsburgh, we saw them infrequently. They were industrious, convivial, solidly Catholic people in the Bavarian tradition. I liked them, and they had some impact on my faith, particularly Anna, a gentle, quiet, deeply religious woman.

During the Thirties, my Father began to drink excessively. As the bouts of drinking became more frequent, the associated behavior became aberrant and at times violent. The effect on the household was devastating, as anyone who understands alcoholism will know. Sadly, he never considered any kind of treatment, and the situation persisted in varying degrees until a stroke gravely incapacitated him in 1971. That my mother survived this long period tells a lot about her strength. For her, divorce was unthinkable and separation unacceptable. She prayed, continued full of hope, and never despaired. God only knows how many rosaries she prayed.

After the stroke, my father became totally dependent on her. She took him to Mass regularly and led him up the aisle to Communion. At least one priest would not give him Communion, so she led him up another aisle to other priests. In the sixty-first year of their marriage, he died at home in her arms.

What was his effect on my faith? Despite his grievous failings, my father worked hard; provided adequately for his family; kept a regular schedule; was honest and patriotic; and took pride in family accomplishments. I doubt that he had any negative effect on my faith, though I wished faith could have helped him with the burden of alcohol. I do not hold him responsible for my failings. Nobody is given a perfect foundation. I clearly had enough to go on. Over the years I became satisfied that my own free will was the reason for my failures and sins. I knew right from wrong. Moreover, in reaction to my father, I learned as a kid to take on responsibilities, to work a little harder at whatever I did, and to grow up faster than other boys. I also saw how my mother's faith helped her to persevere. However imperfectly, I fathomed that prayer and Jesus Christ had something to do with that.

I have never attended a Catholic school; my mother was committed to public schooling. As a result, my education was in the public schools of Washington, D.C., in the Thirties and Forties. This was a superb school system, a national model—as it should be but, sadly, is not today.

Though these were public schools, values and morality were instilled as a natural part of the teaching process, as was discipline. Nor was any effort made to conceal that we were in the presence of God. In high school, a Bible was kept in the front of the classrooms and a passage was read each morning from either the Old or the New Testament, the choice of the student who did the reading. This was never a source of concern despite the fact that between thirty and forty percent of the kids were Jewish. The dominant spiritual caste of the school was solid, main-line Protestant, and the Catholics had no problem with that. I can't resist mentioning that the top boy and girl scholars were Catholics. Yes, I was the boy, and as president of the senior class, I was permitted to select a priest from my parish to give the graduation invocation.

I was proud to be a Catholic, loyal to my team and eager to make my faith public. I had no sense of the real joy and profundity of the faith that had come down to me from the Apostles. It was all perfunctory. I was obedient to my parents and to the Church. I went to confession when prodded by my mother and received the Eucharist. I said my daily prayers without much sense of a conversation with God. I worked at everything with dizzying intensity.

I was on organized football and baseball teams; I got a varsity letter in basketball; I was in the school band and school plays (even in singing roles); I was a soda jerk and scoreboard boy for the Washington Senators; I chased all the pretty girls who would have me; took up drinking and smoking and burned all the candles I could find except those in church. I was a popular kid and going somewhere, even if I had pimples.

The place I was going in 1944 was the United States Navy. I had been admitted to the Naval V-12 Officers Training Program that spring. Ten days after I graduated from high school, I entered the Navy, only seventeen years old. It was a bigger and more dangerous world than I had bargained for, with more than enough temptations for a nice Catholic boy from Washington. Here began the ten darkest years of my spiritual journey.

During that span, I completed my mercifully brief Navy career, got an undergraduate degree from Princeton and a Doctor of Laws degree from the University of Virginia, and went to work for a Wall Street law firm. And I pulled steadily away from the Church. I wasn't even tepid. I gave up the Sacraments completely. I indulged in whatever riotous living came my way. I ran wherever the café crowd ran. And all the while my career flourished—Devil's cunning. What's worse, I was passing up opportunities for marriage that only a fool would have ignored. Pride was master of my ship.

Oddly enough, I went to Mass every Sunday, regardless of inconvenience. I was the Pharisee in the temple. I was blessed by having a group of dedicated Catholic friends who worried about me, as well they might. I was given fraternal advice and a copy of Thomas Merton's bestselling *The Seven Story Mountain*, which had been published only a few years earlier. I didn't know it at the time, but that book was my road to Damascus.

I had never read a book of theology or spirituality. I am sure it was one of those little guardian angel miracles that caused me to read Merton, about whom I knew next to nothing. I certainly could not have told you who the Trappists were. Not that I wasn't a reader—from childhood I had been a prodigious reader, with strong focus on American history, politics, and the Civil War.

Merton's book is his autobiography and confession, taking him from his childhood to his conversion and his reception into the Cistercian (Trappist) Order at the Abbey of Gethsemane in Kentucky. The definition of rapture is to be carried away by joy. I was enraptured by this book. I can open it today with the same effect. Christ passes through these pages, beckoning Merton to the Church, beckoning me into His arms—to His freedom, away from the despotism of sin. I identified with Merton's life in New York, the carefree emptiness of the lifestyle, the concerned friends, the spiritual reading, the tabernacle, Christ hidden there, the backsliding, return to the tabernacle, conversion. It was only twelve years or so earlier. It was painfully real.

Merton first sought his vocation with the Franciscans at their church on West 31st Street in Manhattan. They thought he wasn't ready, and turned him down. I knew the church and began to go there. I felt

Merton's presence there, and more. It was like a story told to me by a priest friend years later: An old Jewish woman approached him in a nearly empty St. Patrick's Cathedral and said, "What is here? There is something here." The priest said simply, "Christ is here." "So that's it; I knew it was something," she said. I began to pray, to really talk to God and to ask for help. I prayed with fervor and humility, as I had never prayed before. Some never find God and wonder why. The only way is to lift heart and mind to Him in prayer. And then lift them again, and again.

It became clear to me that there had to be a real change in my life; doors had to be shut, entanglements ended—for good. Professionally, I continued to work hard and take on new responsibilities. Socially, I began to draw more into myself, not as a hermit but allowing more time with myself alone. It is human to resist being alone. It is also a mistake.

I expanded my reading: Dante, Thomas a Kempis, more Merton, Ronald Knox, Frank Sheed, Church history, even Catholic novels. And I returned to the Church on West 31st Street. This was the summer of 1955. In August, I spent a weekend with friends in the small Long Island village of Quogue and attended the Saturday night dance at the Quogue Field Club. I didn't like big bashes of this type, and was there only to be polite to my hosts. I sat in the bar, drank scotch and soda, and tried to be amiable. We were joined by a startlingly attractive, tall brunette who reminded me of Rita Hayworth. Her name was Luisa Degener. I knew the name through mutual friends but had never met her. While her husband George was socializing and dancing, we talked for quite a while. That was easy; she was an engaging lady.

A month later, George was killed in an auto accident in Manhattan. In October of the following year, Luisa and I were married. That was almost forty-one years ago. It was also four children, eight grandchildren, and quite a number of other things ago, some of which are pertinent to this story.

By dint of prayer and reflection, I had come to realize that marriage and family were my vocation and were essential to my salvation. I did have some romantic notion about joining the Franciscans, but I wasn't really cut out for Holy Orders or bachelorhood. I had certainly conceived that my wife should be a nice Catholic girl from a proper Catholic college and family. That was the old loyalist in me, if not the spiritual man I should be. But the Spirit had other plans for me. Luisa was a cradle Episcopalian with a family background that was hostile to Catholicism. She shared a few, but happily not all, of the modernist notions of her church about which Cardinal Newman had so perceptively warned a century earlier—in vain, as things were turning out. The grand orthodoxies of the Episcopal Church of my youth were on their way into modernist quicksand. This did not give us much concern in 1956, but it did later.

Before our marriage, I took a step I had been dreading: I went to confession for the first time in over ten years. The event is very vivid to me. I went to Our Lady of Victory Church in Manhattan's financial district, near my office. It was one of those blessed churches where the confessional light seems to burn all the time. There was a lot for me to say, and I had prepared carefully and in painful detail. In the confessional, I gave my accounting at length as the priest listened quietly. When I was finished, he commended me for my honesty. Can you imagine? After all those sins, I was commended! I cried as he gave me absolution, and cried on as I knelt in the dark church. Victory!

Luisa had a fine three-year-old son named George and was expecting another child in April 1956. Paul arrived on schedule, as sweet a baby as you could imagine.

We were married in St. Patrick's Catholic Church in Millerton, New York, at the northernmost reaches of the Archdiocese of New York. Millerton was the home of Mary and George Degener, the parents of Luisa's late husband. That the Degeners wanted the ceremony in their town was touching for Luisa and me. Until their deaths twenty-five years later, the Degeners were like second parents to us both. Grandpa Degener became more my father than my own. I am reasonably sure that in his mind, I became more his son than the one who died in Manhattan.

The Degeners were not religious people. The closest they ever got to St. Patrick's Church was in dropping off their ancient Irish housekeeper for Mass. Her name was Bridgit Coen. It was my privilege to attend Mass with her when I was in Millerton. She was a short-spoken person and invariably introduced me to the ushers as "Mister." We made quite a picture. She was tiny, garbed from hat to shoe in black. She came in on my arm, all six feet, five inches of me. After her death, I inherited her most prized possession. Her worn and stained prayer book is on my bedside table.

Grandpa Degener used to say to me, "Kuhn, I would give anything to have a faith like yours." I know he was looking for an answer, but I didn't know how to respond. Moments lost! I think I could do better today.

Before Luisa and I were married, we received a course of instruction from a kind of monsignor in Amenia, the parish seat. Luisa was agreeable to a Catholic wedding and upbringing of any children we might have, but was not comfortable with joining the Church herself or bringing in her existing children and I did not press her. The Catholic Church had too many "musts" for Luisa, too many places where she might lose her individual freedom. Because of my ignorance, I did not explain to her that "individual freedom" was the road to nowhere. Had I pressed her, she and her children would have joined the Church, but it would have been an accommodation, nothing more. I felt with all my heart that time was the solution, and I still do. Forty-one years later, Luisa is still an Episcopalian, bravely trying to keep her corner of that church from falling into shreds, but as one of her Episcopalian friends said some years back, "She votes the Catholic ticket." For her, the once-dark recesses of Holy Mother Church are not so dark today. I wish I could say that I supplied the light, but the truth is that Pope John Paul II did. She admires him more than any other living person. The remaining shadows are cast by my pride.

We were blessed with two more children: Alix, who was born in 1959, and Stephen, born in 1961. But for several miscarriages, there would have been more. Thus, in a few short years, I had gone from being a meandering bachelor to a family man with four children, a homeowner in Tuxedo Park, New York (of all places), and a partner in my law firm with responsibilities everywhere I looked. I loved having a wife and a home full of little children into which I could pour the love that had been pent up inside of me. I was a better Catholic, periodically going to confession, avoiding mortal sin, and making an effort to achieve unity with God. I was aware of Christ in the tabernacle and even paid Him weekday visits, infrequent though they were.

Eight years ago, a perceptive priest gave me a book titled *Humility of Heart*, by Father Cajetan Mary de Bergamo. It contains a Latin aphorism that I have committed to memory: *Hoc arbitror esse superbiam, quae caput et causa omnium delictorum est*: This I take to be pride, which is the chief and cause of every sin. The priest was more perceptive about me than I was about myself. I didn't think much about pride as my family grew in Tuxedo Park. No doubt, the same could have been said for most of the young men in the world around me. In time, I would learn to think about it more.

A key factor in my selecting the law firm in which I worked was that it represented Major League Baseball. On and off, I had worked on baseball matters, and in 1967, I took over, which was fine with the client, because I was well received by baseball people. Two years later, General Spike Eckert was relieved as Commissioner of Baseball. After a short search, I was named Commissioner, a job I was to hold for sixteen years. Let me say here that this essay is not about baseball, except as it affected my spiritual life or was affected by my spiritual life. I wrote a book that was published in 1987 (*Hardball: The Education of a Baseball Commissioner*) and is being republished ten years later. It will tell you more than you want to know about my time in the game.

My baseball career had spiritual consequences—some good, some not so good. The game flourished in my years. It has not done so well since. There is some portion of the American public that attributes the game's success in my time to the style of leadership I gave it. I stressed honor, integrity, and keeping commitments. I talked about the moral nature of these concepts and their impact on young people. Because baseball's impact on the American public was very great in those days, the moral message had an impact. While no one can say how much, I think it was significant.

For example, I fought throughout my tenure against legalized gambling on professional sports. I battled my way through the United States Congress, state legislatures, and the Canadian government. I even took the debate to Las Vegas. I wouldn't let baseball people work for casinos or own stock in them. I did not hesitate to put my objections on moral grounds. The message got through, because I was accused of moralizing on this and other subjects. That was fine with me.

There was another good consequence. Given baseball's age, tradition, and folklore, there was no game that the public and media understood so well or felt more competent to micromanage. The result was that as Commissioner, I could make few moves without drawing criticism. On major moves, the criticism came in torrents. I felt it, I was often hurt by it, and my pride was given useful infusions of humility. At the time, I don't think I understood that these infusions were a benefit, but I did later.

On the negative side, there was never enough criticism or trouble to put more than a dent in my pride. Baseball is prideful business. Everybody's got pride. It's contagious. My faith wasn't strong enough to immunize me. This was bad news for my spiritual journey and for my family, and I began to backslide on both counts. When you're looking for God, you need to keep moving forward, growing. I wasn't growing. And I was cutting back on my family. I had been a pretty good father, if impatient at times, but now I became more impatient and irascible. I wasn't listening well. I wasn't hospitable to conversations initiated by the children. I was Commissioner around the house and in the office. The same was true of my relations with Luisa. It's what pride does. You get remote from what counts.

After sixteen years, baseball and I parted company. It was certainly best for me (conceivably not for them). I was foolish enough to seek reelection, but a "kindly" minority blocked my way. I used to say that I cherished the experience and would have done it all over again. I would not say that today.

I was fifty-eight years old. I was well-off financially and had large houses in New Jersey, Long Island, and Vermont. I was respected, had various jobs, joined boards, and was in demand as a speaker at handsome fees. It should have been time to take a deep breath and look to renew the inspiration Thomas Merton had given me thirty years before. Though my pride would yet lead me into more trouble, a series of providential happenings ensued that reshaped my life. It would take five years for me to get there.

In 1984, my older brother Lou died of leukemia. We had not been close until the years before his death. He was not a practicing Catholic and had little or no use for the Church. After he fell ill, we began spending time together regularly. Whenever possible, I flew to Jacksonville, Florida, where he lived. I prayed for him harder than I had ever prayed for anyone. On one of my visits, as we sat in his living room and he self-administered his prescription drugs, he said, "I've gone down the street and rejoined the Church." His smile was radiant. We went to Mass together, and he received Communion. He kept a rosary beside his bed and died with it in his hands. I had prayed for his life. God heard those prayers.

By 1985, I had returned to my old law firm as counsel. I had an unexpected visit one day from a young priest of the Opus Dei Prelature, Father John McCloskey. To my surprise, he invited me to attend a retreat of the Opus Dei in Amenia, New York, the village where Luisa and I had received our marriage instructions. I did indeed attend, and came away knowing that my life was slipping out of my hands and into those of Infinite Love. Thereafter, Father John agreed to become my spiritual director, and has been since. He began giving me books to read. One was Father Cajetan's *Humility of Heart*.

Providence next took me on a pilgrimage to Lourdes with the Knights of Malta. I was not prepared for the sublimity of Lourdes. It was like stepping back into an age of pure faith. One night, in a rainstorm, I roamed the streets of the town alone, saying my rosary over and over with total indifference to time or weather. I cannot remember leaving any place with such reluctance.

About the same time, John Cardinal O'Connor told me of his visits to the AIDS wards of St. Clare's Hospital. He said he found the patients so painfully alone, and asked if I would organize Knights of Malta volunteers to visit them. I was a volunteer there for almost two years before I left New York. The patients were acute and dying; they couldn't care less about who I was or ever had been. If I physically touched them, was compassionate and ever so gentle, some would discuss with me their spiritual needs. I watched them die, and understood better where Christ was pointing us in the twenty-fifth chapter of Matthew.

My financial providential happening was one I inflicted upon myself through pure, unmitigated pride: I participated in the formation of a new law firm that was ill-conceived and had no chance of surviving. Within two years, it was out of business. I bore the humiliation and principal financial burden of its collapse.

A lady whom I had met at Lourdes heard the story on the radio. Confined in her small apartment, she was slowly dying from the effects of a severe stroke. She called a friend of mine to offer me her life savings of $1,500.

I am a slow learner, but I think I had finally gotten to Damascus.

My Faith and I
William E. Simon

IMUST admit that I have never asked myself why I am still a Catholic; faith has always been very much a given in my life, as I have always believed in the fundamental principles and doctrine of the Catholic Church. These were taught to me in a loving and compelling way first by my family, and then by the sisters in the wonderful Catholic schools I attended.

Although there have certainly been periods in my life when I did not practice my faith as I should have, my allegiance to the Church has never been in doubt, and I have always had a childlike love for the Blessed Mother, perhaps because my own mother died when I was eight years old. My early formation not only gave me a strong sense of conviction and personal connection to Roman Catholicism, but it is the very core of my faith and as much a part of me as my eyes, voice, and skin.

Being Catholic from birth, I did not acquire the foundations of my faith through some miraculous moment of epiphany, like Saint Paul on the road to Damascus. Instead, my spiritual journey seemed to proceed almost insensibly from my earliest years. My parents were a marvelous example of Catholic faith, and I have keen memories of attending Mass with all the family every Sunday in Spring Lake, New Jersey, often serving as an altar boy at the 7 o'clock Mass several days a week in the summer. I became somewhat distracted during my high school and college years, when I couldn't resist the temptation to sleep in and skip

Mass every now and then, but I returned to regular practice as a married man when my wife and I began our family of seven children.

Since that time, there have certainly been periods of greater and lesser religious fervor in my life, and my participation in the life of the Church has ebbed and flowed. For too many years after our family was well launched, my life was defined and guided far less by the Church and its teachings than by secular pursuits. My sense of being a Catholic then was pretty much limited to attending Mass on Sunday, belonging to certain Catholic organizations, and going on an annual retreat. Although my faith never wavered, I had pushed it to the periphery of my life.

As the philosopher G. K. Chesterton once observed, Christianity has not been tried and found wanting but, rather, it has been found difficult and thus, too often, left untried. When I first read these penetrating words, I remember hearing a voice within me say, "Bill, that passage was written for you." And so, recognizing that I am but a failed and flawed mortal, I always approach the subject of religion and personal faith with abiding humility. In fact, I often reflect on the passage in the Bible where Our Lord says a just man sins seventy times seven. And since He gave me a keen mind for numbers, I soon realized the reason He did so was that, with His perfect foresight, He knew I would be sinning in such multiples that I would need superior ability to keep track of the total!

It really was not until I became a Knight of Malta some twenty years ago that I began to explore and live my faith in a more meaningful way. For a time, the Knights of Malta was just another social organization; yes, there was some prestige associated with being a Knight, but we failed to live up to our purpose as Hospitaller Knights and members of the oldest lay order of the Roman Catholic church, whose history extended back to the Crusades. We did not serve the sick, the poor, and those less fortunate than we, which was and is our very reason for being.

In recent years, however, the Knights have undergone a remarkable transformation and begun changing in quite dramatic, positive, and far-reaching ways. We've gone beyond our former emphasis on social gatherings, and focus increasingly on more serious, spiritual quests.

As the Knights have changed, I have changed with them in very important ways. And as it turns out, giving more of my time to the Knights has brought me closer to Our Lord and permitted me to know Him in ways that I had never before dreamed possible.

We are told in Scripture, "No eye has seen, no ear has heard, no mind has conceived what God has prepared for those who love Him." Gradually, as I have strived to commit myself to Him, not just once a week but every day; not just by writing checks but by offering my time and energy and a willingness to do whatever the task is at hand, I have begun to discover His presence in many different places and many different ways.

I have seen and felt God's love at the Grotto in Lourdes and while working at Covenant House in New York City, and in the eyes of the sick and terminally ill at several hospitals: the Cardinal Cooke Health Care Center and Memorial Sloan-Kettering Hospital in New York; Morristown Memorial Hospital in New Jersey; and St. Francis Hospital and Cottage Hospital in Santa Barbara.

I want to describe some of these experiences in more detail, but before I do, it's worth pointing out that as I have set out on this journey, I have felt my own faith strengthen. And by "faith," of course, I mean believing with the mind and heart what the eyes cannot see.

Today, I understand in a more complete way that living our faith is not a sometime thing that comes easily or naturally; instead, it requires that we buckle down and renew our commitment each day. And, as I make this effort, I can be sure that I will all too often succumb to the distractions of the world, for which I will express contrition and be truly sorry. Then I will endeavor to do better, in the sure knowledge that along with confession and repentance comes the promise of forgiveness and reconciliation with our Lord.

And this is most important, because our days on earth are but a speck of time within the giant realm of eternity, and God will surely judge us for what we tried or failed to do to make life better for those less fortunate than we. I would like to believe that there is a growing awareness within our Catholic community that the responsibility to be a soldier of Christ falls on the shoulders of each of us, and that we must take our vows to serve the sick, the poor, and the less fortunate as a personal commitment.

This is especially important for those who, like myself, have been blessed with material abundance, if "blessed" is the proper word—as I think it is, if one uses one's wealth properly. Wealth is always an issue with God, who challenges us to put His commands ahead of monetary concerns. And Christ put it pretty matter-of-factly when he said, "It is easier for a camel to go through the eye of a needle than for a rich man to enter the Kingdom of Heaven."

On the other hand, Jesus also makes it clear in his teachings, such as the parable of the ten talents, that it is not wealth per se that is wrong but, rather, the love of wealth; making it an idol. If a rich man becomes mired in the material and idolizes his possessions, then clearly he is falling short of God's teachings. But if he invests his money intelligently, as did the wise servants in the parable of the ten talents, and deploys it to help others, then I believe he is behaving as a Christian should.

One person who demonstrated this principle well was Andrew Carnegie, one of America's leading capitalists. He wrote about it in *The Gospel of Wealth*, a powerful treatise I have given to each of my children. Essentially, his message was that much good, not evil, has come from the generation of wealth by those who have the ability, ingenuity, and energy to produce it. The key, however, is what we do with that wealth. I believe, as Andrew Carnegie believed, that the person who amasses wealth has a grave responsibility to make sure that it is not squandered, but given back to the community, whether it be by building libraries (as Carnegie did), schools, hospitals, shelters, or parks, or supporting any number of human service charities.

But it is not enough simply to give of one's wealth. Most important, it is only by giving corporally as well as materially—only by giving in abundance not only our material wealth but also our time, energy, passion, and love—that we can begin to fulfill our duty as Christians. A Jesuit I knew many years ago said this well in a little gem that he wrote on a card and gave me: "When God judges the greatness of an individual, he puts a tape measure around his heart."

And so, this is what my fellow Knights and Dames of Malta, as well as many other organizations and individuals, have challenged ourselves to do—to raise our sights and to use every possible opportunity to become a greater force for good, not only by stretching that tape but also, indeed, by breaking it.

I can point to at least three experiences, in particular, that have enabled me to become a better Knight, Catholic, and Christian. I must say that the immediate impact of each caught me by surprise, but each brought with it a light of revelation—a small spark that eventually burst into flame. Its fire warms and inspires me still.

My first experience came when I became involved with Covenant House, an international organization that helps runaway youth, many of whom are alcohol and/or drug addicts. Through the years of working on the chow line with my family, and spending not only Christmas but many other days during the year there, I learned some valuable lessons about a world I had seen little of.

I met some of the countless young people in our nation's cities who had never known love and did not know how to accept it. The Kingdom of God had never existed for them until that moment when they walked through the doors of Covenant House. Gradually they saw a whole new future beckoning as they discovered that God's love was for them, too.

While Covenant House was certainly an eye-opener for me, an even more startling revelation came during my first pilgrimage to Lourdes. To say that trip changed me forever might well be the understatement of my life. Lourdes transformed me in profound and permanent ways that I am still discovering, for it was there that I truly felt in my heart that I was meeting Christ for the first time.

Anyone who has visited Lourdes does not need me to elaborate. But for anyone who has not, I can only say that the spirits of Our Lord and the Blessed Mother truly live in the streets of that incredibly beautiful, moving, and miraculous place.

I would like you to experience, as my family and I have, just how powerful thousands of voices raised in hymn and prayer can be, and to see the miracles that faith can bring. If you go to services each day and stand amid the sick and suffering, or visit the Stations of the Cross and walk down to the Grotto, you will feel that you are being touched personally and directly by the healing hand of God.

All of us have heard the stories about how the blind see, the deaf hear, and the lame walk. Yet there are millions more, of whom I am but one, who discover that the real miracle of Lourdes is the miracle that happens within.

It is an awakening of the spirit—and a feeling of closeness to God—that remains in your heart long after your visit has ended. Lourdes is like a dream, except every time you wake up and pinch yourself, you realize that you weren't dreaming. The dream is real, and you want to run out and share it with everyone you know. And so each year I invite others to experience the wonderment, and then take their loved ones and friends. This spring my son Bill and I will be going to Medjugorje, Yugoslavia, and I know this will be a wonderful experience for us to share, as Lourdes has been for so many years.

And, finally, it was at Lourdes that I received my third revelation, during a conversation with Cissie Ix, an incredible human being, a wonderful woman of God, and one of our leading Dames of Malta. Cissie had mentioned during our pilgrimage that for many years she had been a Eucharistic Minister at Memorial Sloan-Kettering Hospital in Manhattan. This is a ministry that Cissie and the Dames have taken on almost exclusively, much to their everlasting credit. Cissie sparked my interest, and I asked her to take me with her one day. And what a profound effect this has had on my life!

Since then, I have become a Eucharistic Minister at four other hospitals, including the Cardinal Cooke Health Care Center in New York City. Essentially, what I do is spend time with people who are on the doorstep of death. I try to comfort and console them, and let them know that a friend is by their side. I give them Lourdes water and rosary beads blessed there; quite often they are overjoyed, and cry as I pour the holy water on their frail bodies. And, of course, I pray with them and for them, asking that the Lord will manifest His love to them through me, whether through my words, my touch, or my smile. I want them to feel that special peace that is beyond all understanding, the peace that comes from knowing that, where they are going, they will find something infinitely better than the pain and grief of the troubled world they leave behind.

I also offer them the Eucharist, the Body of Christ. This is an experience that I have great difficulty describing, for reasons that go back to my years as an altar boy, when we were admonished that we could never touch the Host, for that joy and privilege were reserved for ordained priests. I have always remembered that stipulation as I watched the priest during the consecration, as he held the Body and Blood of Christ.

So it is an overwhelming experience to be able to give the Eucharist today as a layman. I am awed by the strength the spirit gains, even while the body weakens. The peace that these people, young and old, find in prayer and Communion can be more healing and sustaining than all the medicines the world can provide.

Many are the times I have walked out of a hospital room with tears in my eyes, and I find myself wondering how I could possibly have given the patients half of what they have given to me. One such occasion occurred after a visit at the Cardinal Cooke Health Care Center with Eddie, a young man in his thirties who had contracted AIDS, had lost over half his body weight, and was now too weak to move. His legs were the circumference of my wrist, and he would weep as I poured Lourdes water on his emaciated body. Eddie became a good friend, and I was able to help reconcile him with his family, who were very bitter about his disease and had not seen him in two years. Perhaps the Lord kept him alive much longer than his prognosis had indicated so that this reconciliation could take place.

Once, after I had given him Communion, Eddie looked at me and said, "Bill, would you please do me a favor? I can't turn over by myself, and I don't like to ask the wonderful people here to move me too often because I know they feel a little uncomfortable touching my body with all its sores. Would you turn me over, please—slowly, so it doesn't hurt too much?"

As I looked into the eyes of that dying young man, I was certain that I was looking right into the eyes of Jesus Christ. As I turned him over, I said, "Eddie, how about me asking you a favor? When you get up to Heaven, and you're sitting at the feet of Jesus and the Blessed Mother, would you throw down a rope and pull me up with you?"

And Eddie said, "You bet I will, Bill."

How, indeed, could I ever give as much to people like Eddie as they have given to me?

So these are some of the reasons that I feel honored to be a Catholic, and strive to do my utmost to carry the banner as a soldier of Christ. To anyone who might be considering making a new commitment of his or her own, let me leave you with these thoughts:

Whether you choose to become a Eucharistic Minister or pursue any of the other avenues of Christian charity that help the poor and the less fortunate, you can be sure that you will reap far more than you will sow. Don't wait.

At the same time, I am strongly convinced that just as we must minister to and defend those who struggle with poverty, disease, and hopelessness, so, too, we must defend our Catholic faith against bigotry and the secular mentality that seem ever more determined to tear them down.

My point of view is, however, broader than just Roman Catholic. There is but one God, and people of all religions strive to spend eternity with Him. My meager efforts are magnified a thousand times by so many other people, all over the world, who do much more than I. It is never too late to join their ranks, and I hope that those readers who have not yet done so, will, for whatever you do for the least of our brethren, you do for Him.

Born with Desire
Mario Andretti

I GREW up in Italy during World War II. The war broke out around the time I was born on February 28, 1940. But even when the war ended, there was no peace, because the borders were in dispute, as they always are following war. The peninsula of Istria, which was where our hillside town of Montona was located, became part of Communist Yugoslavia.

My father had been well-off in Montona—he owned seven tenant farms—but the war changed all that. Once the Communists took over, our family, like thousands of others wanting to retain Italian citizenship, fled our hometown and took refuge in a camp for displaced persons in Lucca. From 1948 until 1955, we lived with 5,000 other people. Our "home" was a large room occupied by twenty-seven families. Each family's quarters were marked off by blankets. We children went to school, and my father kept busy doing odd jobs. Although we were not starving or cold, we were just existing. It was in Lucca that I dared to dream.

My father had been orphaned when he was five and was raised by a priest, Father Quirino Ghersa, who later lived with us. My uncle-priest, as I called him, had a great influence on me as a child. He spoke fluent German and helped keep us together after the war. Other than my parents, he was the person I felt the most affection for throughout my youth. There was something special about him, but he was not "holier than thou." He was a good Catholic priest and was very tolerant, especially of kids. When hearing confession, the older priests, to set an example, would have children say a rosary as penance. The longest line was always for my uncle-priest because he would give a lighter penance, maybe two Hail Marys.

I grew up Catholic, I was surrounded by Catholics, and I never knew there was anything other than Catholicism during my childhood—that is, until my twin brother, Aldo, and I discovered race-car driving. Our first exposure was at the movies, where we saw race cars in the newsreels, and racing immediately became our passion and our dream.

In postwar Italy, everyone was infatuated with Grand Prix racing. Drivers like Alberto Ascari were our idols. The 1950s saw the rise to prominence of Maserati, Alfa Romeo, and Ferrari, the leading racing teams in their day. My brother and I were fortunate enough to see the 1954 Italian Grand Prix in Monza, which featured the duel of the Titans: Ascari in a Ferrari against Juan Manuel Fangio in a Mercedes. That race forever changed my life.

The European economy following the war looked bleak, and the future didn't look any better. So our family took a vote and elected to move to America for five years; then we would return to Italy. (We never did.) My mother's uncle, who had lived in the States since 1909, agreed to sponsor our family in order to assure the U.S. Immigration officials that we had housing and work. So my father applied for our visas.

It was three years until the request was granted, but we were ready to start a new life. We had to leave most of our belongings behind, not to mention a lot of close family members, including my beloved grandparents. But my uncle-priest was the toughest to leave. As a teenager, I wasn't the greatest of letter writers, but I always kept in touch with him once we moved here.

On June 16, 1955, my sister Anna Maria's twenty-first birthday, we sailed past the Statue of Liberty and arrived in New York at 5:15 in the morning. My father had exactly $125 in his pocket, and none of us spoke English. But we had our faith and the belief that a better life awaited us. Within two years, my dad built a home for us in Nazareth, Pennsylvania, and we had two cars. We were, far from rich, but we all pitched in and pooled our money.

We went to public school in Nazareth, not to the Catholic school. Although Aldo and I had been well educated in Italy, we were placed in seventh grade when we were fifteen, so that we could learn English. We also had a special tutor to supplement our language studies. I met her at a school dance, and thanks to her, I got an A+ in English. Dee Ann became my wife six years later.

Not long after we settled in Nazareth, Aldo and I discovered the most wondrous noise. It seemed like race cars from a distance, and we set out to follow that sound. We were amazed to discover there was a dirt racetrack practically in our backyard. Although the cars were not the sleek Maseratis and Ferraris that we had known and loved for years, the modified stocks were still race cars. And there was a lot of speed, a lot of action. What's more, that type of racing seemed achievable for two wide-eyed teenagers. Our dream didn't seem so impossible, after all.

Without knowing the odds that were against us, Aldo and I were determined to become race-car drivers and to have our own car. We set out to learn as much as we could about engines, shocks, spring rates, suspension, chassis setup, and so on. Our only option was to build our own car, and we needed about $1,000. My brother and I and four of our friends came up with $500, and the rest we borrowed from the bank. A local businessman cosigned the loan for us and became the primary sponsor of our 1948 Hudson Hornet.

Our first race was on March 27, 1959, and by July, Aldo and I had paid everyone off, including the bank. We were the only owners, but we had to share the race car. Aldo would drive one weekend and I'd drive the next. In fact, each of us won his very first race.

Dee Ann was a tremendous support to me, especially in the early days of my career. She was a Lutheran when I met her, and her family was not too keen on her marrying an Italian Catholic. Her father actually refused to give her away until the day of the wedding. But soon we became great friends, and he later lent me money so I could buy a better race car. Before we were married, Dee Ann became a Catholic, embracing the faith that helps to define us and our three children to this day.

Race-car driving is a very risky business, but it is the only thing I ever truly wanted to do with my life. I had thoughts about becoming a priest when I was twelve or thirteen, which was only natural, having been surrounded by priests, but it was not something I considered once I discovered racing.

Being Catholic has helped me deal with the difficult times in my life. I often say, "I don't know how I am going to get through this without Your help." I always invoke the Supreme Being in times of need. And I'm very lucky to have retired from the sport alive. In nearly forty years of competition, I've been spared serious injuries, but I know I didn't do it alone. I had my faith to rely on. I've been able to achieve some of the things I've accomplished because I had help from "Upstairs."

For many years, we've had a very important tradition before each race. Our close family friend Fr. Phil DeRea, a Missionary of the Sacred Heart, always says a short Mass either before or after the drivers' meeting on Sundays. He hears confession, says Mass, and gives Communion—all in six minutes! Father Phil has an ability to help make sense of everything that goes on around us. Given the way I felt about my uncle-priest, it's very comforting to have such a strong relationship with Father Phil. I'm not sure I could survive properly without the balance my faith gives me. And Father Phil is a large part of that.

He is always there for us, in good times and in bad. He has performed weddings and funerals for our family. He consoled us when our son Jeff was very severely injured in an accident during the 1992 Indianapolis 500 that nearly cost him his legs. Father Phil also christened my three grandchildren.

It has been said that there are no atheists in foxholes. There aren't very many in racing, either. For some reason, the majority of the drivers in Indy car racing today are Catholics, and Father Phil is a source of strength to them.

Besides those race-car drivers I idolized in the newsreels of my youth, my other heroes are priests. They give of themselves to serve the

Church, much the same way a driver gives devotion to motor racing. I have known some great priests in my lifetime, ones who really look after their flock. When I was a child in Lucca, there was a chaplain at the Cathedral of St. Mark, Fr. Renzo Tambellini, who was like a saint. He had boys, urchins, around him all the time, just like Father Flanagan of Boys Town. He created an atmosphere where boys torn apart by the horrors of the war could stay out of trouble and still have a good time.

The life of a race-car driver can be a lonely one, especially with all the time we spend away from home. Faith helps support me, particularly now that both my sons are in the "family business." Deep down, I wish Michael and Jeff had pursued something less dangerous. But it was their choice; I didn't encourage or discourage them. I would give any aspiring race-car driver the same advice I gave my sons. You are not always in control of your own destiny. You have to know what you are getting into; don't look for fame with stars in your eyes. You have to be prepared to deal with what comes. Pain, loss, injury, devastation—all of these can result. There are ways to protect yourself, but the rest is a game of chance.

Race-car drivers are different from other athletes. We take the ultimate risks, and we often rely on luck. There are drivers who are satisfied just to compete, who are happy simply to be in the race. Champions, on the other hand, sacrifice everything—even family and social life—to reach their goal. They are driven to succeed, and devote every ounce of energy to winning.

A race-car driver must possess two vital characteristics—commitment and focus. Both have to be absolute. And then there is passion. No one is born with a steering wheel in his hands; it's the desire that counts. Many of today's young drivers have gone to racing schools. It's similar to learning tennis by having your own pro. Obviously it's better to be taught by a pro.

But beyond these things, you have to truly and passionately want to race. How much do you want to win? You have to move mountains to make it happen. In any sport, there are only two or three athletes at the pinnacle of their sport. It is the same in motor racing. No magic wand will make it happen if you only dream. You have to work that much harder.

Champions want it to happen. I wanted it. I was always testing, testing, testing—driving anything with wheels. Desire, belief in myself, and faith allowed me to accomplish more than I ever should have. Nobody had to tell me to get up early in the morning to go after what I wanted to achieve. That kind of desire comes from within, but your goals also need to very ambitious—almost beyond reach. You can derive inspiration from anyone who is a champion.

My son Michael has that special inner drive that only champions possess. He is totally committed to the sport, and he has the track record to prove it. But it is not just Michael's accomplishments that I am proud of; it's also his dedication and hard work to achieve his goals. The same is true for my son Jeff and daughter Barbie. All of my children are successful in their own right because of their intense commitment and focus. And our Catholic faith sustains all of us in the same way. It provides balance in our lives and bolsters our courage to face the dangers of motor racing and the challenges and obstacles in life.

Testimonies
William Bentley Ball

To ME, the question "Why am I still a Catholic?" is really two questions. One has to do with my personal life. What has the Catholic faith meant to me in the experiences of my life? The answer, I feel, may be of chief interest to readers under thirty-five. The other question may seem to readers above thirty-five a more obvious inquiry: I refer to the events that occurred within the Catholic Church following the opening of its Second Vatican Council and the pulsating of these events throughout the world down to this hour. That period has seen the departure from the Church of multitudes of laity and clergy, and tenacious dissent within the Church. So the second implied question is, Have those events strengthened or diminished your choice to call yourself Catholic?

Let me begin with the first question.

FOR YOU WHO ARE UNDER THIRTY-FIVE

Judge Robert H. Bork, in his remarkable book *Slouching Toward Gomorrah*,¹ paints a very depressing picture of people younger than thirty-five. Bork says you entered the world virtually prefabbed as materialists addicted to consumerism, hedonists transfixed by sex, persons willingly drugged with often outrageous and violent entertainment, people who, having no religious faith as a fixed center of life, happily accept guidance of the major media in professing secularism and its values. All of this, he says, is commanded by our culture, and he does not leave us with much hope that you will be able to swim, independently, free of it. But all that, if true, is good news compared with the prediction he makes of your future. It is that your generation is headed for chaos, a violent breakdown of order in society that will be remedied only by the coming of a police state.

Bork is dead right in his portrayal of our society, but I hope he is wrong about you. That, in part, will depend on whether, carefully putting your life under a microscope, you say he has pretty well described you, or whether you see ways in which you differ from the prefab pack of under-thirty-fives he's talking about. The "microscope" you need, however, is not the usual "self-awareness" stuff peddled by counselors in some high schools and colleges. No, it is one that makes you stop your busy mind and ask yourself, What do I want out of *life* (not just out of today)? What if death, sorrow, and loss of loved ones, health, or job enter that life? Who, *really*, am I? Is it true, as some say, that God exists, that He gave me life, that I'll wind up before Him, that He wants me to live in a certain way?

If you have the guts to ask yourself these hard questions and answer them with candor (preferably writing them all down as a check against the wobbliness of mind from which everyone occasionally suffers), you may have arrived at a point of some curiosity to read what I have to say about being a Catholic.

Like most of us, I have friends who are surprised that any rational person can really believe in God, Jewish friends who cannot conceive of belief in Christ, Protestant friends who cannot imagine a Christian's being Catholic. And then there is the whole undertow of which Judge Bork speaks, our materialist culture that makes it seem absurd these days to live and practice Catholicism (of all things), or at least to be more than passively Catholic.

"Faith"—what is it? What's the "belief" that Catholics profess to hold? I begin by saying what, for me, it is not. I know it to be not mere emotion (though it may occasionally produce glowing feelings). It is not a reaction to fear or anxiety (though it may help relieve these). It is not, for me so far, the result of experiences that some saints (and no end of fundamentalist Christians) say they have had in actual meetings with God or such encounters with Him as would prompt one to say, "God told me to sell the farm," or "God said I should get out of Camden and try for the job at Westinghouse," or "On June 10 He told me to marry Rupert." I have heard, without skepticism, recountings like these, not only by televangelists but by others—people I can personally deem reliable. They are all fortunate—but God has not yet been so direct with me as to show up in my life in such a dramatic way. He moves me by indirection, giving me some very hard kicks (e.g., lung cancer) as a way of making me turn to Him more fervently. Here is how "faith" has been with me.

It begins with the experience of the heart, and is complemented by reasons of the mind. I can't dwell long on the former, which is the experience of being in love. A man who says he loves his wife does not explain that by describing her beauty or listing her virtues. So it is with the love of Christ, which some come to have and in which, by the guidance of the Catholic faith, one can happily lose the baggage of self and find hope, joy, and certainty. The experience of the heart continues as I think of my companions in the Catholic faith over twenty centuries—our brothers and sisters imprisoned, tortured, and executed throughout Elizabethan England because of their heroic practice of their religion, the murdering of our priests and nuns in Rwanda at this hour. Catholics feel a great strength in knowing of the faith of other Catholics of long-gone ages and in places far away or close by.

As to reasons of the mind, what I call my "faith" started with the utterly plausible idea that God exists and that God created the universe, including me (the real me being not only this temporary body but this permanent soul). People who believe those two things are derided by some for their supposed credulity. But it really should be the other way around: it's the deriders who are credulous, who maintain a blind faith in No-God, the "big bang" without a detonator, a universe without purpose. They view the constellations with, at best, open-faced awe. They look at the amazing design of a seashell and deny it had a designer.

Though they may grandly profess themselves "humanists," their view of the human being is mean: man is an organism indistinguishable from the mosquito except in structural complexity. I have never been able to accept such naive and depressing beliefs.

Starting with the practical, rational, commonsense idea of the existence of God, I later read in the Old Testament accounts of God's relationship to man that I found very moving. And here again, I reflected on the shallowness of those who, because they think some stories in the Bible improbable, or find some passages difficult to understand, dismiss the immense story of God's marching through mankind's history as its teacher and lawgiver.

The Old Testament, and especially its pinpoint prophecies, led logically to the New Testament, to Jesus Christ—a believable, happy, glorious outcome of history. It seemed necessary that Christ would not only wish to pass on His teachings and way of life to human beings for all time, but that He would leave with human beings a vehicle for perpetuating them and for preventing their misinterpretation. So His instituting of a church, through Peter and the Apostles, was simply logical. That church continues to exist. But there are hundreds of Christian churches, each different from the other and each claiming to be the one church that Christ founded. The great nineteenth-century English scholar John Henry Newman, tracing the history of the Catholic Church,[2] showed that the authority given Peter by Christ was passed on to Peter's successor, and from him to his successor, and on likewise through the centuries in an unbroken line down to the present. These successors we know as Popes. That the Popes of my lifetime could trace their succession, one from another, back to Peter was a bright line in the Church's tumultuous and glorious history. But, more important, they had maintained, precisely (in spite of the gross personal failings of several of them, including Peter), the teachings of Christ down to this hour.

Here let me talk of seven remarkable gifts that Christ left for us in His Church—the marvelous bonuses of certain outward signs that give "grace," or real spiritual life, to one's soul. We call them the "Sacraments." Once you've tried them, you'll not want to be without them. I'm "still" a Catholic because I could not live without their power.

Experiencing life as a Catholic has been a good experience for me because of other Catholics. Orthodox Christians are mostly fun to be with. Most of the devout, practicing Catholics my wife and I have known are neither gloomy puritans nor effete pagans. Catholicism is a religion of joy. But it is not the phony joy of goody-goody, relentlessly cheery, sanctimonious religion. It is a religion that embraces suffering. As a Catholic studies the lives of those people whom his Church has called "saints," he sees first the meaning, and then the beauty, of suffering. It is his ability to accept all that, symbolized by Christ's cross, that *makes* the Catholic a joyful person. I think this sorrow/joy character of Catholic life is what makes it an interesting life, and one that, however quiet, may be heroic. This aspect of Catholic life *relates to more than self.* In fact, it liberates you from the prison of self and draws you to use your life in praise of God and for the good of others, sharing their joys and helping relieve their pain.[3]

Let me share with you two large areas of my very long life in which my Catholic faith brought great strength to me—World War II and, after that, trying cases in courts all over the country.

Life, as it opened up right after 1939—a time known today to but a few—would be especially important to me in terms of faith. There was a dark tidal wave steadily bearing down on us—a war enveloping the globe that would involve every human being in the nation. Being of draft age and sure to be called, I enlisted in the Navy in July 1940. Soon millions of young Americans would be bobbing about in the heaving sea produced by that wave. Separation from family, neighborhood, and things familiar, and being placed in mortal danger, shoved life into a vivid new focus.

That focus was intensified for me on June 5, 1944, when my ship was slowly moving into position off the Normandy coast, with the long-predicted invasion about to begin. The "focus" was on the very questions I posed earlier in this chapter—questions about life, death, my own identity, and God. I had found strength and peace pondering these at

Mass that day in a gun compartment. On the early morning of June 6, D day, flashes from German shore batteries winked in the darkness, and days and nights of both tremendous excitement and horrible losses ensued.

For me, the war stretched out for two more years after that. As my Navy days were winding down, a void was opening up in front of me that life slowly filled.

For the last thirty years I have practiced law in a multitude of cases, mainly on constitutional liberty.[4] As I ponder why I am still a Catholic, part of the reason lies in the fact that many of these cases have involved not only Catholics but Mennonites, Amish, Jews, Seventh-Day Adventists, and many evangelical Christians as well. How did these cases relate to my Catholicity? The universality of the Catholic faith embraces all that is good and authentic in the beliefs of other believers in God, because a Catholic, faithful to the way of Jesus, should have a heart especially open to people who, for His sake, are victims of injustice. My *own* faith, as a Catholic, was reinforced by my having to exercise it in these cases, applying Christian principles of justice, religious freedom, parental rights, the family, and so many things that are not Caesar's and that belong to God alone. So here was this Roman Catholic working, sometimes almost living (during trial preparation), with people who had grown up with the idea that the Catholic Church was evil, but who found in this Catholic someone they could see loved them (and still does!). But affection was a two-way street: they strengthened my Catholicism by bearing witness to our common Christian beliefs with courage and cheer. I'm still a Catholic because the Church's teachings have sustained me more intimately and completely in work of that sort than would any other teachings.

Our World War II generation was not a generation of heroes and heroines, but of ordinary people who rose to the astounding occasion of war. I really think that happened because ours was then a culture whose roots were in Scripture, with noble ideas of human freedom, self-sacrifice, good and evil profoundly stirring the culture. I think it correct to say that it was *thus* a culture close to Catholic. But these were sentiments distinct from those that dominate the culture of 1997. Millions in the 1940s were willing to risk death to themselves; in 1997 millions are willing to cause the death of others through abortion. As America became engulfed in war in the Forties (a crisis it would survive), it has today become what Pope John Paul II has rightly called a "culture of death." In this culture not only is the sanctity of human life widely denied, but also that of marriage, and hence of the family. As Judge Bork noted, materialism and hedonism saturate our media, and it is not hysteria to predict that our ever-weakening society will reach a state of violence and moral chaos, and a Hobbesian state will be sought for the sake of order.

Christ promised that the gates of Hell would not prevail against His Church. He gave no such assurance to the United States. But His assurance to His Church is closely relevant to our country. To the extent that Catholics bear courageous witness to Christ in these times, there is reason to hope that tragedy may be averted. On a trip to Rome in 1993, my wife and I sat in a vast assemblage in ancient St. Peter's Square. Just behind us were pilgrims from former Iron Curtain countries, radiant not only because of their new freedom but because they could now celebrate their ancient faith. And a sequence of prayers was sung from the high altar in Japanese, French, Swahili, German, English, Dutch, Slovak—on and on. The universality of the Catholic Church, its embracing of all peoples, is a great source of courage to me—and can be to you—as we look upon our country.

But the society we have come into is one that has been slowly disintegrating. Many years ago, G. K. Chesterton wrote a book in which he, too, stated "Why I am a Catholic." There he said:

The problem of an enduring ethic and culture consists in finding an arrangement of the pieces by which they remain related, as do the stones arranged in an arch. And I know only one scheme that has thus proved its solidity, bestriding lands and ages with its gigantic arches, and carrying everywhere the high river of baptism upon an aqueduct of Rome.[5]

That also helps explain why I'm a Catholic.

Now I'm going to turn to those you regard as old folks or, at least, older folks. Read on, if you like. You will see me describing controversy within this Church that I still am in wholeheartedly, but don't be upset. What I've told you up to here really says it all about the Faith (which is indeed my life). But Catholics thirty-five and up are finding the Church in some ways unsettling. Never mind, disturbances of this kind have cropped up before in the Church's long life. That life will continue to continue!

FOR YOU WHO ARE OVER THIRTY-FIVE: BEING CATHOLIC AFTER VATICAN II

I am still a Catholic precisely as I thought myself to be in all the decades I lived before Vatican II—with exactly the same doctrinal beliefs, exactly the same sense of loyalty to the Pope and the Church's magisterium. And so some will judge me a reactionary, an uptight representative of the Church Geriatric, a fraction of an ounce of the dead weight from the past that still seeks to suffocate Church renewal. It will be assumed that I greeted Vatican II with a horror that still has me fully in its grip and that I take obdurate pleasure in reflecting.

But it wasn't that way at all. In my answer to our second question, it will be useful to say why.

As news of the Second Vatican Council broke upon the world in 1960, I greeted all that I was hearing of it with a welcoming enthusiasm. The Sixties! I can still taste the champagne atmosphere of those days. Non-Catholic Christians were suddenly our "separated brethren" to whom we were now to pay heed, not with the competitor's eye but with loving concern. And so, positive accounts of these former strangers now flowed into the Catholic press and the strangers themselves flowed into innumerable interfaith conferences. Catholic priests and Protestant clergy were literally discovering one another for the first time.

"Dialogue" among religious intellectuals and leaders became, if not a virtual mandate, then certainly the vogue. Within the new ecumenical obligation was the duty to seek out—and hear—Jews. Out of many examples, I recall a spirited meeting at Rockford College with the brilliant Phillip Scharper of Sheed & Ward, Rabbi Marc Tannenbaum, and Jewish reconstructionist Arthur Gilbert that ranged, with good effect, I think, across issues dividing Catholics and Jews. While American Catholic leaders were dialoguing up a storm, there was word that, at the highest levels, bridges of "understanding" were being built. At the level of this layman, it was all an exciting thing—positive and long needed.

New, stellar appearances were being made almost weekly in the news from Rome—Schillebeeckx, Rahner, Robert McAfee Brown, and a host of other intellectuals begging to claim our rapt attention.

Immensely helpful to the interfaith rapprochement was the dramatic news of a statement on religious liberty about to issue from Rome. In 1960 John Courtney Murray's *We Hold These Truths* appeared.[6] Not only did Murray's central thesis on the position of the Church's relation to the civil order seem beneficent, but so did his attack on the prevailing secularist interpretation of the First Amendment. We now had good reason to hope that the Church would make clear that it did not insist that error has no rights. She would instead, at Murray's beckoning, point to the United States as the example to be followed in the observance of religious liberty. I saw our hopes fulfilled when, attending the Council in 1965, I heard proclaimed at St. Peter's Basilica the Declaration on Religious Freedom. I could assume that among the good effects of the Declaration would be a deeper appreciation of religious liberty among Catholics, and a reversal of the prejudices that had motivated much Protestant and Jewish opinion in the past.

But most directly touching Catholic lives was the onset of changes in the liturgy. I recall the odd "dialogue Mass" at which our congregation was bade to recite Latin responses mixed with English, along with the dubious attempts to inspire youngsters to embrace Christ by means of "beat" from strummed guitars. Later came the priest's facing the congregation. At this time (the mid-Sixties), reconstruction of altars had not yet been undertaken. Gradually American congregations were participating in Mass wholly in English.

Ecumenism, religious liberty, liturgy: Did we greet the momentous happenings in these with consternation? For me, at least, just the opposite: with joy. These were the actions of the Church, the Church of our allegiance, the bishops from all the globe assembled, the Pope. The changes were all necessarily good and right. "If the Church wants it, I want it" seemed to be the mood of priests, all the clergy, the laity everywhere. We were not borne along by a love of change, and certainly not by an anticipation of a future of endless change. Instead, the feeling was that the Church (and all of us) had simply arrived at a new plateau. Life on this new level would be better than ever before, but it would not be a life of uncertainty or experimentation. The rock of Church doctrine was unchanged, the means of spirituality would be augmented. We welcomed Vatican II, not because it changed anything essential but because it affirmed everything essential.

And all of this was starting to happen at the very time that Americans had elected their first Catholic president. The Kennedys fascinated the public. The turbulent and dramatic thirty-four months of John F. Kennedy's presidency, his brother's actions on behalf of civil rights, the exciting (historically dubious) confrontations with the Soviets all combined with the stir over the remarkable news unfolding at Rome to give American Catholics a heady sense of pride as Catholics. This sense was actually augmented by events immediately following the assassination of the President on November 22, 1963. Even today, replays of the films of the funeral are deeply moving—the assembly of the world chiefs of state to honor our slain leader, the beautiful dignity of Jacqueline Kennedy, the sight of the stricken family, the Mass at St. Matthew's, the old Cardinal at the graveside, the whole nation joining in mourning the death of its first Catholic president and, in a sense, led, in that mourning, through a Catholic observance.

A high moment, and one would have wished that the country could have been justified in retaining those noble images of the first family and, left with a wide respect for the Faith to which that moment contributed. Alas, just as that was not to be, so the highly positive first reaction to the work of the Second Vatican Council was not to continue.

In 1964, signs had begun to appear that aroused concerns of many persons above forty in age, who had been reared in the Church, loved it, and accepted its fundamental teachings. There was, for one thing, a tidal flow of rumor, speculation, and dissent—the cumulative effect of which presently conveyed the impression that the Church might be riddled with conflict, that her historic teachings on many things might not be true, or need not be obeyed. Doctrinal interpretations and changes in practice were being proposed by some that, by necessary implication, informed the world, and Catholics in particular, that all the Popes and saints from 1563 (the Council of Trent) to 1965 had lived in considerable darkness and were guilty of all sorts of errors.

Perhaps the most disconcerting development of all, in our country, was the response of a brace of Catholic scholars to the great encyclical of Paul VI, *Humanae Vitae*. This attack came close to me personally because of my involvement as a lawyer in mapping the resistance that I felt the Church in the United States should mount against the first major effort to establish population control by law.[7] This episode was my first experience in discovering that within the Church there now existed a spirit of rebellion profoundly threatening to her. I refer to it here briefly because my reaction to it is one reason why I feel it important to stay Catholic and to say why.

In 1997 the Church in the United States (and perhaps elsewhere) appears to be in a state of uneasy and unstable division. The *nominally* Catholic population of the United States is huge. Lost to many who call themselves Catholic are (1) knowledge of the teachings of the Church, (2) unswerving fidelity to its teachings, and (3) a profound sense of the sacred. This is due in part to the spirit of rebellion to which I have referred, but even more to the ally of that spirit—the view that doctrine is "up for grabs": pick and choose what suits you, rely on feelings. All this, and the impact of materialism and the pervasiveness of the media's pushing of pagan values, means that today's Catholicism presents a very mixed picture.

A powerful influence within the Church, loosely called (by itself and its critics) "progressivism," expresses testy impatience with John Paul II and, indeed, with papal authority. It has converted colleges that bear a Catholic name into colleges that, asserting the importance of free inquiry, are reluctant to inculcate the Catholic faith. It affirms evangelizing, of a sort, but believes it should be subordinated to an unbounded ecumenical spirit. In this view, we should never refer to the Catholic Church as "the one true church," and one dares not attack the Protestant Episcopal church or the American Jewish Committee for its support of "abortion rights." In liturgy, this voice often promotes "inclusive" language, phrasing said by some to be mere contrivance to appease feminists but, in any event, somehow never before deemed requisite.

Much progressivism is seemingly attached to the idea of continual *change* in liturgy as the mark of renewal of worship. Critics of progressivism say that liturgical change is not some progressivists' main aim; rather, it is new views of *doctrine*, including doctrine relating to priestly ordination, the morality of contraception, the Real Presence of Christ in the Eucharist, and, ultimately, the idea of doctrine itself. As to doctrinal matters, some prominent progressives seek a "common ground" within the Church, a dialogue in which differences in doctrine may be resolved—a congregational polity, in other words, not unlike that obtaining in most Protestant bodies. Some also promote the inconsistent "life ethic" of equating the evil of abortion with various other social evils.

The media typically portray the opponents of all this liberalizing trend as "conservatives." By and large the "conservatives" reject the main features of "progressivism." They are ardently supportive of John Paul II—in particular, his great encyclicals *Veritas Splendor*, *Evangelium Vitae*, and *Ut Unum Sint*. Without arrogance and solely out of love, they candidly embrace the Church as "the one true Church." They encourage Catholic elementary and secondary schools, insisting that these resume inculcating Catholic doctrine and pursuing traditional spiritual formation. Their view of ecumenism is limited to receptiveness to representatives of other faiths, and earnest and prayerful exchange of views with them. Your typical conservative, unlike some of his progressive counterparts, will not hesitate to make the sign of the cross at a public gathering. He accepts what changes have been made in the liturgy but would now stabilize liturgy and, more important, seek reversal of the trend in Catholic progressivism to turn churches into bare assembly halls devoid of sacred and moving symbolism. The conservative position is deeply concerned over intrusions of government upon religious freedom. It encourages private effort, the growth of "mediating structures" as buffers between the individual and the state—subsidiarity, in other words.

Yet both the "progressive" and conservative trends present varied pictures. Within the ranks of Catholic progressives are people with genuine and ardent concern for the poor—a range of servants of Christ like the late Dorothy Day. The U.S. Catholic Conference by and large supports the social policies of the congressional Left (excepting only the latter's abortion stands), but whether ill advised or not, the motivation appears to be one of compassion for the distressed and disadvantaged. Within the ranks of Catholic conservatives are those who express their enthusiasm for the Faith at black-tie dinners where like-minded prestigious Catholics gather to raise money for the Church, to promote ethical practices in corporate life, to encourage each other in orthodoxy, and to endeavor to present to the nation a favorable image of a vital, unified Church. More populist Catholics, also called "conservative," are found performing humbler tasks for Christ as well—serving in soup kitchens, working in hospitals, organizing prayer groups, marching arm in arm with evangelicals in pro-life demonstrations, giving personal testimony without undue concern for "image," or fear of embarrassment, on behalf of the moral positions established by Pope and magisterium.

I have no standing to advise our Church leaders, but I do have the advantage of a long perspective. That perspective is one that remembers pre–Vatican II days well, and quite differently from the crude caricatures of them now so widely popularized. Even to say "Those days weren't all that bad" is to diminish, needlessly, the then-glowing reality of American Catholicism, its courage to be "different," its boundless charities, its familiarity, intellectually, with the wellsprings of Catholic tradition. I say that with no purpose of setting the clock back and scrapping all that has been good since Vatican II. It is not a matter of setting the clock back but of setting it right—that is, according to the real perils of the times we are in. These times are thrusting us into barbarism. The Church alone can change the times.[8] The means is *not* to avoid confrontation or "get along by going along"—attitudes now too often too observable in the Church, in particular with respect to governmental regulation and taxation.

I am still an adherent of the Church, believing in God's providence and trying to see, always, whatever good I can in views advanced by either of the mixed "progressive" and conservative sides. I am always encouraged by the truly Christlike priests and nuns vitally present in our midst today. But some duties, in 1997, appear to be of the essence for the leaders of the Church to pursue. The first need is the realistic promotion of a return to the sacred. The restoration of sacramental life and prayer life among Catholics is the obvious substance of that promotion.[9] The second calls for encouraging *personal* sacrifice on the part of Catholics, not only for the support of charitable works but also in the rendering of charitable service (a thing quite different from mere advocacy of, or participation in, government welfare programs). Many Catholics today, unlike their immigrant predecessors, are not generous givers but welcome government as national caretaker. And Catholics are deeply a part of the consumerist culture. The third of these duties is the pursuit of orthodoxy in doctrine.[10] This will necessarily involve use, for example, of both pulpit and confessional in condemning contraception.[11] It calls for official and public protection of the sacred name and identity "Catholic," and the resolute avoidance of the cancerous scandal that now metastasizes in the actions of "Catholic" politicians who, unreproved, support such evils as abortion.

The failure to move decisively on these essentials, along with the effort to promote "*change*" as though it were a value, will result in a further decline in of Mass attendance, loss of religious vocations, the exodus of younger Catholics (longing for certainty and faith) into evangelical religions, and, in fact (as the least of evils), the Church's financial bankruptcy.

I am still a Catholic in order to be one small voice, not on behalf of much that is bruited as "renewal" but on behalf of the real thing.

NOTES

1. Regan Books, HarperCollins (1996).

2. *Apologia pro Vita Sua*, J. M. Dent & Sons (1934).

3. The French writer Léon Bloy in 1914 spoke of this. "When you die, that is what you take with you: the tears you have shed and the tears you have caused others to shed—your capital of bliss or terror. It is on these tears that we shall be judged, for the Spirit of God is always borne upon the waters." L. Bloy, *Pilgrim of the Absolute*, Pantheon Books (1947), 18.

4. Among these was the defense of Amish parents *Wisconsin* v. *Yoder*, 406 U.S. 205 (1972).

5. *The Thing—Why I Am a Catholic*, Dodd, Mead (1930), 26.

6. Sheed and Ward (1960).

7. The story of this appears in my article "Population Control: Civic and Constitutional Concerns," *Religion and the Public Order*, 4 (1968): 128; and in E. M. Jones, *John Cardinal Krol and the Cultural Revolution*, Fidelity Press (1995), 248–300. See also J. Kasun, *The War Against Population*, Ignatius Press (1988).

8. And happily *is* doing so in dioceses in Pennsylvania.

9. I point to the serious and prevalent decline among Catholics of respect for, and comprehension of, the Real Presence of Christ in the Eucharist in my article "Him, Not Hymn," *Homiletic and Pastoral Review* (May 1997).

10. It may be that those moves need not wait for action by the hierarchy. Russell Shaw, in a perceptive commentary on "our secularized, decadent American culture," urges the creation of faith-based communities to counter "the uncritical acceptance of secular standards and values on the part of Catholics." R. Shaw, "Back to the Ghetto: A Prescription for Evangelization," *Lay Witness*, 18 (January/February 1997): 6.

11. About which today there is appalling ignorance. I strongly commend the reader to Dr. Janet Smith's *Humanae Vitae, a Generation Later*, Catholic University of America Press (1991); and Uricchio and Williams, eds., *Proceedings of a Research Conference on Natural Family Planning*, Human Life and Natural Family Planning Foundation (1972).

As Well As I Could

Fr. Theodore M. Hesburgh, C.S.C.

I CAN never remember not being, or not wanting to be, a Catholic. While I attribute this constancy to the grace of God, and a rather complete Catholic education from the first grade to the doctorate some twenty-three years later, my life has been singularly free from doubts about my religious faith. There is nothing very romantic about this, perhaps not even exciting. However, it is the bald truth. This simple statement is a central fact in my life that I have recognized gratefully as I have grown older and encountered people who had a different life, full of doubts and wavering religious commitments. I can take no pride in an unbroken life of faith, but I do thank God for it as a special blessing I did nothing to deserve. The simplest statement I can make about it applies to faith generally; it is a pure gift of God, not something one earns or deserves.

Part of the blessing was, of course, growing up in a good Catholic family, with an Irish mother from the Bronx whose father had been born in Ireland and was strong as a rock in his faith, and a German-French father from Brooklyn who had had a difficult family life in childhood and yet practiced his faith with an unemotional steadiness that was a great example to all of his children. I also have three wonderful sisters and a brother who have never ceased to be faithful, despite all kinds of difficulties that might have overpowered them or shaken their faith. My older sister died in her early forties, leaving four small children, but her passing into eternity, which I shared closely with her as a priest, did nothing but edify me and strengthen my own faith considerably. Eternity was as real for her as the sun rising in the morning.

I suppose my first of recollection of being Catholic was when I received my First Holy Communion on my seventh birthday. I also remember that day because I received my first baseball, baseball glove, and bat—presents for my birthday and the celebration of my First Holy Communion. My dad was a great baseball fan who had a lifelong devotion to the New York Yankees and the Notre Dame football team. I assume his dedication to the Yankees came first, because I got that baseball equipment instead of a football.

I grew up in Most Holy Rosary parish in Syracuse, New York, where my father was manager of the Pittsburgh Plate Glass factory. We lived in a brand-new house in a development on the edge of Onondaga Park. Despite my father's good job, with the advent of the Great Depression we were never in a class that could be called affluent. We had everything we needed for a good family life, and that was enough.

I spent twelve years in elementary and secondary education at no cost except what my parents put into the collection at Sunday Mass. I owe this blessing particularly to the Sisters of the Immaculate Heart of Mary, headquartered in Scranton, Pennsylvania. During all of those twelve years in the parish school, I had only one lay teacher. All of the others were religious sisters who received thirty dollars a month for everything they needed. Practically all of them had master's degrees, and we all did quite well on the New York State Regents Exams that we took each June, at the end of our high school courses.

While I had a class in religion every year during those twelve years of parochial schooling, unlike many of my friends who went to public schools, I don't remember those classes as more than a gradual maturing in the teachings and practice of the faith.

The only other constant in those years was again a grace for which I will always thank God, that I never thought of being anything but a priest. Perhaps this was because we had a great Irish pastor and wonderful young priest assistants who understood us and kept us steady in our adolescent practice of the faith. Father Harold Quinn, who was a special adviser of mine, always insisted that I live what he called a "normal life" for a high school student. There were plenty of dates and dancing, sports and picnics, school plays and a good many opportunities to practice oratory. We went to Mass and received Holy Communion every day without thinking twice about it, except that it seemed the thing to do in that environment. At Confirmation, all of us took the pledge, which meant that we would not drink alcohol until after our twenty-first birthdays. Again, it was something that one did at that time, and I thank God we were spared the problems of drugs and promiscuity that most young people face today.

My wildest adventure was to skip school with my friends and go pheasant hunting on the first day of the season, a really big deal in upstate New York. We were suspended from school for a day and became ineligible for positions as class officers. It was a bit ironic, because at graduation in June 1934, the good guy who went to class that day was unable to give the graduation oration and I had to substitute for him. I also remember having the lead in a play on the life of Christ. It was a bit uncomfortable, taking the role of Christ, but I did have to learn practically everything He said in the New Testament as part of the play. The only other thing I remember about the experience was getting an infection from gluing on and taking off a beard every evening for a week.

All of us were very active in athletics, mainly baseball and football, although I was never spectacular in either sport. I dated the prettiest girl in the class, Mary Eleanor Kelley, who was not too popular with the nuns because they thought she would distract me from the vocation they thought I had. We kept in touch after graduation, and years later, I had a midnight call from Mary Eleanor, who was dying of cancer. She requested that I officiate at her funeral and see her into eternity.

When I was in eighth grade and an altar boy, four Holy Cross priests came to our parish to give a mission. While one of the missionaries was out giving the men "hell and brimstone," another sat in the sacristy with the altar boys and regaled us with wonderful stories. One of the priests, Father Tom Duffy, decided that I probably did have a vocation, and showed up at our house to talk to my mother. He told her I should go to Notre Dame and attend high school there in the seminary. When she told him, "No way," he said, "But if he doesn't do this, he may lose his vocation." (Maybe he had seen Mary Eleanor.) My mother, with her typical Irish bluntness, told him, "If he goes to a Catholic high school and lives in a practicing Catholic family and loses his vocation, then it is very simple to me—he doesn't have one." Thank God for her wisdom.

The September after my high school graduation, my mother and father, elder sister, Mary, and I drove to the University of Notre Dame, where I had been accepted in Holy Cross Seminary. My freshman year at the university was full of learning and fun, although I never did get used to that wake-up bell at 5:30 A.M. We had the normal freshman humanities courses of Latin and Greek and English literature, chemistry, drama, and speech. It was a very cold winter, so I had some great ice skating on Saint Mary's Lake. I acted in a play or two, sang in the choir, waited tables, and played football and baseball. I had a good dose of homesickness in September and October, but I guess it just meant that I had had a good home life and missed it.

At the end of freshman year, we were allowed to go home for six weeks. Then I returned to begin my novitiate year on a farm just west of the university, near a village called Rolling Prairie. That year was far more difficult than Marine boot camp. It began with twenty-nine novices and ended with seven. All seven of us were ordained priests years later. After the novitiate, clothed in my religious habit, I moved to Moreau Seminary, across the lake from Notre Dame and completed my sophomore year with more Latin and Greek, biology, literature, speech, and education courses. After a year of silence and intensive prayer in the novitiate, it was great to get back to the university and look forward to what I knew would be my favorite courses—I was to major in philosophy.

That summer I suddenly began to practice the vow of obedience that I had taken at the end of the novitiate, together with the vows of poverty and chastity. I was told that I was going to Rome for eight years, to get a doctorate in philosophy and theology at the Gregorian University.

Thus began three years in Rome. It would have been eight, but the blitzkrieg intervened, and we students were ordered back to Washington to finish our studies at Holy Cross College. My first year in Rome, I had all of my philosophy classes, and others as well, in Latin. I had to speak French in the house and Italian in the streets, and I learned to understand Spanish because I had a friend from Mexico who was too lazy to learn Italian. For a summer vacation they took us to the Tyrol, where everyone spoke German. I didn't go to Europe to study language, but I ended up learning five or six at once. I had had plenty of Latin, of course, but it was all classical and only reading, with no speaking and not much writing.

All this time, while there were the usual difficulties one faces in his early twenties in a completely new setting, I never had any thoughts about being anything but a priest, even though it was a bit tougher than I had imagined, given the educational process and the strict daily regime (now we were rising at 5 A.M). I just thought that if this was what one has to go through to be a priest, I was going to do it. In the summer of 1939, I took my final vows of poverty, chastity, and obedience. I did so with great gratitude that I had been accepted for a life into the Congregation of the Holy Cross. I would never be wealthy, I would never be married and have children, and I would do what they told me to do, but I knew it was a good life, a chance to serve God and others, the great joy of being a priest who can offer Mass each day, forgive sins, baptize, officiate at marriages, and, of course, give the final sacraments to the dying. In prospect, it seemed like a wonderful life, and indeed it has proved to be so. I have now been sixty years in the religious life and fifty-three years a priest. I attribute it to what we sing of as "Amazing Grace." But there it is, and I am grateful it has worked out that way.

By 1943, I had completed my four years of theology and was ordained at the University of Notre Dame with my parents and siblings in joyful attendance. Since the war was on, I hoped to become a Navy chaplain, but I was told to get a doctorate in theology at Catholic University. I did the next three years' work in two and then applied again to become a chaplain. The Provincial of the Order simply said, "We have more Navy at Notre Dame than they do on any ship in the Pacific, so come back here and teach theology. You can do all the chaplaining you want with five thousand Navy ROTC cadets here." I showed up for my first teaching assignment, six classes in those days, in July 1945. I guess the Lord has a good sense of humor, because two summers later, I was able to spend the summer as a chaplain on an aircraft carrier in the Pacific, which I enjoyed greatly.

During all of those years of formation and early priesthood, my faith was still growing, as I am sure it does in all of us as we pass through life in different circumstances. It carried me over every difficult situation I faced. Now I was in a different world, a world of university life, but there were plenty of chances to exercise my priesthood with long hours in the confessional, morning Mass at an ungodly hour, chaplain to the returning veterans, especially the five hundred married veterans. We had never had married people at Notre Dame before, so this was an especially exciting apostolate. I baptized two or three babies each Sunday and spent a lot of time in the maternity ward as well. All of these were new applications of the Faith, in different and often difficult circumstances, but I saw that it really worked. That was the one bright light that kept people going despite the problems that life brings.

Soon the practice of faith had to come into play again. I had done doctoral studies instead of being a chaplain, which would have been my preference, and then I had come back to teach when it seemed more promising to be a chaplain in war, but curiously I was immensely enjoying those early years back at Notre Dame. Teaching was a joy, and working with the returned veterans was an even greater joy as they struggled to rearrange their lives.

One day I passed the President of Notre Dame, Father John Cavanaugh, on one of the campus walks. He stopped me and said, "Ted, how would you like to be an administrator?" I told him frankly, "That is the last thing in the world I want to be." But, again, I had that vow of obedience. The next year, I became chairman of the Theology Department and rector of one of the largest residence halls for freshman on campus. A year later, I was Executive Vice President, and three years after that, in 1952, President of the university. I had turned thirty-five the month before. However, in those days, the term of the President was limited to six years because I was also religious superior of all of the priests on campus. When six years had passed, the administration decided to change the rules, so I had to go around that six-year course about six times, finally retiring at age seventy in 1987.

What about the Faith in all those years? It had a lot to do with fulfilling the many duties that come to a priest each day, some difficult, all satisfying. I enjoyed being a priest in those early days, and I still do. It is marvelous to see so many examples of faith in action in the lives of ordinary people. They make one a better priest by being so faithful in their lives and so loyal to their beliefs.

My world changed considerably after I become President of the university. I was now thrust into a much larger world of higher education, of government, of social action, of world problems, and of so many other challenges that it would be difficult to list them all. I found myself traveling hundreds of thousands of miles each year, abroad several times each year. And, as time went on and appointments to commissions and committees multiplied, I was spending up to half of my time away from the university, yet managing to meet all of my obligations there. I suppose what really kept me going was offering Mass each morning wherever I was, reciting my Breviary every day, managing to fit in the other prayers that bring our days together.

At first I feared that my faith would be greatly challenged. I was being thrown into a completely new world, often the only Catholic in the group working at this or that national problem, spending long hours each day on very secular subjects that were important to the world of education and justice and peace. Maybe it was the nobility of the task that kept me focused. But beyond that, I must pay homage to the wonderful people with whom I worked.

I was almost always the only Catholic in the group, not to mention the only priest in most of these national and international activities. It was pioneering, and yet, looking back over all those years in so many different secular circumstances, I cannot remember a single instance when I was not received graciously and amiably by the other members of the commissions and committees. They were always supportive and conscious of my special obligations. They knew I was offering Mass each day, early in the morning before the meetings or late at night after them, squeezing in the Breviary whenever there was a free moment, working as conscientiously as I could to learn about each new situation and problem. There was never a nasty glance or word, never a challenge to the faith they knew I practiced; indeed, they were always looking for a word of inspiration or an ethical principle, if the moment required it.

As the years passed, it became clear to me that most of my friends outside the university were not Catholic, and that I was the only priest they had ever known or called a friend. People speak of prejudice and discrimination, but I never felt a single moment of it. I respected the non-Catholics in the task we were doing together, and they always respected me more than I deserved. Often I became chairman of a commission or committee, and I always received full understanding and support from all of the members. Maybe this is unusual, but I must say that it was the norm in my own life outside the university. In a curious way, I think non-Catholics were more impressed by my celibacy than by my prayer life. One day one of them said, "Why do all of our wives love you more than they do the other members?" I responded, "Maybe it is because I am not a threat to them. They know I am promised elsewhere."

I never felt uneasy as I joined dozens of committees and commissions where I stood alone as a member of the Catholic faith and as a priest. I learned much from all of them about human cooperation, human decency, human dedication to the task at hand, and the kind of understanding that makes democracies work. I do not want to sound like Pollyanna about all of this because it is a simple fact that I think needs to be recorded. My faith was indeed bolstered by my association with so many good people who, especially in the scientific community, had no real faith at all, and many others in the international community who belonged to a variety of faiths. I even got along well with the Russian and

Chinese Communists, who somehow did not see me as a threat but, rather, as an unusual friend who was really interested in them and worked with them as fellow human beings.

On an entirely different plane, I must say that I have enjoyed the Church of Vatican II much more than I did the pre–Vatican Council Church. In many ways, the post–Vatican Catholic world seems much freer, much more open to others, more understanding in the face of conflict, more seeking of peace among different faiths and the promotion of ecumenism. As far as the practice of the Faith or the priesthood goes, the post-Vatican world is much easier. One can hear confessions everywhere, not only in one's diocese. One can celebrate Mass at any hour of the day or night, without fasting from midnight and without having to be in a church, as previously required. I enjoy the Breviary in English much more than I did in Latin, even though I had many, many years of Latin studies. Somehow it seems more reasonable to pray in one's own language. There is a certain openness to the post–Vatican II Church that I welcome and in which feel I can exercise my faith much more broadly and understandingly. Thank God for John XXIII and Paul VI, the one who initiated the Council and the one who saw it through to completion.

We will probably need another Council one of these days, but the benefits of Vatican II were and are beyond compare in revitalizing and making the practice of the Faith more human, more open and compassionate, and more satisfying. I have disagreements with decisions of higher religious authority at times, but I believe that is quite normal in a world of constant change and of the interplay of conservative and liberal points of view. I have always been in the latter camp. I believe that one can be very faithful to basic truths and standards while being very liberal in the way they are applied and practiced. I do not take this difference of approach or understanding as a matter of faith but, rather, as one of finding the best way to live and apply the Faith in each person's life. Each person has to decide that for himself or herself. In no way does it mean disloyalty. My greatest faith these days is in the working of the Holy Spirit. In the end, He will bring all to a happy conclusion.

If I were to begin life all over again, I would hope and pray that I might be born into and nurtured by this same faith. I am under no illusions that I have served the Faith as much as I should have, which only leads me to trust that the Faith has pulled me through life with no particular merit on my part except to recognize the gift for what it is, and to hope and pray that I might persevere in the Faith and serve it as best I can until my death.

Faith has enlarged my intellectual life and my profession as a priest and educator. I never felt that faith impaired my search for all knowledge on a rational basis. On the other hand, I am happy for the insights that can come only from the Faith because they are not revealed or accessible by reason alone.

I never felt that I had to apologize for my faith, but neither did I try to flaunt it in the face of others who might disagree with it. I simply tried to live it and be grateful for the light it shed upon the understanding of a difficult world and the making of difficult decisions.

I have never felt obliged to hide my faith, certainly not to force it on others, since only God can give faith. The happier moments of my life have been when I lived the Faith as well as I could.

I end with a prayer: May I die in the Faith and may I awaken in eternity to see those things that I have taken on faith as open and clear and splendid as the morning sunrise, as a smile on the face of a friend.

Roots and Reform
William X. Kienzle

WE KNEW they had hands. We knew they had faces. And we knew they jangled when they moved. The rest of their bodies were covered with yards and yards of religious habit, with headgear whose main objective was torture. They wore a larger-than-life, five-decade rosary—whence the jangle. They were (for they now are an endangered species) Catholic nuns, religious women.

They are part of the first of two reasons why I'm still a Catholic.

Not to say that small roots cannot nourish plants and trees; still, it doesn't hurt to have strong, extensive roots. And my roots in Catholicism are substantial.

Back when families were nuclear, without knowing they were, our family hung together closely and shared a strong Catholic faith. There were no others of differing sects; everybody was Catholic.

My mother, Mary Louise Boyle, had once toyed with the notion of becoming a nun. Then she caught sight of a tall, good-looking guy, Alphonso Kienzle, who managed the department store in which she worked.

She demonstrated sheet music, the only drawback being that she was still learning to read music. When a new piece came in, her supervisor would bring it to Mother, who would improvise. She was very good at that. Later, she would painstakingly learn to read and play the piece.

Al Kienzle was smitten with Mary Louise. However, Al was Lutheran—no small impediment in those days.

On his own initiative—and without telling Mary Louise—Al visited a Catholic rectory to check out Catholicism. The priest asked at the outset if he had any questions. Yes, Al said, he wanted to see everything—church and rectory—from top to bottom. On the tour, Al opened every door, examined every room, and looked in every closet. Curiosity piqued, the priest asked Al what he was looking for. Armaments. Al had heard of the "Catholic plot" to take over the country and the world by force.

Once satisfied that Catholics were mainly concerned with survival, Al took instructions. He was received into the Church—still having told Mary Louise nothing. On the first Sunday of his Catholicism, he received Communion along with Mary Louise and her family. A maddeningly typical surprise.

Everyone attended Mass every Sunday and Holy Day of Obligation. Mother attended Mass daily when possible. I have no clear memory of when they first took me to Mass. But I am aware that I never made them regret it. I took to church and Mass as a squirrel to a tree. Whenever I was in a church, it felt natural. I loved it, every minute of it.

When it was time for me to enter first grade, we moved to southwest Detroit, into a parish famed throughout the city. Holy Redeemer was gigantic, both in size and in institutional buildings. Within its boundaries were three national parishes: Polish, Lithuanian, and French. In addition to a mammoth church and rectory, there were three huge schools, an impressive home for the teaching nuns and another for the teaching brothers, an auditorium, and a full-sized gym.

The parish was staffed by priests of the Redemptorist Order. As I recall, there were ten confessionals—and confessors to spare. The grammar school was staffed by nuns, Servants of the Immaculate Heart of Mary (or IHMs—which we kids perverted to mean I Hate Men). The IHMs also taught in the girls' high school, while the Brothers of Mary taught in the boys' high school.

Someone, I know not who, had decided that boys and girls should not be together in school. Thus, from the first grade and throughout the rest of grammar school, the sexes occupied separate rooms. In high school, they occupied separate buildings. The result of this, plus the fact that I entered the seminary in the ninth grade, was that in what would have been my high school graduating class of 1946, I knew only one young woman—my cousin. The result of *this*, plus the fact that I spent all my summers as a counselor at a Catholic boys' camp, was that I was a prime candidate for the celibate life.

Today there is nothing to match the parochial school of my day because there is nothing to match the teaching orders of nuns. Without those heroic women, I suspect that no one would have seriously considered establishing a Catholic school system.

For the most part, Catholics were not wealthy back then. Against all odds, and at great personal sacrifice, they built schools for their children and homes for their priests and nuns. There was little money left over for teachers. But parents knew where the perfect teachers of religion were to be found.

Nurtured by the parochial schools, young men and women flocked to the religious life. The nuns let us know that "first class" boys went to the seminary and became priests. "Second class"—because females were genetically incapable of being first class—girls ended up in the convent and classroom or hospital. The rest—those unable to control concupiscence—got married.

In 1934, I began a Catholic education that would last twenty years, from the first grade through the theologate. I was nowhere near perfect. In the fifth grade, a nun in frustration loudly admonished me, "Mr. Kienzle, you would make Job chew carpets." Her message was lost on me. It was several years before I learned that Job, an Old Testament character, was the quintessential patient man. This discovery cast new light on just how disconcerting I could be as a student.

One of my earliest lessons in parochial school was that I was there to learn—not to question. That approach to the philosophy of education was to endure through all my education. And it held radical consequences when things changed—as I will explain shortly.

For the first eight years of my formal education, we studied geography, history, English, and the like. But of far greater effect on us—and what separated us from our non-Catholic friends—was our study of religion. Very definitely the Catholic religion. Even today, Catholics of that era do well on trivia questions based on the Baltimore Catechism.

"God made me to know Him, to love Him, and to serve Him in this life and to be happy with Him forever in the next." That, at least, is how I remember it. The Baltimore Catechism has been remaindered to extinction.

About this time, we Catholic kids were scheduled to select role models. A fair number of us chose a particular priest—or the priesthood in general.

Already I had adopted the Church as my home away from home. Of course I became an altar server (formerly "altar boy," but my raised consciousness won't permit a sex change). Those were the days of Latin responses to Mass prayers.

Peripheral observation revealed a vocation that offered everything I wanted: priests wore a distinctive uniform, were addressed as "Father" even by people two or three times older, and officiated at Mass—my most fervent desire. A priest was a personified employment agency as well as a provider of emergency housing, food, and/or clothing.

These yearnings occurred several years before one of the great recruiting films of all time, *Going My Way*. After that movie came out, even more Catholic boys wanted to grow up to be "Father" Chuck O'Malley (Bing Crosby). No matter what your need, "Just dial 'O' for O'Malley" and your troubles would be gone.

But even before that, I wanted to be "more" than a Catholic. To do that, one went to a seminary. As far as the types of priesthood available, I knew there were Jesuits and I knew there was Maryknoll. And of course there were Redemptorists. But I was unaware of the bread and butter of the priesthood—the diocesan clergy, aka parish priests, aka secular priests. In the nick of time I learned not only of the existence of diocesan clergy but that their seminary was a streetcar ride away.

And so, hopeful that God wanted me, I enlisted. And my Catholic roots deepened measurably. The seminary in the Forties and Fifties was, arguably, at its zenith. Hundreds of boys and young men jammed the corridors, the chapel, the study halls, the classrooms, the dormitories, the private rooms.

Absent from our lives and our futures were females—with one exception: several Sisters of St. Joseph, of Nazareth, Michigan, lived in the convent annex and worked in the kitchen, the chapel, and the infirmary. The average age of these lovely ladies was approximately 104. The seminary was taking no chances. The Sisters provided a touch of graciousness. A flower or two on the refectory tables helped inject an atmosphere of some slight civility into what might have gone from horseplay to an all-out food fight.

The most common characteristic of all the nuns I've come to know is dedication. They testified (and still do), sometimes silently, to a deep and motivating faith. Their example contributes to why I'm still a Catholic.

The theater occasionally pokes gentle fun at Catholic nostalgia. Some time ago, we attended a performance of *Do Patent Leather Shoes Really Reflect Up?* In the next row, during the performance, was a lady pounding the seat in front of her and screaming, between tears of laughter, "That's the way it was! That's the way it was!" That *is* the way it was. There was humor to be found in the unique combination of the nuns' dedication and naiveté.

In our seminary, for example, the nuns, for their *recreation*, did our laundry and repaired our clothing. One of the nuns—I'm sure not all of them—was in charge of replacing buttons lost in the laundry. For reasons known only to her, when she could not find the right-sized button, she sewed the buttonhole shut. At one time I owned a white shirt that had neither buttons nor buttonholes.

We seminarians were encouraged to send our soiled clothing to the laundry weekly. There was, however, one item that was forbidden to be included: the athletic supporter. No reason was given for this exception, but then seminary discipline did not include reasoning. Inevitably, one of my classmates mistakenly deposited his athletic supporter in the wash. Weeks passed, but the item did not come back. Finally, it was returned. It had been washed, starched, and ironed. Pinned to it was a note in the tiny, spidery handwriting so typical of nuns. It read, "This pair of undershorts is beyond repair." The incident gave us some understanding as to why the proscription.

I have rarely been disillusioned by a nun. By and large, they are models of credibility. For a little more than three years, as a young priest, I was assigned as a regular confessor (meaning I heard confessions every week) to a convent of some twenty Sisters. Each week I came and listened to a recitation of small imperfections. Their lives consisted of prayer, study, and work. Some of these nuns are among my closest friends today.

Also among close friends are the men who inhabited the seminary with me. Those of us who entered the seminary at our earliest opportunity—the ninth grade—soon learned that only a very small percentage of our group could hope to survive the coming twelve years; the dropout rate was extremely high. However, others—delayed vocations, they were called—joined our ranks. Even many of these left before ordination. Boys left the seminary of their own volition, or were advised to leave.

There were so many of us that the faculty reacted quickly when they spotted trouble. Fortunately, they were slightly more tolerant of trouble*makers*. For that was my contribution. Demerits were awarded by college prefects. A certain number of demerits meant assignment to the work crew. I estimate that I came very close to having sufficient demerits to be dismissed. In any case, I have the impression that I worked my way through school on demerits.

Ours was a class that produced some outstanding achievers: a Cardinal (Edmund Szoka); a best-selling author and poet (James Kavanaugh); a principal of the first diocesan high school (Thomas McAnoy); others who became chancellors of some of the Michigan dioceses, as well as chancery personnel; and two editors of the *Michigan Catholic* newspaper.

Many of us boarded in the seminary. Thus, we shared our adolescence as well as our young adulthood. In relationships at times painful, at times rewarding, we bonded. Beyond our September-to-June togetherness, some of us were summertime counselors at a Catholic boys' camp. Toward the end of our time there, someone took count: out of the twenty-some counselors, twelve of us were classmates. Even during Christmas and Easter vacations we frequently met for movies, ball games, and other activities. It was as if, literally, we could not get enough of each other.

Of all the things we shared over so many years, of all the bonding that took place, nothing was more elemental for each of us than our Catholicism and the dream and desire to be a Catholic priest.

I remember those associations with family, dedicated nuns, larger-than-life priests, and seminary buddies as roots of my Catholic faith that intertwined and became ever stronger and a source of stability.

Also contributing mightily to the depth and strength of my Catholic roots were the irreplaceable men, women, and children who made up the laity. For excellent reasons they were known as the Faithful.

Young married couples, in the early years of my ministry, generally had many more children than they would have planned. Moral theology of that day gave two—and only two—methods of family planning: the rhythm system and abstinence. In both city and suburban parishes I served, women referred to their "eternity clothes."

Still, the laity supported their parishes unstintingly. They attended Mass each and every Sunday. They turned out for meetings. They taught catechism. They were attentive, respectful, and obedient.

No one questioned the shape of the Church. It was a pyramid. On top was the Pope. The next layer comprised bishops. Then came priests. Finally, as the fundamental foundation of it all, was the laity, bearing all on their shoulders.

The Pope could, and did, formulate both dogma and morality. It was the Pope who, in 1950, promulgated the doctrine of Mary's assumption into Heaven. This may or may not be the sole infallible statement, properly defined. Shortly after that, it was the Pope who, in an address to midwives, formulated the morally acceptable method of rhythm for family planning.

There was little difficulty keeping up with subtle changes and developments in Church doctrine. The wheels of the Church ground very slowly.

In all of this, the lively faith of the laity was a challenge to me to believe more securely. Their faith was one more reason why I'm still a Catholic.

What I have chronicled thus far was a quiet time. A time of unchanged faith, of unquestioning fidelity.

Then came the Second Vatican Council. Change stormed through the window to the future opened by the beloved Pope John XXIII.

Before 1962 and the beginning of Vatican II, Catholics usually had rather frivolous reasons for abandoning their Catholic faith. The story is told of an FBI agent spotting Father Philip Berrigan among the nine activists who burned draft records in a parking lot in May 1968. The agent (a Catholic), recognizing the priest from a similar event at the Baltimore Customs House seven months earlier, exclaimed. "Him again! Good God, I'm changing my religion."

Waging peace was not necessarily a natural outcome of Vatican II. But differing from or being scandalized by one or another priest was a classic, if nonsensical, reason to quit Catholicism—before or after Vatican II.

A popular columnist for one of Detroit's metropolitan daily papers made no bones about it. He had been drafted near the end of World War II. A Catholic, he was made assistant to a chaplain who was not only a priest but a redneck racial bigot. That was the end of Catholicism for that columnist.

This sort of story is all too common. I have never understood why someone would abandon something as important as a religious affiliation because some member lacked humanity, or because of some disagreement in how to confront a delicate situation. Is it because the defector's roots were too shallow?

No right-minded person should expect perfection from any Catholic, any priest, any bishop, any Pope. But there are those who would discard me for suggesting that a Pope could be imperfect, Borgia Popes notwithstanding.

When we come to Vatican II, reasons for staying in or leaving the Church become more exotic and interesting. In January 1959, Pope

John XXIII called for a Church Council and for the reform of canon law. He got his Council, which ran from 1962 to 1965.

Vatican II, I believe, was a divider almost on the order of B.C. and A.D. And it gave relevance to the topic of this essay—why I'm still a Catholic.

For the once-a-week Catholic, the Council changed the language and liturgy of the Mass. Gradually, like the birth of an elephant, English supplanted Latin. In the distribution of Communion, the priest no longer said, "Corpus Domini nostri Jesu Christi custodiat animam tuam in vitam aeternam [May the body of our Lord Jesus Christ guard your soul into eternal life], Amen."

Now the priest said, "Corpus Christi [the body of Christ]." To which the communicant responded, "Amen." (Except on at least one occasion, when, to the priest's "Corpus Christi," the distracted communicant responded, "Texas.")

This liturgical change most affected the weekly attendees at services. That was the aim of the liturgists, who were perhaps the best-prepared group at the Council. (And it has been said that the difference between a liturgist and a terrorist is that one can reason with a terrorist.)

"Community" was a very "in" word. Almost nothing could be done unless there was a community aboard. Gone was the solitary Mass witnessed only by a server in a private chapel or at a side altar. I was about to do that very thing once, when the seminarian sacristan observed, "You gonna say one against the wall?" Contempt for the procedure dripped. But I did it anyway.

"Participation" was an equally "in" word. Damned was the practice of attending Mass on Sunday—or any day, for that matter—and listening, observing, and praying privately. By bringing the altar closer to the congregation and facing them, the priest was now part of the participating community.

Church music suffered the cruelest blow. Hundreds of years had been spent developing Church music. There never was a musical expression to match the polyphony of Palestrina, Perosi, and others, as well as the ethereal quality of plainchant (witness the recent sales of CDs of monastic song). The problem was not with the music. I can remember listening, without any compulsion to participate, to the seminary choir's magnificent rendition of this glorious music. If all parishes could have experienced that soaring beauty, they would never have tolerated what was to come. One does not have to pray and sing aloud to pray and sing.

But classical Church music had been butchered by parish choirs and was a cripple waiting for the coup de grâce. Enter Church music composed after the Council. It was intended to help form community by encouraging active participation in the liturgy. By and large, the music is puerile and badly rendered. About the only time it rises to the level of what we've lost is when we borrow some of the majestic melodies of our Protestant brethren—music that, not unlike our lost treasure, has developed and proved itself over much time.

Catholic congregations have found post-Council liturgy to be a contributing factor to the statement "This is why I'm still a Catholic." Or "This is why I'm not." While I think we could at least have preserved and perfected the pre-Conciliar liturgy, our present form of worship would never drive me out of the Church.

However, I believe there is a deeper question in the case of thousands of priests worldwide: Why are we not still priests? It is a source of mild irritation when people ask me, "Why did you leave the Church?" I didn't leave the Church; I left the priesthood. But why?

I spent the major part of the first third of my life looking forward to being, and preparing to be, a priest. Ordination day, June 5, 1954, was, and remains, the happiest day of my life. So why, though still a practicing Catholic, am I no longer a priest?

The reason, in two words, is "canon law." Vatican II did its work over a four-year span. It issued sixteen painstakingly developed documents. In one of those documents it is stated that the Church is "the People of God."

An interesting concept. But if the Church were the People of God, we would have women priests and married priests. The results of Father Andrew Greeley's surveys clearly demonstrate that. The People of God are boxed in, just as they always have been, by Church law.

Recall Pope John XXIII, way back in 1959, calling for the reformation of canon law. Twenty-four years later, the new code was published. It substituted 1,752 laws for 2,414. But I believe the presumption in all of that law—former and present—favors the institution and protects God. I'm not sure why.

Several years before the promulgation of the new code, I met an internationally recognized expert on Church law. A Trappist, he was a charter member of the commission in charge of the reform. He told me that the only way he had of knowing he was still a member is that every few years he received a notice of some sort. He thought it might be good to scrap codified law entirely and move to constitutional law. The next question, of course, would be: Who would write the Constitution?

For me, far more than its sixteen documents, Vatican II left its spirit behind after it ended. Until that Council, almost all of us learned. We did not question. However, the Council encouraged testing, reasoning, questioning. Prior to this, we were presented with dogmas or moral teachings *and* the proof and reasoning underlying them. All this we memorized and entered on examination papers.

Now there was a fresh and scholarly approach to Sacred Scripture. And with that, we more deeply understood the human authors of all the books that make up the Bible. These writers gave the Word of God to their readers. How could they do otherwise? They were not writing to or for us. However, we read these books centuries after the ancient teachers wrote them. A modern study of the Bible needs not only a translation from Hebrew and Greek but also from ancient cultures to today's world. With this knowledge, this insight, we are able to more perfectly interpret the Scripture that formulates dogma, law, and morality.

Of course that has made it possible for some scholars, once the bit was in their teeth, to run away from a traditional position to teach near insanity.

For many, laity and clergy alike, even the orthodox interpretation of Scripture was disquieting. So many of us had been taught that nothing in the Church ever changed. Now "change" was the relevant word.

Church law perhaps took the most serious blows. And rightly so. Few things affected Catholics in troubled marriages more devastatingly than those canons that dealt with marriage—especially with regard to divorce and remarriage.

A Catholic planning marriage, if either party had been previously married, had to zero in on an annulment, which meant that the previously married person had to prove, to the Church's satisfaction, that no marriage had truly existed. There had been a ceremony and the exchange of consent, but for a reason on the canonist's list, a valid marriage had not occurred. The simple, honest statement, "It didn't work. We gave it our every effort. It was a nice try, but it fell apart," was not enough.

In my early priestly years, the Church would accept only a few reasons for initiating a nullity process. And that was only the start. Once the case was accepted, the burden of proof was entirely on the petitioner.

Today, in the distant wake of Vatican II, the Church accepts more reasons. Still, one is moved to wonder whether the Church should be in the business of granting or withholding declarations of nullity. It's like the motel guest who, on complaining, "There's a shark in the swimming pool," is assured by the manager, "The shark is quite friendly." Yes, but the point is that there shouldn't *be* a shark in the swimming pool.

In the light of all this, there arose a concept called "the pastoral solution," the purpose of which was to acknowledge that there are reasons for a dissolution of attempted marriage beyond the scope of Church law. In effect, canon law, as it is presently constituted, cannot address some of the reasons why marriages break down.

In the "pastoral solution," a priest encourages such petitioners to follow their conscience. They have been married, say, by a judge rather than a priest because canon law bars the priest as official witness in such cases. However, the couple sincerely believe before God that they are married. The pastoral solution then tells them to behave as though they were married by a priest. They are encouraged to take the Sacraments and live Catholic lives.

I once read a transcript of a debate on the pastoral solution between the head of a marriage tribunal and a widely respected moral theologian.

The monsignor keeps stating, "You can't do that. It's against Canon Law." And the theologian patiently explains, "Yes, you're right. We are saying that this is beyond the scope of current Church law. So the matter is settled through this pastoral solution." *"But you can't do that. . . ."*

The point of all this—and more—was stated years ago by the then Bishop of Lansing, Michigan, in his column in the *Catholic Weekly*. Bishop Kenneth Povich wrote of me and my books that although I saw all her warts and blemishes, I loved the Catholic Church. And that, I think, says it.

I have a priest friend who likes to say, "Catholicism is the product. Sell it. Don't knock it." To a degree, I could accept that. But it is clearly possible that the Institutional Church can be mistaken. Very recently, for example, the Vatican agreed that the earth really does revolve around the sun. And there was the classic confrontation in Antioch when Paul, in no uncertain terms, corrected Peter, who was waffling over dietary customs important to Jewish Christians but meaningless to Gentile converts.

It seems not only possible but natural to love the Church even when not agreeing with every Institutional word. That very love may lead to charitable dialogue. The ancient dictum still holds: The Church is ever in need of reform.

We want sinless Presidents, congressmen, mayors, police, parents, and others in authority, but we are never going to get them. There may be those who insist on a sinless Pope, bishops, and/or priests. But we're never going to get these, either.

Jesus promised that His Church would be indefectible ("I will be with you until the end of time"), not impeccable (sinless).

So, after all these years, why am I still a Catholic?

- Because of all the training and examples I've received from my parents, my family.
- Because of the selfless Sisters who taught so eloquently by word and example.

- Because of the priests who inspired me to follow them into one of the most glorious vocations imaginable.
- Because of the enduring friendships made in the seminary and in the priesthood.
- Because of the marvelous and sacrificing laity it was my honor to serve. (Incidentally, having gone through the process of laicization, I have been "reduced to the lay state"—the Institution's expression, not mine. However, no person or thing can erase the "mark.")
- In spite of—no, *because* of all those warts and blemishes. The Institution needs help, not desertion. As a priest, I could and did keep the Church's rules without undue problem. But as a representative of that Church, I found it increasingly impossible to inflict the chains of Church law—law on which Church theologians themselves could not agree—on the laity. The sheep look to the shepherd to protect and guide them, not to confuse and inflict torturous strictures upon them.
- Finally, I am still a Catholic because I need the Church. I attend Mass not out of obligation, but out of need. I need the Eucharist. I need Christ's presence in my life. I need the peace, pardon, reconciliation, and love that I know I can find in the Catholic Church. A Church that is not static, but growing, moving, evolving, loving, trying.

To borrow from Martin Luther, who, sad to say, did not remain within the Church: "Here I stand; I can do no other. God help me. Amen" (speech at the Diet of Worms, April 18, 1521).

I Like Being Catholic
Fr. Andrew M. Greeley

I AM still a Catholic because of the beauty of Catholicism, beauty being truth in its most attractive form. It is the beauty of the images and stories of Catholicism that keep me in the Church, not the wisdom or intelligence or virtue of the Church leadership.[1] Beauty, truth in its most attractive form, is not weaker than prosaic truth but stronger.

I am also still a Catholic because of the warmth of the social support that the Catholic community provides, most often, though not always, through the neighborhood parish.

I'm still a Catholic because I was born Catholic, raised Catholic, educated Catholic, and like being Catholic. I'll never stop being Catholic, despite the fact that many of the current leaders of the Institutional Church are corrupt thugs, from the parish right up to the Vatican. The word "still" might be construed as suggesting that we who remain in the Church are somehow a declining minority. In fact, 85 percent of those who were raised Catholics are "still" Catholics. It is those who depart who are the exception. Moreover, the departure rate has not changed in the last thirty-five years, despite the enormous turbulence that has shaken the Church since the end of the Second Vatican Council. If the idiots who are running things (most notably bishops and we priests) have not driven the lay folk out with thirty-five years of insensitivity and stupidity, then I suspect that they will never drive them out.

But surely "thinking Catholics" have a harder time staying in the Church?

About 2 percent of the American population can be classified as "intellectuals"—writers, artists, teachers, professors, scholars, researchers, musicians. Two percent of American Catholics fall into the same category. Their defection rate from the Church is *lower* than that of other Catholics, and their Mass attendance rate is higher.

One does not justify one's Catholic allegiance by counting noses. But one can refute the foolish myth that Catholics, especially well-educated Catholics, are leaving the Church, and clear the ground for a discussion of a more serious subject: Whence Catholic loyalty?

Catholics like being Catholic. Why should they leave?

I once had an argument with Sam Donaldson (a nice man) on the *This Week with David Brinkley* program about whether a Catholic who disagrees with the Pope is no longer Catholic. Mr. Donaldson said that he had "always believed" such was the case. I'm not sure that I persuaded him. In fact, one stops being Catholic only when one formally renounces the Church or joins another church. Of those who leave the Church, about half do so at the time of marriage to someone who is not Catholic and who is stronger in his/her religious faith than the Catholic party is. The other half leaves for reasons connected with sex or authority.

"If you don't like being a Catholic," a right-wing kook recently wrote me, "why don't you join a Church in which people don't think birth control is wrong, support women clergy, disagree with the Pope, think a woman has the right to an abortion, and approve of married clergy?"

I didn't reply to him, because I don't waste my time replying to right-wing kooks. But if I had, I would have said that I belong to such a Church, and its name is Catholicism.

To which he would have said that such people are not good Catholics. Perhaps, but judgments of that sort should be left to God.

Doubtless some of the authors in this volume will say that they are Catholics because Catholicism provides certainty, that papal authority gives them the confidence that their convictions are right, that they possess the "Truth."

Ask such folks whether they believe slavery is moral, that coeducation is against the natural law, that the sun revolves around the earth, that those who are not Catholics cannot be saved, that the theory of religious freedom is wrong—all doctrines that Popes have taught, most of them in the present century. They avoid the question because they define papal infallibility far more broadly than the Church does, because they are ignorant of history, and because their personalities require an absolute certainty that the human condition cannot provide.

For such men and women, (misunderstood) infallibility is more important than the core doctrine of Christianity: that God is reconciling, forgiving Love—the central truth about God that Jesus came to teach.

Such rigidity is most like to occur among converts who came to the Church seeking total and absolute certainty, or among cradle Catholics who find in such religious rigidity confirmation of their own radically conservative political convictions, the kind of persons who feel that when they use the word "liberal" against someone else, that person is dismissed from the list of those who are entitled to civil discourse and respect for their human integrity.

I am not denying that there are certain clearly specified times when Popes are immune from mistakes. I am, rather, asserting that such times in the history of the Church are rare, and that far more frequent are those times when Popes, like everyone else, make terrible mistakes.

I have been called an incorrigible liar for my list of papal mistakes. Events like that, it is said, never happened. That is the way the integralist responds to the facts of history.

Most of us who are still Catholics remain so for these two reasons—the stories and images the Church discloses and the community support Catholicism provides. This is an assertion based on reflection of what appeals to us in the Church and not a spontaneous answer. For most of us, not being Catholic is unthinkable. What else would we be if we were not Catholic? We may drift to the fringes of the Church in our late teens and/or young adulthood, but when it comes time to marry, and especially time to raise our children, we look around and say to ourselves,

"It might not be much of a church right now, but it's the only one I have, and I don't want to be anything else." This might not seem like rational behavior. It might, rather, seem like instinct, "feel," habit, inertia. Yet, if religion is story before it is everything else and story after it's everything else, then feel and instinct for the quality and the attractiveness of the story are all-important.

Before we reach grammar school, before our formal religious instruction has begun, our imaginations have been filled with Catholic images and stories, pictures of God and Jesus and Jesus' mother that will never be extirpated from our imaginations. In this sense, the dictum "Once a Catholic, always a Catholic" is true. We might leave the Church, temporarily or permanently, but we cannot escape the images and the stories.

I tried to make this point in my first major novel, *The Cardinal Sins*: the key scene in the book occurs when two childhood friends who were once very much in love, and will always love each other, meet, one wanting to go to confession to the other. "I focused on all the ugly things and forgot about Father Conroy and Sister Caroline and First Communion and May crownings and High Club dances."

This scene is patently the core of the book, for it articulates the book's major theme and explains the lifelong relationship between Kevin and Ellen. None of the mean and nasty critics who attacked the book commented on that scene. Somehow they missed it.

Yet that scene tells why I am still a Catholic and why most of us, at least when we come to think about it, are still Catholic; why even the most arrogant, ignorant, insensitive leader cannot drive us away from our Catholic heritage.

We were taught in the seminary that the Mass is the center of Catholic life. I found that hard to believe, because it was so boring in those days. Yet now I am convinced that our teachers were right, though characteristically for the wrong reason. When people who have been away from the Church for a long time—whether for reasons of the Right or the Left or for what some damn fool priest has said to them—return, the first thing they usually say is how happy they will be to participate in the Mass again.

When one considers that for many of them, the Mass they knew was mumbled in obscure Latin, and even today is often celebrated in a monotone and accompanied by semiliterate lectors, rotten music, sinfully bad homilies, and insulting commentators, the appeal of the Mass is astonishing.

The other story that has incredible power for Catholics is the story that "constitutes" Catholicism (and Orthodoxy) over against the other religions of Christianity—in the sense that it sums up, at the level of metaphor and story, the Catholic conviction that our reconciling, forgiving God lurks everywhere in the objects, events, and persons of our life experience.

It is, of course, the story of Mary, the Mother of Jesus, who represents the mother love of God, the truth that while God loves us in many different ways, She also loves us the way a mother loves a newborn child she holds in her arms. Any religious heritage with such a story is well nigh irresistible to its members. If the love of the mother for her child, to whom she has given life and whom she is about to nurse, is a valid metaphor for what creation and life and death are about, then that is very good news indeed—perhaps too good to be true, but true nonetheless.

So some of our stupid ecumenists, having no idea what the metaphor of Mary means (and not caring about it, either) have been willing to sacrifice it on the altar of Church unity. The May crowning that meant so much to Kevin and Ellen is passé, unfashionable, and neither politically nor liturgically correct.

Liturgy, properly carried out, should be a *représentation collective*, as Emile Durkheim called such celebrations, an experience that creates an "effervescence" of happiness and joy among the congregants. No matter how discouraged or depressed I am when I begin the liturgy, at the end I am filled with hope and joy.

That's not the purpose of liturgy, the liturgical purist protests.

Isn't it? Why else do we call it a celebration? Why else is it a continuation of the family celebration of the Jewish seder?

Why are most Catholics still Catholic? Why am I still Catholic? As a quick, shorthand explanation—on which there could be much commentary—because of the Eucharist and the Madonna, and because of God's reconciling, forgiving, ever-pursuing love that both stories make flesh. We Catholics know that, even if we are not used to articulating our answer in that form.

The second appeal of Catholicism is its communal emphasis, which in the Ellen-Kevin scene is closely related to the sacramental imagery. Catholics are much more involved in community than are Protestants, a phenomenon that is revealed in their attachment to neighborhoods, their involvement in parish activities, their social and political attitudes, and their family lives. (Catholics, for example, are more frequently in contact—personal and telephonic—with parents, children, siblings, and other relatives than are Protestants.)

For the purpose of the present essay, the issue is not whether this difference is good or bad (I think the Catholic way is better, but I'm a Catholic), but whether it is true. In my research on religion around the world, I have found in every country I have studied that Catholics place more emphasis on community relationships than do Protestants (net of all other background variables).

One would expect such difference in imagination if theological perspective still matters: for the churches of the Reformation, salvation is essentially an individual activity. For Catholicism, it has always been essentially a communal activity.

I discovered how the combination of the two works (and a proof that they do work) in a recent research exercise. The first finding was rather surprising: Catholics are more likely to attend symphony concerts, operas, dance performances, and art exhibitions than are Protestants. The second finding was even more surprising: church attendance correlated positively with fine arts participation for Catholics and negatively for Protestants. It was precisely among regular church attendees that one found the difference in artistic involvement between the two denominations. Liturgy, even bad liturgy (and most Catholic liturgy in this country is bad liturgy), affects Catholic behavior.

As I looked at the models that emerged from this analysis I heard Kevin and Ellen talking again.

I grew up in a neighborhood parish in the 1930s and the 1940s that was more progressive than most because we had the dialogue Mass. I lived each year through the cycles of the liturgical seasons and devotions to the saints. I knew the warmth and comfort of this environment long before I went to school. While the Catholic school I attended celebrated both community and story (better at some times than at others), there seemed to be little connection between the religious environment and the doctrines I learned from the catechism. We lived the sacramental (incarnational) imagination, but we really did not know what we were doing or why. Only later, when, heavily influenced by David Tracy and John Shea, I began my several decades of sociological and later storytelling work on the religious imagination, did I begin to grasp what we were doing and why, and the enormous appeal that the sacramental imagination possesses.

It is why people like being Catholic and stubbornly refuse to leave. When I explain my theory to the laity, they are rarely surprised. Of course that's why we stay, they say. Have you just figured that out?

I confess that I have not been very successful in persuading bishops, priests, and theologians of the advantages of this perspective. In general, such people are prosaic. They consider metaphors to be a distraction.

Nowhere in this rationale for "still" being Catholic do I mention doctrine; I say nothing about infallibility (which everyone knows is the most important Catholic doctrine!) or primacy or authority or resurrection or life after death.

In fact, doctrine results from reflection on experiences and images and stories. It is essential because we are rational, reflective beings, and we must articulate our experiences and our insights in prose sentences and in systematic organization of such sentences. We cannot do without creeds and catechisms and theology. But the origins and raw power of religion are found in the stories.

Catholic stories are incarnational; they speak of God incarnate in the human condition at Christmas and God going down to the Valley of Death with us and returning alive with us on Easter. They speak of a community of the followers of Jesus bonding with one another to pass on the heritage that is formed by the stories. The doctrines are latent in the stories. Both are necessary, but the stories come first. Alas, for much of what passes for Catholic religious education, the stories are discarded in favor of the doctrines. All the Trinitarian and Christological controversies in the early Church, as important as they may be, do not have the appeal or the value of the image of Madonna and Child.

(As the Orthodox seem to know better than we do, the story of the Trinity is the story that God is a relationship, and our task is to reenact for those around us the mystery of the Love that binds God together. It is not an optional and unintelligible story for them, as it seems to have become for us.)

The doctrines help us to stay in the Church when we find ourselves reflecting on religion (as least when the doctrines are properly explicated), but the stories make us want to stay in the Church.

I'm "still" a Catholic because of the stories I heard while I was growing up in the 1930s and 1940s in St. Angela parish on the West Side of Chicago. I have reflected on the stories and on the doctrines I learned in my various educational endeavors and, with the help of Fathers Tracy and Shea and my theory of the sociology of religion, I see how the stories (now embraced in what Paul Ricoeur calls the second naiveté) and the community still drive my religious life and underpin my religious faith.

The only difference between my experience and that of most other Catholics who are "still" Catholic is that my various professions (priest, sociologist, storyteller) have forced me to make more explicit the link between St. Angela in 1934 and the present than has been necessary for them. They also tend to think that my explanation, when I offer it, is self-evident.

Where does the Institutional Church fit into why I am a Catholic? Do I think that the stories are more important than the Church? That is a foolish question. The Church exists to tell the stories (and, as Father Shea says, to break the bread, to preside over the community). It also exists to protect the stories from misunderstanding and distortion down through the years and the centuries. That is not an option; it is essential. But the Church is not a proper object for worship. It is made up of human beings with all the faults of human beings, and through the centuries some of these faults have been horrendous. The men who hold office in the Church have great responsibilities, but they are not sacred persons. We honor them, but we do not worship them. We worship only God.

Only those who are unaware of history think that Church leaders are sacred people. The leadership of the Church has not improved all that much since the time of the Apostles—and they were, on the record, no prizes. It is time, and long past time, to desacralize Church leaders.

On the other hand, those who leave the Church because they have discovered how flawed many leaders are, are ignorant of history. Jesus never promised us saints. Nor did he promise that the saints who on occasion might be in charge would be either effective administrators or wise leaders.

Peter was not a sacred person and didn't act like one. Whenever Popes began to think they were sacred, they made a catastrophic mistake. We worship the God we encounter in the stories, the God we reflect on in our doctrines; we do not worship our institution or our leaders. We acknowledge the necessity of the former and the modest respect due the latter. And nothing more.

If I had been born a Baptist or a Presbyterian, would I still be one? Probably. Americans tend to settle for the religion of their parents in their own adulthood. I might think that Catholics are idolaters because of their angels and saints and souls in Purgatory, and their worship of the Mother of Jesus. I might think that their blind obedience to the Pope makes it impossible for them to think for themselves. This essay is not an attempt to refute anyone else's religion; rather, it is an explanation of why, given my background and experience, I like being Catholic.

There are problems with the Catholic imagination. Precisely because

it believes that God lurks everywhere, that everything can be a sacrament, and that all is grace, it is prone to superstition, folk religion,
idolatry, and institution worship. It can easily succumb to what sociol-
ogists call the Iron Law of Oligarchy: means become ends and the ends
are forgotten. When Catholics worship the Church instead of God, they
become victims of that law. The Church has become an end in itself and
not a means for the revelation of God's reconciling love. The familiar
phrase "for the good of the Church" becomes an excuse for much evil.
As the late Jesuit John Courtney Murray once remarked ironically of a
prominent archbishop, "He's a perfectly honest man. He would never
tell a lie except for the good of the Church."

The Church must always, therefore, be involved in the process of
reforming itself, "*Ecclesia Semper Reformanda.*" That constant reformation must occur everywhere, from the papacy on down.

The demand that the papacy and the whole Institutional Church always be in a process of reform will be shocking only to those who think
that the perfection of the institution and its leadership is the proper object
of faith. But our faith is not in an institution or in institutional leadership
(despite the Catholic conservatives in this book); it is in the God of Love
revealed in the teachings of Jesus, in the stories He told and the stories
we tell about Him—the stories that are passed on by our heritage. The
institution exists for the heritage (indeed, is essential for the transmission
of the heritage); the heritage does not exist for the institution.

Doctrine never exhausts the truth and the beauty of story. Thus, if I
am asked whether I believe in the Madonna and Child or the Incarnation,
my answer is that they are one and I believe in both. The doctrine of
God become human is surely true, though it is an abstract statement of
the truth contained in the story that begins with a journey from Nazareth
to Bethlehem.

It is worth noting that it took four centuries to make the doctrine
reasonably precise, while the story was there at the beginning. Each
requires the other, but it is the story that appeals to the total human. It
is the beauty of the story that holds Catholics to their heritage.

I'm still a Catholic because of the beauty of the Catholic stories.

So are most of us Catholics.

An appeal to beauty may seem a weak argument; surely it will seem weak to many Catholic conservatives. Again I remind them that we were Catholics for several centuries before the doctrines acquired some precision. It was the beauty of the stories and the lives inspired by the stories, particularly the Christmas and Easter stories, that appealed to those who heard them. Whatever appeal our idiot leaders have left us is still to be found in the beauty of the stories.

Beauty is not opposed to truth. It is simply truth in its most attractive form.

I wonder how I would be able to explain why I am still a Catholic to Sam Donaldson. If I said to him it was because of the beauty of Catholic stories, he wouldn't know what I was talking about.

Or to the ineffable Phil Donahue, whose main concern seems to be whether masturbation is a mortal sin. Or to those Catholic conservatives for whom a list of doctrinal assents is the proper measure of Catholicism.

One of which assents is NOT to the notion that God is love, a notion they find dangerous.

Too bad for St. John.

They are the heretics, the falsifiers of the tradition, the scribes and Pharisees of our time, the false prophets.

Pay them no heed.

NOTE

1. A consideration of some of the classic blunders of Catholic history should be enough to establish that leaders make terrible mistakes, often because of a lust to sustain their own power. Thus the Vatican's termination of the work of the Jesuits in India and China was a disaster, as has been its more recent policy in the Netherlands, which all but destroyed Dutch Catholicism. An example of a wise policy that was approved, though just barely, was Rome's support for the innovations of Cyril and Methodius among the Slavic tribes. If most Slavs are Christian today and many of them Catholic, and few Chinese and Japanese are Christian, the reason is a wise Vatican decision in the former case and an intolerably stupid decision in the latter. History will probably conclude that the birth control encyclical of Paul VI and the reinforcement of it by John Paul I was

similarly catastrophic. It had exactly the opposite of the desired effect: Catholics in the United States (90 percent) and all over the world decided that the Church had no right to intrude into their marital relations and their sexual habits. This represented a complete loss of the Church's credibility as a moral teacher in this aspect of human behavior. The point here is not (necessarily) that the Church should change its teaching, but that both Popes should have listened more closely to the experience of the married laity (whom Pope John Paul said elsewhere had an indispensable contribution to make to the Church's self-understanding in sexual matters) before they tried to change the laity's minds on this subject. Patently the laity dismissed the reasons for the ban on birth control imposed by both Popes as unconvincing.

A Woman's Place
Mary Ann Glendon

I AM always amazed when I read of Catholics of my generation who complain that they felt stifled in the Church of the 1950s. For me, as a girl in a small Massachusetts town, pre–Vatican II Catholicism was a window opening out to the wide world that lay beyond the Berkshires. Its ceremonies spoke to me of a history before Plymouth Rock, and its liturgy linked me to every living Catholic on earth. The words and gestures of the Latin Mass connected us parishioners of St. Agnes to villagers in places where it never snowed, to inhabitants of great cities like Rome and New York, and to our own ancestors buried in faraway lands. The rituals; the sacramentals; the crimson, green, and purple vestments; the stories of saints and Apostles relieved the drabness of everyday life in the land the Pilgrims made. The Church enabled the sons and daughters of mill workers and mill owners alike to find themselves in the rich tapestry of world history, and in the unfolding mystery of salvation. Small-town life in former times was sometimes stifling, but Catholicism was liberating. It enlarged the spirit, gave wings to the imagination, and lent meaning to suffering.

A stranger driving through Dalton on Route 9 might well have taken our little white church for a Protestant meetinghouse. It was a graceful wooden building of the type often seen on New England village greens. But anything more than a superficial glance would have told you that there was something special about it. The steeple was topped with a cross rather than a weathervane; there was a stained glass window, rather than a clock, over the entrance. The interior was crowded with statues and pictures that prompted little children to ask questions: Why does St. Agnes have a lamb? Why is Theresa carrying red roses? What are those men doing to Jesus? That old wooden church has long since been replaced with a modern brick structure, but in my memory it is as lovely as Chartres.

Directly across from St. Agnes on Main Street was the First Congregational Church, an imposing gray granite structure. As the child of a mixed marriage between an Irish Catholic and a Yankee Congregationalist, I was fully immersed in both cultures—destined, I suppose, to be a comparatist. My mother's parents, Julia and Theodore Pomeroy, went out of their way to support her in her promise to raise her children as Catholics. My grandmother Pomeroy gave me a rosary for my First Communion and a little book about different religions called *One God*.

By the 1950s, the Dalton Congregational Church functioned mainly, but vibrantly, as a social organization. The Congregationalism of those days bore not a trace of its stern Puritan origins; the church was a beehive of fraternal and charitable activities. Unlike the Catholics, who took the obligation to attend Sunday Mass very seriously, most of the town's Protestants confined their church attendance to Christmas, Easter, weddings, and funerals. My mother's relatives were typical in that they rarely attended services, but the women were active in the church's many social clubs. Protestant church ladies organized a never-ending round of events and benefits that the whole town, Catholic and Protestant alike, thoroughly enjoyed: bake sales, potluck suppers, white elephant sales, talent shows, clambakes, and so on. In the war years, these good women knitted socks for our soldiers. After the war, they packed care packages for the children of Europe. During Lent, Congregational families saved spare change in little calico sacks to be brought to church on Easter and sent to some worthy charity.

The groups and events at St. Agnes's Church had a very different focus. There were no suppers, no sales, no shows, but many novenas, recitations of the rosary, Benedictions, and adorations of the Blessed

Sacrament. In the war years, we prayed for our soldiers and for the conversion of the bad guys. After the war, we prayed for the conversion of Russia. During Lent, we prayed and fasted, confessed our sins, did penance, and tried to amend our lives. Exactly contrary to the oft-asserted theological distinction, Dalton's Protestants were virtuosos of good works; the Catholics were virtuosos of faith.

The Catholic Church was, of course, not the only window through which one could glimpse the great world of people, places, events, and ideas beyond the Housatonic River valley. There was also a *Time* magazine, which came every week, and the Dalton Public Library. It was through a *Time* article on Graham Greene that I first became aware of a more intellectual side of Catholicism. I do not recall what it was about that article that impelled me, at the age of eleven or twelve, not only to read all of Graham Greene's novels that I could find, but to seek out works by the other authors mentioned in the article, Evelyn Waugh and Fyodor Dostoevsky. That began a series of lifelong "friendships" with a circle of writers who took religion very seriously. T. S. Eliot and Gerard Manley Hopkins were soon added, and promoted to the head of that list.

Curiosity led to me to other books that some of the authors I liked seemed to treat as very important. Thus, works by Freud, Marx, and Darwin were duly checked out of the Dalton Public Library.

Freud and Marx enabled me to torment my brother with observations about the Oedipus complex, and to annoy my parents with questions about the exploitation of man by man. By the 1950s, Darwin's evolutionary theory was uncontroversial in our milieu, and Darwinism as a proselytizing ideology was unknown. In the period when I was becoming dimly aware of the pretensions of psychological, economic, and biological theories to become total philosophies, I was fortunate to come across an essay in our local newspaper by Theodore Hesburgh, then the President of Notre Dame. One sentence jumped out at me, and it is no exaggeration to say that it had a transformative effect on my life. "When you encounter a conflict between science and religion," he wrote, "you're either dealing with a bad scientist or a bad theologian."

It was a joy many years later to have the opportunity to thank Father Ted personally for that gift. That single sentence from a newspaper column not only helped me on the perilous journey from childhood beliefs to adult faith; it also served to channel some of my adolescent rebelliousness toward a dialectical and critical engagement with the natural and human sciences (not that I didn't find other ways to be a pest to my parents, brother, and sister).

I count it among my blessings that a full scholarship enabled me to pursue that engagement at the University of Chicago. Indeed, improbable as it may seem, the University of Chicago deserves a good deal of credit for "why I am still a Catholic." Though Robert Maynard Hutchins was no longer its President when I entered, the core "great books" curriculum he had installed was still in place. Hutchins himself had a great respect for the Catholic Church, once referring to it somewhat enviously as having "the longest intellectual tradition of any institution in the world." He, Mortimer Adler, and their colleagues drew freely from that tradition in constructing Chicago's mandatory core of courses. Not only did Catholic students become acquainted with our own greatest thinkers, but we observed that those thinkers were honored by the best Chicago teachers. Works by Augustine and Aquinas were taught by the likes of Richard Weaver, Leo Strauss, and Richard McKeon. Catholic luminaries like Jacques Maritain and Martin D'Arcy were frequent visiting lecturers. Wags of the day used to joke that Chicago was the university where Jewish professors taught Thomas Aquinas to Marxist students.

I like to think that, thanks to Father Hesburgh and Saint Thomas, I absorbed a little of the confident approach to knowledge that enabled Thomas to engage the minds of the ancient Greeks without the slightest worry that his faith would be unsettled. Thomas understood the intellect as a gift from God—a gift whose use not only need not threaten faith, but may advance the ability of each new generation to know, love, and serve the Creator in this world. Paradoxically, the same Chicago education that reinforced a critical and dialectical approach to learning helped to put an intellectual platform under the religious habits and practices I had acquired in Dalton.

Like many Catholics of my generation, however, I entered the 1960s with a livelier appreciation of the spiritual and intellectual riches of my religion than of its social mission. The Second Vatican Council and the encyclicals *Mater et Magistra* and *Pacem in Terris* thus came as a revelation and an inspiration. In the mid-1960s, I was a young lawyer practicing in a large Chicago firm, but also active in the pro bono defense of indigent prisoners and in the burgeoning civil rights movement. But I did not really connect my public service activities to my Catholicism. In the Dalton of my childhood, after all, it had been the Protestants who were most conspicuously involved in social causes. When my sister, Julia, and I traveled to the March on Washington, where Reverend King gave his famous "I Have a Dream" speech, it was with a group organized by the Unitarian church in Pittsfield. As Vatican II unfolded, however, I realized that Catholic social thought had been sorely neglected in my education. I came to understand that my religious experience thus far had been rather self-centered—overly aesthetic and intellectual.

In the three decades that have passed since the Second Vatican Council, Catholic social teaching has come into its own, attracting increased interest and study by non-Catholics and Catholics alike. We American Catholics are more aware than ever of the 300,000 educational, health care, and relief agencies that the Church maintains around the world, serving mainly the earth's poorest inhabitants.

As a law teacher specializing in international and comparative legal studies, I have watched with pride as the post–Vatican II Church has developed into the world's most influential institutional champion of social justice in international settings. As a member of the United Nations, the Holy See has adopted a distinctive approach to the human rights that were declared fundamental in the Universal Declaration of Human Rights of 1948. Most U.N. members have taken a "cafeteria" attitude to the human rights menu, with some favoring the traditional political and civil liberties, and others focusing on the newer social and economic rights. The Holy See has consistently affirmed both human freedom *and* solidarity.

The idea that social justice can, and must, be harmonized with traditional political and civil liberties has been the touchstone of the Holy See's advocacy in the United Nations, as well as a central theme of the social encyclicals of John Paul II. Amid the tug-and-pull of special interests and power politics, the Church has stood clearly, and often alone, for *all* the freedoms that flow from the common principle of the innate dignity of creatures made in the image and likeness of God. (Needless to say, those of us Americans who are passionately convinced of the rightness of that stance find it somewhat difficult to fit into conventional American political categories!)

On the fiftieth anniversary of the founding of the United Nations in 1995, John Paul II took the occasion to remind the nations that the promises they made in the wake of the horrors of World War II are mutually reinforcing. He celebrated the freedoms of which the liberal democracies are rightly proud, saying that humanity has been "inspired by the example of all those who have taken the risk of freedom." But then he asked: "Can we not recommit ourselves also to taking the risk of solidarity—and thus the risk of peace?"

Thanks to the flowering of Catholic social thought, I am not only "still" a Catholic, but an enthusiastic Catholic. And thanks to John Paul II, I am a Catholic who is immensely proud of her Church and its role in the modern world.

I should say, too, that this seems to me to be a tremendously exciting time to be a Catholic woman. When I hear women complain about "sexism" in the Church, I always want to ask, "Compared to what other institution?" Back in the 1950s, Flannery O'Connor gave what I consider to be the perfect response to a friend who asked her how she could belong to a church that treated women as second-class citizens. "Don't say the Church drags around this dead weight," wrote O'Connor, "just the Rev. So&So drags it around, or many Rev. So&Sos. The Church would just as soon canonize a woman as a man and I suppose has done more than any other force in history to free women."

Alas, many contemporary Catholics are unaware of the ways in which the advance of Christianity strengthened the position of women in the ancient world. When we read the Apostolic writings today, we can easily overlook how radically Our Lord departed from the customs of his time when he befriended a variety of women, including public sinners. It is striking how many important conversations Jesus had with women, and how many of his teachings were first confided to his female friends.

As for the early Church, one can only stand in awe of its counter-cultural accomplishments where women and the family are concerned. It boggles my mind to think that she succeeded in gaining wide acceptance for the idea that marriage was indissoluble—in cultures where men had always been permitted by custom to put aside their wives! She introduced the ideal of monogamy where polygamy had been the norm. In her rules governing separation *a mensa et thoro*, she introduced standards of fidelity and decent treatment that were unknown to the secular law. Later, despite pressures from princes and merchants, the Council of Trent stood firm against marriages arranged without the consent of the spouses.

Not even Flannery O'Connor guessed, however, that the Church would one day become one of the world's most vigorous advocates of the freedom and dignity of women. Vatican II began that process with a few cryptic statements rich in implications. The Council said that political and economic orders should extend the benefits of culture to everyone, aiding both women and men to develop their gifts in accordance with their innate dignity (*Gaudiam et Spes*, 1). And in their Closing Message, the Council fathers proclaimed: "The hour is coming, in fact has come, when the vocation of women is being acknowledged in its fullness, the hour in which women acquire in the world an influence, an effect and a power never hitherto achieved."

That the Church would be more than a passive observer of women's progress became clear in the 1970s, when she emerged as a vigorous proponent in international settings of social and economic justice for women, especially poor women, refugee women, migrant women, and mothers everywhere. In international debates, she has avoided ideological extremes, combining respect for women's roles in the family with full support of women's aspirations for participation in economic, social, and political life.

As of the time of this writing in the late 1990s, it is already clear that one of the most significant achievements of the papacy of John Paul II has been to give increased life and vigor to the Second Vatican Council's fertile statements on women. In a remarkable series of writings, he has meditated more deeply than any of his predecessors on the roles of women and men in the light of the word of God. In *Mulieris Dignitatem* (1988), which contains the main theological basis for his messages to women, he labeled discrimination against women as sinful, and repeatedly emphasized that there is no place in the Christian vision for oppression of women. The tone of all these writings is dialogical. Their author invites women to help him and the Church reflect upon the quest for equality, freedom, and dignity in the light of the Faith—and in the context of a changing society where the Church and the Faithful are faced with new and complex challenges.

As time went on, the Pope embraced the cause of women's rights in ever more specific terms. His Apostolic Letter to Women, written prior to the 1995 Beijing Women's Conference, stated: "[T]here is an urgent need to achieve *real equality* in every area: equal pay for equal work, protection for working mothers, fairness in career advancements, equality of spouses with regard to family rights and the recognition of everything that is part of the rights and duties of citizens in a democratic State." A few months later, he urged all Catholic educational, health care, and relief organizations to adopt a priority strategy for girls and young women, especially the poorest, with a special emphasis on education (Letter to the Holy See Delegation). He pointedly included in this strategy the education of boys "to a sense of women's dignity and worth." In the same document, he made a special appeal that will challenge women and clergy alike for years to come—he appealed to women of the Church "to assume new forms of leadership in service . . . and to all institutions of the Church to welcome this contribution of women."

The vocabulary of these writings came as a surprise to many. In aligning himself with women's quest for freedom, the Pope adopted much of the language of the women's movement, even calling for a "new feminism" in *Evangelium Vitae*. In his 1995 World Day of Peace Message he observed, "When one looks at the great process of women's libera-

206 · Mary Ann Glendon

tion," one sees that the journey has been a difficult one, with its "share of mistakes," but it is headed toward a better future for women. In his 1995 Apostolic Letter to Women, he added, "This great journey must go on!"

No one who reads the Pope's writings to and about women can fail to be impressed by the evident love, empathy, and respect John Paul II holds for womankind. This is especially manifest in his compassionate words to unwed mothers and women who have had abortions. The image that comes through is of a man who is comfortable with women, and who listens attentively to their deepest concerns. After meeting with the Pope prior to the Beijing conference, Secretary-General Gertrude Mongella told reporters, "If everyone thought as he does, perhaps we wouldn't need a women's conference."

Where women's changing roles are concerned, the Pope's writings contain no trace of the dogmatism that often characterizes the rhetoric of organized feminism and hidebound conservatives alike. He affirms the importance of biological sexual identity, but he is no biological determinist. In particular, his writings give no comfort to those who believe men's and women's roles are forever fixed in a static pattern. On the contrary, he has applauded the assumption of new roles by women, and stressed the degree to which "cultural conditioning" has been an obstacle to women's advancement (Apostolic Letter to Women, 1995).

Unfortunately, many Catholics receive their information about these matters secondhand or thirdhand, often from dissenters. Many are unaware of these ongoing reflections about the roles of women, and of the role of the Holy See as a defender of women's interests in society. Many women, like Flannery O'Connor's correspondent long ago, complain that the Church has been slow to examine her own structures and the behavior of her own representatives in the light of the Holy Father's meditations. A glance at recent developments, however, shows that significant changes have occurred under his leadership. More important for the long run, he has provided a powerful impetus toward further and deeper transformations. Squarely confronting past injustices and the problem of all the "Rev. So&Sos" throughout history, he has written: "And if objective blame [for obstacles to women's progress], especially in particular historical contexts, has belonged to not just a few members of the Church, for this I am truly sorry. May this regret be transformed, on the part of the whole Church, into a renewed commitment of fidelity to the Gospel vision" (Apostolic Letter to Women, 1995).

Modeling this rededication to the Gospel vision in his own sphere, John Paul II has taken a number of steps to raise the level of participation of religious women and laywomen at all levels of the Church. In 1995 he appealed in strong terms to "all men in the Church to undergo, where necessary, a change of heart and to implement, as a demand of their faith, a positive vision of women. I ask them to become more and more aware of the disadvantages to which women, and especially girls, have been exposed and to see where the attitude of men, their lack of sensitivity or lack of responsibility may be at the root" (Letter to the Holy See Delegation). The following year, he reiterated his call upon all the institutions of the Church to welcome the contributions of women: "It is . . . urgently necessary to take certain concrete steps, beginning by providing room for women to participate in different fields and at all levels, including decision-making processes, above all in matters which concern women themselves" (*Vita Consecrata*, 1996). He himself has made an unprecedented number of appointments of lay and religious women to pontifical councils and academies, providing an example for cardinals, bishops, and other priests throughout the world.

Those who take a legalistic, formal approach to the study of institutions can easily underestimate the profundity of the changes that are presently under way. The issue of women's ordination is apt to loom large in their thinking. But an organization's formal rules can give a very misleading picture of the actual status of women within the group. (One need only think of the United Nations as an example of an organization whose practice has fallen far short of its official commitment to sexual equality!) In the Catholic Church, the tradition of an exclusively male priesthood has in practice been accompanied by an extraordinary increase in female participation in the life of the Church since Vatican II.

Pastoral and ministerial roles today are more open than ever to women. Indeed, the Church in many places desperately needs and seeks the contributions of lay people in these areas. All over the world, laywomen and religious women currently are serving in many roles that were once confined mainly or exclusively to priests, men, and boys. Women are performing a variety of pastoral duties in parishes. They are swelling the ranks of missionaries. Perhaps not since the first century have women been so actively and visibly involved in the life of the people called together by Jesus Christ.

As for leadership roles, I know of no religious group that ordains women that even comes close to the Church's outstanding record in promoting women's progress. The Church's health care system, the second largest in the world, is managed almost entirely by dynamic Catholic women executives (mainly religious Sisters). Catholic women, religious and lay, are superintendents, principals, and trustees in the world's largest provider of private elementary and secondary education. Women are high-ranking officers in Catholic colleges and universities. (And let us not forget that the Church long ago pioneered in women's education, opening up opportunities for young women in countries where others paid little or no attention to girls' intellectual development.) In other words, there seems to be no correlation at all between the ordination of women and the advancement of women within a given religious organization. The Catholic Church has no comparative need to apologize in this regard.

Church agencies also compare favorably, where progress for women is concerned, with large secular institutions such as corporations, governmental bureaucracies, universities, and the United Nations. The latter remain slow to welcome the contributions of women, especially at higher levels. Unlike many secular institutions, moreover, the Church does not expect laywomen to sacrifice their family lives. When Dr. Janne Matlary, a member of the Holy See's Beijing delegation, announced she had to return to Norway before the end of the conference because her youngest child was having difficulty adjusting to kindergarten, she left with blessings and good wishes. Many a woman's progress in the business world has been permanently impaired by resolving such a conflict in favor of her family. But the Church takes a different view. John Paul II subsequently appointed Dr. Matlary to the Pontifical Council on Justice and Peace.

All in all, the Church seems to have entered a period of great vitality for women (and laypeople) who are willing and able to "think with the Church" as she enters the new millennium.

Has the Church done enough to conform its own structures to the principle that men and women are equal partners in the mystery of redemption? Of course not. Flannery O'Connor had it right. When her protofeminist friend railed against the Church's shortcomings, O'Connor replied, "[W]hat you actually seem to demand is that the Church put the kingdom of heaven on earth right here now." She continued:

> Christ was crucified on earth and the Church is crucified by all of us, by her members most particularly, because she is a church of sinners. Christ never said that the Church would be operated in a sinless or intelligent way, but that it would not teach error. This does not mean that each and every priest won't teach error, but that the whole Church speaking through the Pope will not teach error in matters of faith. The Church is founded on Peter who denied Christ three times and couldn't walk on the water by himself. You are expecting his successors to walk on the water.

Four decades after those wise words were written, a Catholic woman impatient with the pace of change might consider asking herself: Where in contemporary society do I feel most respected as a woman, whatever my chosen path in life? What body of thought takes most seriously my deepest concerns? What organization speaks most clearly on behalf of all women, including those in poverty? Catholic mothers might consider asking as well: Where do I feel most supported and encouraged in the difficult task of raising children under today's conditions? For my own part, I cannot think of any institution that surpasses the Catholic Church in these respects.

Finally, no reflection concerning what binds me to the Church would be complete without mention of my friend and teacher Joseph Flanagan, the longtime Chairman of the Boston College Philosophy Department. Father Flanagan loped into my law school office one day in 1976 and asked me to join an interdisciplinary group that was working on a new core curriculum. Among the many benefits I received from being associated with that remarkable collection of scholars was an exposure to the path-breaking thought of Bernard Lonergan. Just as Thomas Aquinas performed an inestimable service for the theology of his day by assimilating the best of ancient and contemporary thought, so Lonergan has laid the foundations for a twenty-first-century theology that both learns from and challenges the modern natural and human sciences. For many years, I had the exceptional good fortune to read and discuss Lonergan's works with Father Flanagan. It was a kind of second Sunday school that opened new intellectual horizons for me and, I like to think, endowed me with a bit of Ignatian spirituality.

So, why am I still a Catholic? By the grace of God, and aided by many relatives, friends, and teachers—some of them dead for centuries, several of them non-Catholic. Thank you, Martin Francis Glendon, for keeping the Faith of your forebears. Thank you, Sarah Pomeroy Glendon, for the Protestant rectitude that kept you faithful to your promise to raise your children as Catholics. Thank you, Holy Mother Church, for not dumbing down your demands to suit the culture, and for holding us sinners to a high standard. Thank you, Edward Lev, for our comradely marriage in which, like my mother, you supported the Catholic upbringing of our children. Thank you, Lord, for the utterly inestimable gift of faith, and for the privilege of having lived in the time of John Paul the Great.

Confessions of a Semi-Pelagian
John E. Coons

EVERY CATHOLIC writer over sixty knows the temptation to commit religious autobiography; this atrocity is prevented only by his paralyzing fear that old friends might discover and read it. Therefore, he temporizes, scratching a private line or two for his grandchildren, hoping meanwhile that, by some miracle, the misdeed will become a duty. This state of suspension is generally terminal, and thereby the indiscretion is averted. Now, however, come the Ryans, cleverly disguising opportunity as responsibility, saddling me with a cross that I can gamely shoulder with secret delight. Their call must be answered, however great the pleasure.

Are there not enough stories about "Why I Left," "Why I Returned," and "How I Received the True Light"? Precisely; that is the point. It is the Ryans' insight that merely staying the course can also constitute religious adventure. All that is unclear is how such a premise could include me; bourgeois tranquillity makes my story a pale proxy for the real thing. Still, when I consider the ideological desert about me, even Catholic banality has something to recommend it.

Was I a cradle Catholic? You be the judge. About 1889 my mother was the firstborn in a Kentucky Catholic family, bearing genes French, Irish, and Whatever. The French, we were told, had been Huguenot. The daguerreotype of my great-grandmother's face inclines me to believe it.

Mother had completed maybe a year of high school when her

mother—my grandmother—died, leaving young Jill in charge of four little sisters. (There had been a brother, who drowned at the Presbyterian picnic!) For the five girls there ensued a brief nomadic period with grandfather (a railroad man, also gone before my time), followed by a general diaspora as each set off with her first—but in no case last—husband. All these marriages terminated, none in death. Eventually the total swelled to thirteen, Mother accounting for two, a number sufficient to flout canon law.

My father supposed himself to be English and German. In *The American Language*, Mencken uses my name twice to exemplify the corruption of German spelling that was typical at Ellis Island. Roughly the same age as Mother, Dad left a central Missouri farm with his mother, brother, and two sisters at about age six after his father was killed in a harvesting accident. He had a year of public high school, either in Kansas City or in the state of Washington, where his mother and family reappear—and where he met Jill, circa 1916. If he had seen the inside of a church, there was little to suggest it beyond the occasional eruption, "Jesus, Lover of My Soul!" (when he had hammered his thumb or dropped a paint can). Still, at Christmas and Easter we detected blips of a disposition toward a Christian God; in a difficult environment something in him was struggling toward the surface.

What Mother originally told Dad about her prior marriage—about her son and daughter and her religious status—remains a matter of speculation among her descendants. All that is apparent is her frontier faith in a fresh start, even for Catholics—and, in any event, for herself. In some internal forum she pursued a kind of religious bankruptcy—its discharge would allow her to reembrace her old creditor, the Church. For this she needed a clean slate, and she secured it her way. Resurfacing in Minnesota in 1918, both my mother and her daughter (my splendid Catholic half-sister, now eighty-eight) had my father's name, and nobody seemed the wiser. The son (my lovable Methodist half-brother, now ninety-one) was with his father and remained discreetly and distantly so, somewhere out West. Mother patiently played the part of a good Catholic until nature eventually made her one through the demise of her ex (plus, I assume, the cooperation of the Church and my father).

Meanwhile, with the zeal of guilt, Mother sent my two full brothers (today members of the Church Triumphant) to the school of our parish in Duluth, where she quietly worshipped. In due course I followed, by ten years the youngest of my tribe. My father, taciturn on all subjects, specialized in silence about religion; still, he paid our tuition and approved the support of our church from his modest resources—even when out of a job during the Depression.

Apart from Mother's passion for surface orthodoxy, there was nothing in all this that was uniquely Catholic. My salient images of the two of them feature hard work and personal tension, plus authentic generosity to kids, tramps, and friends out of work. But before all else stood their resolve to spoil me to the limit of their modest time and budget. I can't specify their social class; they had a decent house and indecent debts. When I was little, Dad was a kind of Willy Loman, home on weekends, otherwise driving the roads of the far North, selling Perfection kerosene stoves. When he got fired, my parents cranked up the mortgage, opened a corner grocery store, and operated it themselves sixteen hours a day, seven days a week. All the while, their determination to overindulge their baby never flagged. I think they liked me.

When I was six, their ambivalent religious influence merged with the clearer mission of Holy Rosary School and the Dominicans; even now the place retains its subtle grip. This is strange, for these nuns obviously had missed the point of Catholic school, at least as this is interpreted today by the typical middle-aged apostate. Sometimes I suspect that these women were misfits exiled to Duluth for flunking their basic training in knuckle-knocking, humiliation, and puritanism. In any event, my cohort missed all those treats. I concede that, in their outlandish garb, they were never Our Miss Brooks and but middling athletes; they excelled only in orderly energy and an occasional outburst of irony. I cite the celebrated case of the fifth grade wise guys who followed Sister Aquinata's counsel to "go jump in the lake." Her order was promptly executed in the cold waters of Lake Superior. The principal presented the half-frozen nitwits to our eighth grade class as examples of Christian obedience. We appreciated the gag.

The nuns liked me because I could blot up what they poured out. But at the deepest level, they liked us all—and equally—as the Baltimore Catechism seemed vaguely to require of them. The idea that smart kids had by nature the stuff to be better human beings never crossed their minds. They assumed that they were backed up in this judgment by their great Dominican hero, Thomas Aquinas. They pictured him as some sort of theological democrat who would find a place even for Stalin, on the sole condition that he acted out of "invincible ignorance." On this particular point I now suspect that they had read more of the Catechism than of Aquinas. Fate, it seems, had made me a schoolboy during a sea change in the Church's theological understanding of who the good people really are. America had considerable to do with this, helping the Church recognize a specific part of her own identity that from time to time tends to submerge. I return to this theme at the end of the essay.

After eighth grade, half a dozen Rosary boys, including myself, enrolled for a year in the neighboring public junior high, where the shop teacher dubbed us "Holy Rollers." Victims of false consciousness, we never knew that we needed a lawyer; in our innocence we saw (and still see) nonsense of this sort as essentially funny. So far as I am concerned, the only crime of East Junior High was to be thoroughly conventional. The regnant value was a rather blind patriotism—this was 1943–1944. Rosary had also managed to be patriotic, with a singular difference; a Catholic was supposed to have reservations about how he characterized his enemies. In certain cases he could shoot his opponent, but he was always bound to respect him.

The next fall my cadre of Catholic pals headed off to Cathedral High. The bishop had just ejected the Christian Brothers, who had graduated my two older full brothers (in itself a sufficient crime). Against the Christian Brothers' tradition the bishop made the school, housed in an old four-story firetrap downtown, coed. Father Michael Hogan and the Benedictine nuns were to execute the transition. Many of us still correspond with Hogan, who was tough, just, and—after our time—successful at bringing the boys to reasonable order. To be fair, it was not all chaos even in my own years. There were ideas being transmitted, and some of them were distinctly Catholic.

For example, a really smart and thoroughly respected priest taught us religion. It turned out to be rather serious stuff, including Catholic social justice and "subsidiarity." Twenty years later, I made subsidiarity a core theme of my first major book, in which my students Bill Clune (a former seminarian) and Steve Sugarman and I attacked the system of taxes and subsidies by which public school districts are treated so unevenly by the states. In the process I discovered that even the Jesuits had nearly forgotten this concept that I had learned as a kid. Today subsidiarity has become a staple in the law of the European Community and is widely discussed by legal scholars in this country, most of whom have no consciousness of its source (I think the word was coined in a papal encyclical around 1930).

I'm not certain where (or if) I learned to write English prose, but my high school (specifically, Sister Ruth) gets much of the blame or credit. Sparing the details, this woman—and these women—were literate; what is more, their attachment to language qualifies for remark here as a peculiarly Catholic virtue. Apart from profound theological puns about The Word, for them language was in itself a representation of human community. To reach out with symbols of mutual intelligibility is to counter the centrifugal pull of individualism. Language is an integrating and necessary vehicle of faith, whether the symbols are deployed as Scripture, preaching, teaching, or merely as human reciprocity. My teachers knew this.

So did my favorite human icon, who had first appeared in Duluth when I was in the seventh grade, and leavened all that followed. Patrick Lyons remains a legend in my hometown. A fortyish bachelor lawyer and former seminarian, he created a Boy Scout troop at Rosary that became a howling success and a fixture in our lives. None of us seemed ever to grow out of this enterprise, for the thing constantly evolved into new forms, most notably a very ambitious choir. Pat early discovered that a number of us could sing. He educated himself in the basics, and soon the boys were mastering the gorgeous Latin stuff that would be slaughtered in the Sixties. The choir packed the nine o'clock Sunday Mass, traveled a bit, and even did some turns in a fancy nightclub. (Imagine Arcadelt at The Flame.) But Pat also encouraged Tin Pan Alley—the kind of stuff I was to sing with a band in college, and still do on Saturday night at the local piano bar. I claim to know every song written before 1950, and the Church must accept some of the blame for this.

Pat pushed my latent lawyer button, and this, too, is relevant. As court-appointed counsel, he rescued a Chippewa boy just my age from a charge of patricide. It was the right result, but in any event it was a nice piece of work. I watched him enjoy doing good things well. Soon he found himself voluntary legal counsel to the Chippewa at Nett Lake, to my intense admiration. His pro bono relation to the tribe ended in a surprise that October when his clients delivered their counsel's first annual retainer of wild rice, stacking the bulging gunnysacks in his office. However, Pat's instinct for "legal aid" found alternatives; among other things, he lawyered a lot of us out of jail (myself included), but that's not an especially Catholic part of my story. The Chippewa thing had to do with justice, and mine only with pull.

One of the intensely Catholic things about Duluth was our easy access to the diverse Protestant majority and the suppleness of that relation. One encountered the rare troglodyte bigot, and, even among close Protestant friends, there was misunderstanding about Mary and the Pope. But, to tell the truth, this sometimes vivid ideological competition did us less harm than good. There was a synergy about it that made us more than the sum of our contrary parts. Nor was this a function of our being forced to sit side by side as students mastering the same ideas; quite the opposite. It was outside of school that we constituted this teenage marketplace of ideas; each came as a salesman of concepts learned from adults who believed and cherished them. In this juvenile intellectual scrimmage the Catholic kids had the advantage of an elementary training in apologetics that included a set of relatively clear premises; still, the Protestants were well enough prepared for battle, and a good time was had by all. Our few anathemas were reserved for those officious Prots who at midnight would remind us to skip the burgers and/or start fasting.

This tale of mine is mostly atmospheric—and fifty years after the events. Nonetheless, if I have gotten it more or less right, the benign principle that was operating is clear enough. We Lutherans, Presbyterians, Catholics, and Methodists were far enough apart in our convictions to make the fight interesting but close enough to grasp what the fight was about and—when that failed—close enough to recognize the humanity of our adversary. I suppose there is a limit to the chasm that can be bridged by such "dialogue," but we never reached it. For the Catholics, I think it was a precious reality check.

Meanwhile, where were the Jews? They were few in my town, and we got to know most of those our age in a variety of ways. Catholic school taught us to respect the Jews both as the foundation of our own identity and simply as fellow humans—but not to marry them; that sort of mixed marriage was even more complicated than one with a Protestant (as a veteran of such wars, I wondered!). Outside, the world was more ambiguous about the Jews. I recall a nasty set-to in my silly high school fraternity over admitting a certain boy. The fraternity had no religious or school connection and was perhaps half Catholic in membership. Sam was admitted, and then other Jews. They were thereafter treated on their merits. We had our Jewish jokes; I still hear them, mostly from Jews. My parents seemed to like the Jews they knew, and I remember one whose company they especially enjoyed. It all seemed unimportant to me, though later it came to be consequential in subtle and mostly benign ways, both in law and in the academy.

A strange feature of our teenage Catholic life was a fascination with alcohol. One couldn't in this case blame the Irish; stereotypes aside, the Irish were few enough in Duluth that we must exonerate them. I mention it only to blame the Church itself in this one respect. Somehow, excess was discouraged only enough to make it a distinction. I can still name the local bootlegger who would deliver a pint of Four Roses on call. The display of it was important enough that we learned subtle pretenses of drinking and went on spurious benders just to be one of the boys.

But the real thing went on with gusto, producing its harvest of chronic dipsos, some of whom heroically reformed. Our Catholic mentors seemed sufficiently concerned about every sin but this one.

I have allowed the sequence to become a bit fuzzy. Let's make it 1947 and time to go to college. This part is short, containing little that is specifically Catholic. Our circumstances kept me at home, enrolled in the newly converted state teachers college—now a campus of the University of Minnesota. The student body was sprinkled with Catholics, many with Slavic names fresh from the Mesabi Range. They skated me straight off the hockey squad, but I got to play football with Danny Devine, which ought to count as a Catholic gig. Indeed, football was a kind of religious experience; there were so many Romans in any given huddle that those inclined could easily manage a Hail Mary. I worried about the First Amendment until the statute of limitations had run. In any case, if these prayers were heard, the answers seldom came as touchdowns.

This is not a bad point—if there could be one—to consider the question of women. Our friend Andrew Greeley continues to paint us Catholics as a lusty crew, and I know nothing to the contrary. Most of the girls I dated are still alive, and for their sake I solemnly affirm that—concerning the crucial question—the answer in our town was always the same, anticipating Nancy Reagan by thirty years. I will not claim that we achieved the Church's ideal of sanctity, but only that this ideal was and is correct, quite apart from any utilitarian concerns about health and pregnancy. It would have been fun to be a part of the sexual revolution, but all in all we had a better deal. My wife, Marylyn, agrees.

Duluth had its barbaric charms (our paper reports minus 27° F there as I write), but it was never wholly secure from learning and the arts. I sometimes think of San Francisco as the Duluth of the West Coast—cold water, hills, boats, and (well) culture. In any case, I soon found the history curriculum at U.M.D. packed with sophisticated religious themes taught by a subtle and scholarly faculty. I still maintain ties with James F. Maclear (in 1996 he had a book published by Oxford University Press) and Ellis Livingston (Marine tank commander at Okinawa). Protestants both, they helped me to clarify and appreciate the Catholic ideas that were becoming my own religious identity. Livingston and his sainted wife, Edith, worked tirelessly to get me a fancy scholarship for law school, a typical good work of theirs that eventually becomes relevant to my theme.

For the moment, however, I want to focus upon book learning and to reaffirm my fifty-year apprenticeship to the most original Christian apologist of the century. Oddly, the literary form in which I first encountered him was not yet Catholic. *Orthodoxy* appeared in 1908, long before Chesterton converted. The copy I hold in my hand is tattered. Inside the cover is a salutation dated 1/1/56: "Chesterton had a great reverence for God and for beer . . . I suspect you of similar tastes." It was from Marylyn. I have not pursued Chesterton quite as I pursued her, but it is fair to say that whenever I lack the one, I tend to seek the other. If Chesterton is not wife to my mind, he is midwife, calling forth the best I have, even when I disagree with him. And that is seldom enough, though he wrote more than I could ever read.

Behind GKC in importance for me is the standard cast of Catholic writers who have had their hands on most of our minds. John Courtney Murray, Karl Rahner, Bernard Lonergan, Walker Percy, Thomas Merton, Etienne Gilson, Jacques Maritain, Georges Bernanos, Léon Bloy, Graham Greene, François Mauriac, Hilaire Belloc. It's fair to include C. S. Lewis. Though he is not a Roman, it is hard to tell the difference. Lewis, I think, emulated Chesterton; it shows in the paradoxes, the inversions, the weird juxtapositions. Unlike GKC, however, Lewis could not bear disorder; his trim, prim prose was yoked to his apologetic task. I think it was sometimes a weakness in him, for it makes otherwise rich stuff sound like a lawyer's brief. Chesterton, by comparison, was an intellectual slob who wrote too much and too fast, a spring thaw that spills over the banks. This exuberance gives his work an animal energy. Chesterton was the personification of his own celebrated image of the Church as a great chariot hurtling down the track of history—rocking and swaying, constantly at the point of a cosmic and final capsize that never occurs. Such was GKC himself. Many of us have kept upright in his colossal wake.

My generous scholarship got me through three years of law school at (Methodist) Northwestern. I roomed, of course, with Chesterton, but also with my college classmate and boyhood neighbor, Don Ames. For three years we carried on the wars of religion, and still do; neither of us has changed much, except that now he'll take a drink and I'll concede a point or two to Calvin. It's all very catholic and surprisingly Catholic. At law school, Don and I became close to John Bodner (who would have been a better choice to write this essay). Like my father, John doesn't talk much, which is perhaps the secret of his huge success as a trial attorney. What he has done for forty-seven years is draw me out on the subject of this essay, a subject he has understood better than I. (Being outed as my theological crutch will strike John as bizarre and more than a bit embarrassing. When he commissioned a statue of St. Ives for our law school, he managed the whole thing as an anonymously given surprise.)

After law school, coincidence landed me at the Pentagon, doing trial work with the Army Judge Advocate General in government contracts. The whole military experience lasted less than two years, being cut short by what were called "hardship" discharges for those of us bound either to Supreme Court clerkships or—as in my case—back to an academic post. Nonetheless, in a year of night classes at Georgetown, I learned scraps of Plato, Augustine, and Descartes in a university that was still profoundly Catholic. It was a jump start for my life as a philosophical autodidact. Meanwhile, at work I found myself chumming with a set of Pentagonian Mass-goers—they, daily; I, when in town and pursuing no frolic of my own. The military was crawling with Catholics, most of them admirable and emulable. I think I met John Noonan during those days, but neither of us is sure.

The return to Northwestern in 1955 was, as intimated, a major piece of good luck from the perspective of this essay. I was the only Catholic on a faculty that was distinguished and lively but already verging upon the religious ignorance that was to paralyze much of the academy. It was a lovely collection of smart but gentle WASPs and Jews who must have wondered what was sustaining my intellectual bondage to the Pope. They were full of natural charity and squandered it on me. Most are gone now. An exception is Vic Rosenblum, faithful Jew, long a pro-life guru—and my good confessor. The school now has at least one youngish Catholic who has become an authentic *peritus* on the role of religion in American Society.

Marylyn comes on stage just as I return to Northwestern in 1955. Her family story is oddly complementary to my own: South Side of Chicago Irish mother—thoroughly lovable; WASP father, a friend to me but not an admirer of the Church, an attitude that had been exacerbated, I fear, by some of his in-laws. Whether their marriage was originally canonical seems a mystery. The four kids were raised vaguely Protestant, but the mother was at Mass on Sunday. Marylyn identified with the South Side and joined the Church in college. We had our Mass discreetly in the morning, the marriage in the afternoon to shorten the pain for her father (he and my own father must have felt some peculiar kinship). Like me, Marylyn proved to be an uncomplicated believer, though after five children and various medical problems, we did have some difficulty with *Humanae Vitae*. Were we "pick and choose Catholics" or simply bad ones—or neither?

About 1958, one of my WASP colleagues got himself demonized in a bizarre article in the Chicago diocesan newspaper. I wrote the chancery in the feeble hope they'd publish my letter. To my surprise, the Chancellor himself called and said, "Let's talk." Within a week I found myself part of a radiating Catholic conspiracy aiming to undermine social evil in all its modern forms. The spark plugs were Fathers John (Jack) Egan and Daniel Cantwell; they had assembled a cast of lay and clerical characters to implement a battle plan of their legendary mentor, Father Hildebrand. Over my remaining years in Chicago, I was to share a good deal with this crew of social busybodies—Russ Barta, Matt Ahmann, John McDermott, Ed Marciniak, Tom McDonough, et al.—as they threatened to make the world safe for justice.

I recall black and white squads from the Catholic Interracial Council strolling along Roosevelt Road on steamy summer evenings. We couldn't undo yesterday's machine-gunning of the projects, but we could show up and . . . what? That part was never clear, but it was Catholic in spirit and good for me. Occasionally these racial calamities had a legal dimension, and I was of some practical use; through working for the U.S. Civil Rights Commission, I had learned the devilish ways of the Chicago public schools, which were implicated in the general racial balkanization of the city. I won't pretend that all Catholics saw it our way, nor even that we had it straight. Standing in the cross fire, the official Church was reasonably steady and overall a force for civic peace.

Our most memorable caper was a weekend in Selma, Alabama, in mid-March 1965. A Yankee minister, Reverend Reeb, had just been murdered, and Dr. King's new gang intended to march from the Old Brown Church to (as I recall) the courthouse. Those Chicago whites who wore Roman collars were set in the vanguard to confront the police line while remaining peaceful, persuasive, and obvious to the press. As the sole legal hope in case of arrests, I was sent to the rear; to my intense relief (and the marchers' good fortune), no one had to depend on me. Next day the *Selma Times* had us on the front page; a close look at the faded photo reveals Mike Royko and me—far to the rear and roaring with laughter.

I did get near enough to the front line at one point to catch a memorable signal of religion's peculiar role in Selma. It was the exclamation of an unhappy local fellow who admonished one of the priests, "You God damned nigger-loving son-of-a-bitch—and you call yourself a Christian!" So did we all, and I have had no reason to reconsider. Later, back in Chicago, at the request of Jack Greenberg of the NAACP Inc. Fund, I advised Dr. King and his lieutenants regarding the legal risks of Operation PUSH. The advice was graciously received, but King was already committed to disregard it. That night, my two older sons and I went to hear him at a jam-packed South Side church. He didn't show, but Bob, John, and I felt the exhilaration of the speeches and Gospel. Enthusiasms of this sort are in general not my style. For me, religion draws more of its strength from intelligible form; even the most exuberant gargoyle finds his voice as part of the cathedral. Still, a little charisma doesn't hurt, so long as we don't expect it to perform on cue.

Our Chicago conspiracy published *New City*, a professionally competent journal that peddled our trendy Catholic messages. I suppose none was more liberal than my own "Why I Belong to the A.C.L.U." A few years earlier, my review of a book on censorship had caught the favorable attention of Bernie Weisberg, Chief Counsel of the Illinois division of the ACLU. By 1997 standards, my conclusions were puritan, but this was not the ACLU we know today. I joined the board of directors and became Chairman of the Committee on Freedom of Communication. That experience was, and still is, good for me; I mean specifically that it is good, qua Catholic, to have been a part of that once-noble organization whose cofounder was Monsignor John Ryan. Its spirit of neutrality is wholly lost, and I see no present hope for it. Nor do I see much more for the Catholic League for Civil and Religious Rights, from whose board I resigned some years ago. America desperately needs an all-purpose Civil Liberties Union that takes human responsibility seriously. It is a work deserving of Catholic energy. If the Church is now at war with the ACLU, it is not she that has abandoned the cause.

In 1967 we left Northwestern to visit Berkeley. The law faculty at Boalt Hall was good and aspiring, and we were willing to sacrifice Chicago weather for the one academic year that has turned into thirty. Though I had vaguely grasped that the presence of John Noonan and David Louisel would be interesting, the last thing we expected at Boalt was a Catholic atmosphere. The place swarmed with Romans. Of a faculty of twenty-five at this public university, at least seven were identifiably Catholic; I cannot recall as many WASPs. Sadly, it was only a statistical anomaly—no conspiracy. Nevertheless, this cadre was a critical mass that was to give special meaning to yet another random miracle—the Robbins money. A Protestant San Francisco lawyer and his wife had left Boalt $12 million (today grown to perhaps $50 million), essentially for books on canon and religious law. Boalt has the world's largest collection, the Vatican not excepted.

I mention the Robbins collection not because I am qualified to use it, but because it brought us the great Stephan Kuttner, who then held the Chair of Catholic Studies at Yale. Kuttner and Noonan between them were to attract a stream of interesting visitors, mostly Catholic. But not all! We had long coveted the great Talmudic scholar David Daube, then Regius Professor at Oxford. When Kuttner said yes, the law faculty approved the following telegram (I had nothing to do with this):

Catholics are fine
But so are Jews
Kuttner's coming
How about youse?

Daube came. He and Kuttner were my friends and colleagues.

In the late Sixties and Seventies the Berkeley campus Catholics—not all of them from the law school—met occasionally for dinner at the Newman Catholic Center, joined often by religious scholars, such as Daube, from outside the Church. There were also faculty from the Berkeley Theological Union—then a new institution; scattered on "Holy Hill," north of the campus, the GTU is the largest collection of religious schools united in one association. I sometimes use its splendid library. The evenings at Newman stopped during the demoralized Seventies and Eighties, but have recommenced in the Nineties to become a monthly expectation of perhaps thirty academics; of these, roughly half or more show, depending on the subject. Among those who may appear are Ceslaw Milos, William Bouwsma, John Noonan (now a federal judge), and a smorgasbord of young academics from a dozen disciplines. Their friendship and wisdom would in itself be a sufficient answer to the question "Why am I still . . . ?"

Over the past fifteen years the Catholic seasoning of Boalt Hall has been somewhat diluted by death, departure, spiritual defection, and sheer expansion of the faculty. There remain, nonetheless, two whose distinguished scholarship is borne upon a consciously Scholastic framework. By chance (I suppose) my office is next to that of Michael Smith, who teaches Dante's theories of punishment both at Berkeley and at the University of San Francisco. This is a lawyer who spent his sabbatical at the GTU studying Thomism (and who greatly aided me with this essay).

The other is James Gordley, who has written *the* most readable and convincing précis of Aquinas's theory of natural law.

The Catholic experience in California was to be only partly academic. Noonan promptly betrayed my activist past to local lay folk looking to do their duty in the Vatican II Church. It became a Mack Sennett crew of which I was for a time president. We christened ourselves the Bay Area Council of Laymen. The survivors still see each other for parties but no longer have a corporate existence or annoy bishops with cheeky proposals. It was a cheerful bunch, lacking the hubris that is necessary to sustained activism. Most of us see the current afflations of the Catholic Left and Right as self-indulgence.

I hope the same won't be said of my thirty years of writing, litigating, and politicking on behalf of parental choice in education. Curiously, I don't think of this as a Catholic thing (though it brings out ferocious bigotry); nor have many of my confederates been believers. Preeminent from the beginning has been that fixed star of my conscience, Professor Steve Sugarman. My student at Northwestern, my colleague at Boalt, he has kept me standing steady in the tradition of *Rerum Novarum* (which he has had no reason to read, having its content somehow encoded in his genes). I might forget, but Steve never does, that the point of school choice is to arm poor and ordinary families with options and self-respect, and not merely to ease the burden of the middle class.

Over the last quarter-century, Sugarman and I have had much experience with the Catholic bishops, in California and elsewhere. We watched the pastoral letter on the economy duck the issue of school choice in order to accommodate the teachers' unions. We were not surprised. In 1981 the Cardinal had strongly and personally urged his California colleagues to give robust financial support to our proposed statewide popular initiative. This encouragement lasted just long enough for us to secure major Protestant and secular alliances, all of which collapsed when four of the bishops huddled to tell me, for their colleagues, "Our people are not ready." Who in fact was unready may have been unclear; nevertheless, today I can once more view the California bishops as persons, and my pique over this farce has evaporated. These are good men trying to be good pastors. When at last they and their people are ready, Steve Sugarman will probably still be alive to write the new organic law for school choice in California. I'd settle for that.

My hope for episcopal leadership over the long haul is objectively justified by the bishops' work and sacrifices for inner-city parish schools, those paradoxical refuges in which suburban Catholics subsidize the tuition of low-income Baptists. (Here I can praise my own bishop, John Cummins.) I have known these islands of hope as a board president, writer, lawyer, parent, and observer of our daughter and her pupils. For several years Mary has taught seventh grade at St. Cyril's in Oakland; the school has one white student, two white teachers, and a faculty and student body that want to be there in spite of the financial sacrifice. I wish that Walt Whitman could know St. Cyril's and the generous people—and that Church—whose fidelity sustains it. In these halls one can still hear America singing.

A last word about bishops. Gone now is the late great Bishop James Carroll of Sydney, Australia, titular Archbishop of Amasea. Carroll brought choice and equity to the Australian schools; he brought Marylyn and me there to see it work; he brought himself often to Berkeley, ostensibly to refuel but more in fact to sustain us. How he did it eludes me; he said very little but, though he might be engrossed in prayer or music, even our dogs sensed his gentle power. Jim, who was big in Sydney opera circles, was also at home in our local piano bar, a refuge where tax collectors and prostitutes were few but sinners of every other sort were common. He loved them indiscriminately.

In the winter of 1991 a wiry—and wired—young fellow visited my office at Boalt: Brennan, Patrick McKinley. I'd been appointed his adviser, and he'd come to see what sort of thing Providence had thrown his way. He discovered a sixty-one-year-old lawyer who'd been chasing a philosophical idea for fifteen years but lacked the horsepower to finish the book. The lawyer had forgotten most of his Latin, and Greek to him was Greek. But he needed both for his project—and Brennan had them, partly from classics at Yale, partly from the Pontifical Institute in Toronto. He had a good deal more that I needed, and I had a thing or two for him.

Patrick asked about my idea. He criticized my manuscript on human equality, saying I had misconceived some aspects of relational reality. He was right. By summer he was scoping the GTU library for religious aspects of what had become our book, and discovering enough red meat to restore my powers. The book took another four years. Religious publishers are ready for it, but we still seek the imprimatur of a secular press. As to that, we shall see. Is this typically Catholic—courting the secular?

I'll describe the book's central idea later; here I want only to describe Patrick, who is a major Catholic force in my old age. My own kids describe him as the academic son I secretly wanted (but I also wanted a circus clown, a nun, and a U.S. Marine). Academic he is, and in the years ahead, you will hear from him. He talked me into taking a course on Karl Rahner with him at the GTU; it was taught by an exceptional Dominican, Richard Schenk. The following year, Patrick, Schenk, and I taught a seminar together at Boalt Hall for a mix of law and theology students. Schenk has become our good friend, our worthy theological opponent, and still another providential crutch for me.

In these and many other ways Patrick has refocused my energies, and I find myself currently publishing theoretical stuff about children's religious rights, natural law, Bernard Lonergan (whom I knew slightly through Andrew Greeley), feminism, and now this thing—whatever it is. To my good fortune, Patrick has hovered geographically near—now more adviser than advisee—clerking in San Francisco for John Noonan, backpacking with me, and most recently off to be professor at the very fine and creative law school of Arizona State, not so inaccessible as I had feared. We plan several more articles together and a short book on the nature of personal goodness. He has refilled my Catholic tank.

Where can I stop in this litany of luck? I will end with the Paulists, who have tolerated us for thirty years at Newman Hall; though sometimes provocative and upsetting for me, with rare exception they have dignified the Church's mission. The present staff seems to appreciate what the Pope is trying to do and the awesome difficulty of consistently doing it right. This may sound condescending, as if I know what I myself am doing. I do not, nor—except for occasional inspiration from the Paulists—is my spiritual life much to write home about. I have a gift for the intellectual, hence the more trivial, parts of Catholic life. My last retreat was in 1954. My excuse is that, like C. S. Lewis, "I tend to find the doctrinal books often more helpful in devotion than the devotional books." I try to persuade myself that I am one of the "many who find that 'nothing happens' when they sit down, or kneel down, to a book of devotion [but] find that the heart sings unbidden while they are working their way through a tough bit of theology." Still, I feel the moral weight of my own tepidity; and such guilt at least is Catholic.

Perhaps the higher things—the real prayer, the deep emotional connection—are for those who get knocked down and dragged to their spiritual fate, like my father during his last and difficult days. Having no experience of religious incandescence, and never seriously tested, I could be at the edge of some spiritual chasm. But, faith being a gift, who isn't? An Irish priest once remarked that I was simply stuck with my faith. I hope so.

But if I am stuck, it must be in part because I accept the historical and philosophical grounds of Catholic Christianity. Like any responsible adult, now and again I take a fresh look at the evidence; when I do so, I am struck by the simple credibility it imparts to the most profound and awesome claims. Comparing the plausibility of those claims with that of assertions that pass in the academy as "fact," I marvel at the credulity of intellectuals regarding anything called science. Still, the reality is— and must be—that there are no knockdown "proofs" for Christianity. Were it otherwise, we would be enslaved by our own vision, leaving no room for freedom, and hence none for faith. The proofs that are allowed us carry the right measure of persuasion; in any case, they have allowed me the freedom to be persuaded.

But were I able to say precisely *why* I believe, how would the reader know *what* I believe? The editors imposed no definition of "Catholic," and that word is not altogether transparent. Maybe I have tipped my hand regarding certain propositions; had I a mind to dissemble, however, I could still shelter under the Catholic label while actually leaning so far to port or starboard that anyone who knew my real views might say I had slipped right off the barque of Peter. I will not deliberately waste the time of any reader by remaining bland and ambiguous. Wanting the story to bite, I will locate my place on the barque.

I take a rather conventional and uncomplicated view of what is Catholic, standing roughly amidships and satisfying the magisterial litmus test. That is, I am content not only with the recognized versions of the creed but even with papal infallibility, though wanting the wit to grasp exactly what it is. To my credulous mind, Scripture and common sense conspire toward some unique species of authority within the Church. If I am sometimes unclear about its nature, and just when it has been used, I am nevertheless prepared to honor it up to that final barrier called conscience that no Pope would ask me to betray. So there you have it. Count me in.

In the interest of a full answer to the Ryans' question, however, I want to identify a specific element of the faith that is important to me, and that justifies our using the word *Catholic*. The point was long contested within the Church, the question being whether all rational humans are born and remain equal in their hope of salvation. The Church's answer appears to be yes. First of all, she maintains a view of baptism that allows all *good* men to be saved. This, of course, is crucial to the possibility of human equality; but it is not sufficient, leaving two questions unanswered: What does it take to be a good person? Do we all get issued the same equipment for this task?

The ascendant answer to these questions focuses upon the intention of the individual, as he or she chooses among good and evil behaviors. It holds that personal goodness is achieved by being diligent in seeking right conduct; conversely, personal corruption consists in the free choice to ignore (or not to seek) correct behavior. The emphasis is on the conscientiousness of the actor, not upon his deeds; he must *seek* the right way, but honest mistakes are irrelevant to his own goodness. The bungler must follow his conscience; if he does so, he is justified personally, though his behavior is incorrect.

The medieval expression for this view of personal goodness was *Facienti quod in se est Deus non denegat gratiam*, or, roughly, God will grace the person who does what he can toward finding and doing the right thing. Vatican II adopted a version of this proposition in two basic texts:

> [T]he human person is to be guided by his own judgment and to enjoy freedom.
>
> Through loyalty to conscience Christians are joined to other men in the search for truth.
>
> [I]t often happens that conscience goes astray through ignorance which it is unable to avoid, without thereby losing its dignity.

The competing historical position in the church would limit personal goodness (hence salvation) to those who successfully identify the correct behavior and go on to do it. In this second view, goodness is an achievement of the intellect; and those who are best equipped by intelligence or education to discover right answers have a greater chance for sanctity and salvation. Because of its emphasis on brainpower, Brennan and I call this position "moral Gnosticism." It echoes President Kennedy's curious (and I think un-Christian) association of "the best and the brightest."

The Gnostic position has practical consequences that I will presently note, but first we must be clear about the scope of the conflict. The opposing sides on this question agree that there is a real good to be sought and a real duty to seek it. The only difference between them concerns the effect of one's failure to find it. Vatican II seems to have settled the point. The conscientious actor is morally perfected by his honestly mistaken choice of evil behavior. The Muslim marries four wives; in Catholic eyes this is seriously wrong behavior, but it is morally fulfilling for the diligent, well-intending Muslim. In an analogous case, the Catholic idealist volunteers to fight in a war that he wrongly perceives to be just; he commits unjustified homicide—a grave evil—but he achieves the saving good of his own diligent conscience.

If the Church agrees, why am I making such a point of this? One answer is that in considerable part I am still here because I have with hope and, finally, great relief watched my Church as she has struggled to clarify this essential truth. In the end she confirmed the possibility of human equality, thereby providing the world an answer to what no other religion or philosophy has understood even as a question. While modern positivism (and parts of Christianity) sinks unconsciously into the Gnostic illusion that brains and knowledge determine one's capacity for moral self-perfection, my Church has seen and solved this problem. In doing so, she has become the only community that completely deserves the name Catholic.

The opposite outcome would have had very troubling consequences for theology, for the Church—and for me. I will give three examples of the doctrinal havoc that proceeds from the Gnostic view. Consider, first, the fate of the concept of "dignity." Today, the official Church can scarcely clear its throat without uttering this word that comes down to us as the remote but direct descendant of the image of God in Genesis. God gave man a finite participation in his own infinite intellect and freedom. Our dignity consists in having reason and will, hence the capacity for a free morality. The Gnostic would relativize this fundamental and defining human property. People with the luck of high intelligence or a good education are better able to find the correct answers and to advance toward moral self-perfection and salvation; they possess this crucial power in a superior degree. Dignity, which begins as a human excellence, thus becomes the medium of a moral hierarchy. Woe to you, ignorant savages. You have dignity, but we philosophers have so much more.

Second, as dignity is transmuted into moral aristocracy, human equality perishes. Even in its debased and relativized state, dignity can survive; the moron is allowed his shred. By contrast, equality simply dies; unless each human has the same capacity (in the same degree) to embrace or reject association with God, the relation of equality evaporates, a casualty of moral Gnosticism. Such doctrine would come as discouraging news to those moral pilgrims (our "brothers") who happen in good faith to disagree with the Church about this or that. Demotion to moral inferiority is not what they have been led to expect from Rome.

Third, as the belief in Gnostic morality eliminates equality and relativizes dignity, so does it exterminate the possibility of human community. However we may define community, one of its necessary elements is the mutual perception by the members of the cluster that all stand the same in their opportunity for moral self-perfection. Gnostic inequality, by contrast, makes human association a matter of condescension and even contempt. In a Gnostic world, deals may be possible; community is not. And when the question arises—What sort of rights belong to so-and-so?—the lawyers will discreetly inquire about the quality of so-and-so's brain.

The Church has carefully avoided these calamities. Indeed, she has provided all the pieces for a full theory of moral human unity. But *why* did this specific theological outcome become such an anchor to my belief in the first place? Apart from the sheer truth of the matter, within the tangled web of my stories is there some trace of cause and effect? Did my parents' ways with kids and tramps subtly prefigure my feverish conviction that the kingdom of Heaven is as accessible to honest bunglers as it is to punctilious bishops? I suppose so, but I'll never be able to sort it all out; so I depart with one loose generalization.

I was conceived in the unique historic conjunction that is Catholic America. The two parties to this union remain distinct. One is definitely America; the other is definitely the Church. For a long time the world perceived the two as engaged in a deadly intellectual duel. As Chesterton shrewdly observed, America was itself very much a church, and to observers on the remote banks of the Tiber, the creedal themes of this ecclesial competitor could appear—as sometimes they were—idolatrous.

In retrospect, however, my own experience suggests a profound if peculiar symmetry in the spirit of these apparent adversaries. The confrontation seems less a duel than a dance. America and the Church were performing a cosmic pas de deux. At first, it was freestyle; but as the dance proceeded, each began to sense an ideological synergy. There were false steps, as in the temporary muzzling of Father Murray, but the show went on to conclude with Murray's own grand finale, much to the relief of most Catholics. Indeed, America had helped the Church at last to clarify the full human and religious implications of the Council of Trent; in return, the resolute Catholic attachment to a natural and biblical responsibility helped America, at least sometimes, to put the brakes on rampant individualism.

Put in historical-theological terms, Catholics had begun invading the United States in serious numbers just as America was becoming the land of Pelagius, that fifth-century monk who preached that man could achieve salvation by his own will and works. Pelagian hubris was fast constituting the core of pioneer America, both collectively (in our "Manifest Destiny") and in those ardent and struggling individuals who were "forging their own identity." To a surprising extent even organized Calvinism, in fact if not in form, had thrown its lot with Pelagius. The Catholic Church, by contrast, had already come to terms with this temptation, taking its repose—as usual—amidships. I won't try to define semi-Pelagianism, but merely note that the Church has neither condemned it by name nor even clearly defined it. While keeping one foot carefully planted upon divine omnipotence, the Church allowed her American partner to let man "make himself" within the terms of a moral responsibility set by God.

Almost unconsciously these strange ideological confederates were groping together for the meaning of the "self-evident" truth that we are, indeed, "created equal." The natural offspring of the union of America and the Church was the mutual perception that every rational human being has the same freedom to accept (or reject) God's invitation to permanent and loving association. The free choice is exercised affirmatively simply by doing the best one can to discover and execute the content of the real good that in justice belongs to our neighbor and our community. And doing our best is something we are all equally good at. America, the Church, and I somehow learned this together.

This is only the murkiest explanation of my persistence. In the end, faith is a gift, and there are no guarantees of it, even when the human actor freely plays his part. However, play it he must, because that is the way it pleased God to make us. And whatever my free part may have been, it was constantly prompted by the rich reciprocity between my Church and my society. The Church declared me responsible to seek what is an authentic personal goodness that is open to all on equal terms. In its chaotic and sometimes pathetic way, the civil society is still probing for the same thing. I have loved both this country and this Church that in so curious a fashion have sustained the truth that every human can choose salvation by accepting the invitation to responsibility.

But, if orthodoxy insists upon the possibility that I have cooperated, mine is still not much of a story. I have no consciousness of any great Christian leap into the void—hoping that God will catch me. For those who have made that leap with reckless courage, I have nothing but admiration. As for me, I am grateful for the saints who stood both before and behind, cheering me on. They made it easy.

On Having Green Hair
Michael Novak

MANY YEARS ago I was attending my first faculty reception at my first formal faculty appointment, at Stanford, and was met at the receiving line by the sponsoring dean with a warm handshake and the baffling words "I want to tell you that I have the greatest admiration for your church." The two of us had never met, so I remember looking about me to make sure the words were meant for me, and trying to capture the reference. Did I have the template "Catholic" stamped on my brow? It was well known, of course, that I was the first Catholic hired in the Religion Department (then called the Special Program in Humanities). But here I was, in one of the professional schools, at some remove from my own department. How did he know? I hadn't thought my being Catholic was that obvious, especially to strangers. I hadn't thought of being Catholic as a problem about which I needed reassurance. Should I have?

One thing I did know is that the dean was a famous man, well known nationally, and that his eyes exuded an unmistakable warmth; he meant to express a certain generosity of spirit, and he wanted even to suggest that he knew a little about me, and was happy that I was at Stanford and had come to his party.

At Harvard two years before, a fellow graduate student whom I much admired, a very clever fellow and witty writer in the English Department, commented that in discussing a recent universitywide survey, those of his contacts who were religious and actually went to church fairly regularly said that they were made to feel that being religious at Harvard, and especially being Catholic, was like having green hair. You seemed a little odd, and everyone knew it.

That night at Stanford, I felt I had green hair. It wasn't altogether a bad feeling. It got you noticed, and if that which was noticed was also true, what the hell? Enjoy it.

Ever since then, it has both amused and annoyed me that that little adjective "Catholic" keeps getting inserted in front of my name in the press, in the most irrelevant and discriminating of ways: "Sidney Hook, Norman Podhoretz, Robert Nisbet, and Catholic philosopher Michael Novak were among those . . ." and "according to Catholic writer Michael Novak. . . ." This adjective keeps barking at my heels, pursuing me, while most of my friends and associates seem to be adjective-free. What can this mean? It is not purely personal to me. I note that it also happens to many other Catholics who write or teach. Does this giveaway adjective tell us something about our society?

There is, in this respect, one parallel to keep an eye on. At least four times I have had to write a letter to the editor or publisher of a major newspaper to point out that the adjective "conservative" keeps creeping into news stories that purport to round up a range of opinions, even in immediate contexts in which no other adjective—such as "liberal," "left-ist," or "social democrat"—appears. The names of all those to the left of freakish are unadorned, pristine, bathing in the sunshine of reality. The opinions of those to the right are always draped. Like Michelangelo's cherubs.

In due course, I have always received apologetic letters from such editors or publishers, after engaged attention has obliged them to confront the unbalanced reality placed in front of their eyes by the copy of the offending piece that I take care to enclose, or at least to specify by date and page. It truly is inexplicable: six experts cited, two of them by an adjective ("conservative") and four of them not at all. The "authorities," to employ a conservative's term, always promise that an instruction will go out forthwith, and that the practice—for that is what it is, not a mere coincidence—will be amended. For about six months it always is. (At this very moment, I owe such a letter to the editor of the *Washington Post*. The time has come again.)

People whose minds are gifted with an internal tuning fork, who register in perfect pitch, will understand full well what such signs mean. Reality needs no adornment, and the common assumption of intelligent readers today must be that sensible persons are secular and liberal. They are enlightened. Moreover, it is a service to slower readers to point out that opinions that might seem sensible, if not carefully reflected on, are always signaled tremolo for the discerning ear. They should not take as enlightened opinions that truly aren't, even if they seem to be. Lest it be unclear whether the reporter, at least, discerns the difference, the reporter will signal tremolo.

One side of me, the idealistic side, would wish that the world were a fairer place, that is, not the world. I would like to see ideas allowed to join battle on the jousting field without the referees doing combat on behalf of one side. I would like the referees simply to allow ideas to stand by themselves, and render their own account of their strength in open blow and counterblow. I have every confidence that not much more is needed. My friends and I will win some of these battles, maybe more than our share. For we fight where we do because we were once bested by better ideas, from which we have learned.

Another side of my nature finds vindication in fighting on the outside of the conventional wisdom of our secular, liberal, enlightened age. To be a voice of the accepted wisdom would be uncomfortable. During my second (of nine) years of graduate school, a good friend noted that for many months he had been testing me. First he would take one position, and I would demur, pointing out what was wrong with it. Then, having waited a little while, he would take the point of view he had heard me put forth, only to discover me again demurring and pointing out deficiencies. He had done this several times, he said. "The only consistent thing is that you are an *aginner*," he said. "Whatever position I take, even if I borrowed it from you, you will be against."

I had no rebuttal. It was more or less true, and still is. Unless they really know a lot more than I do, and command a height that I have not yet climbed, I don't want to be where others are, even if that is where I have been until now. When everybody is getting the point, it's time to move on. I would just as soon be at least a little on the outside—more, if I can—ahead of the curve. Every position is a point on a pilgrimage, not a lasting settlement. A journey, a pilgrimage especially, has its own integrity, its own kind of consistency—not the kind that, in the aphorism, is the hobgoblin of unformed minds, but the kind that is like that of the survivor in the wave-tossed lifeboat, who leans first right, then left, and back again, in the ever-threatened struggle for balance and pitch.

Being a Catholic is a voyage like that. Not for nothing is the favorite metaphor for our communion a barque, a wind-thrown barque whose earliest sailor, Peter, through fear sank in the waves until the Lord took pity.

No one can be a Catholic in our culture without being battered daily. Practically everyone in our society defines herself, or himself, *against* the Catholic Church. Most feminists surely seem to. When ACT-UP acts up, as often as not they do it in a Catholic church. Even in a more benign sense, what do Protestants "protest" if not the deformations of Rome, and from what are the Enlightened "enlightened" if not from the Dark Ages of you-know-who? If scientists pride themselves on being the opposite of "dogmatic," who do you think *is* dogmatic? When Jews recount the horrors of pogroms, it must be mainly Catholics, more or less, who were doing the pogromming—either Orthodox Catholics, or Roman, or both.

Here's the type of paragraph a young Catholic will read a thousand times during university years:

Generally the state of mind of a believer in a revelation is the awful arrogance of saying, "I *know*, and those who do not agree with my belief are wrong." In no other field is such arrogance so widespread, in no other field do people feel so utterly certain of their "knowledge." It is to me quite disgusting that anybody should feel so superior, so selected and chosen against all the many who differ in their beliefs or unbeliefs. This would be bad enough, but so many believers do their best to propagate their faith, at the very least to their children but often also to others (and historically there are of course plenty of examples of doing this by force and ruthless brutality). The fact that stares one in the face is that people of the greatest sincerity and of all levels of intelligence differ and have always differed in their religious beliefs. Since at most one faith can be true, it follows that human beings are extremely liable to believe firmly and honestly something untrue in the field of revealed religion. One would have expected this obvious fact to lead to some humility, to some thought that however deep one's faith, one may conceivably be mistaken. Nothing is further from the believer, any believer, than this elementary humility. All in his power (which nowadays in developed countries tends to be confined to his children) must have his faith rammed down their throats. In many cases children are indeed indoctrinated with the disgraceful thought that they belong to the one group with superior knowledge who alone have a private wire to the office of the Almighty, all others being less fortunate than they themselves. (quoted in Paul Davies, *God and the New Physics*)

Every reader will see a sliver of truth in that paragraph, perhaps even shudder as parts of it hit home, particularly in reference to materials one has read and even in recalling some narrow-minded believers in one's own life. One suspects that the author of that paragraph was brought up as a believer, quite possibly a Catholic. In these days, however, it is the *secular* person who seems so certain of himself, in just the way the author of that paragraph does. For him, it seems clear that religion is a lie. (When quoting him, Paul Davies described him as a scientist who holds that religion is a "serious and habit-forming evil.")

These days, the religious person feels very much under attack, at least in university circles, in most of the arts, and in most journalism. In the circles in which the symbolmakers of our society set the tone, that tone is antithetical to religion. Many secular persons one meets seem surprised by signs that religion is still taken seriously by anyone they know; some are amazingly innocent of any intellectual contact with it, and at times are hyperalarmed by the emergence of a politically significant religious movement. Some can hardly believe their eyes concerning the upsurge of religion around them. It frightens them.

Is it true that the believer today feels totally certain in his belief? In one sense of the word, yes, and in another sense, no. Around me are so many intelligent persons whom I admire, who do not believe as I do, that there is no possible way, psychologically, that I can believe with certainty that I am right and they are wrong. (I do accept the premise that we cannot all be right; only one position can be true, or more true, and the others must be less so. I put it this way because experience shows how difficult it is to get these matters right, and I am quite willing to allow that the closest any of us gets in real assents is only an approximation, never the whole truth. Although I try to be as deep and serious a Catholic as I can, ready always to inquire further, I would never dream of holding that I have the deepest and best understanding of the Catholic faith ever attained; the best I can hope is not to fall too far short. And so also, I think, for others who hold other ultimate commitments.)

Among these ultimate commitments, experience further shows, there always is a certain degree of overlap, particularly in their operational or practical implications. And this is true even when these beliefs appear, by naked and unadorned assertion (on the level of abstraction), to be antithetical. In 1964, for example, there were Christians, Jews, and unbelievers among those who risked their lives in Mississippi in defense of the civil rights of blacks. Their *reasons* for so acting diverged, but their diverse commitments led all of them to the same practical conviction about what was demanded of them. This similarity in practical implication suggests a certain, often unexamined, "overlap" in their ultimate commitments as well.

It is this visible overlap in practice, and this usually unexamined overlap in ultimate commitments, that I was exploring in two early books of mine, *Belief and Unbelief* (1965) and *The Experience of Nothingness* (1970). My claim is that in the West, or at least in the United States, the practical differences between serious believers and serious unbelievers, in certain weighty matters, are not what historic rivalries would lead one to expect. There are very interesting, and pregnant, convergences, even amid ob-

vious differences. Among all of us, exact consistency between our the-
oretically stated commitments and our actual actions is seldom what we
think it is. Put otherwise, a really thoroughly examined life is exquisitely
rare. Stealthily and unself-consciously, we borrow rather a lot from one
another. And why not? We share the same planet and many of the same
searing experiences, and we often do so as companions in arms, after the
battle raising our glasses to one another in genuine admiration for deeds
well done.

Not to put too fine a point upon it, a Catholic in the United States
today would have to be most insensitive not to recognize that most of
his or her beliefs seem preposterous, out-of-date, or even immoral to a
preponderance of the professional people with whom he deals. It can
hardly help entering into our heads daily that we might be wrong in
what we believe. For to maintain one's faith in the face of unremitting
lack of cultural support, if not overt hostility, is to accept a steady diet
of criticism, skepticism, and disbelief from others. That many millions
of Catholics have abandoned the faith of their fathers is not, in the
circumstances, surprising. What is comforting is the millions who have
not, and the steady stream of converts, particularly the acute and critically
intelligent converts, who keep swelling the ranks. Comforting, too, are
the hard lessons of experience that are forcing many unbelievers to come
to positions far closer to ours than was common thirty years ago. All in
all, our faith seems more in alignment with the cutting-edge forces in
international life than has been the case for centuries. Let me mention
four or five cases, not as an exhaustive analysis but simply as illustrations
and suggestions.

Not very significant, maybe, but as a straw in the wind, consider the
high reputation in which Catholic schools are suddenly being held, especially those in inner-city neighborhoods. Consider also the reasons for
this high reputation, as advanced by secular, Protestant, and Jewish observers: a sense of discipline, order, faith, family, hard and exact work,
care, respect, and service to others. Results in test scores and graduation
rates, and success with students deemed irremediable by public school
systems. Consider the fact that when we were young, in the Forties and

Fifties, observers mocked the uniforms worn in Catholic schools as a sign of conformism and cryptofascism (subtlety was not a strong suit in interreligious comment in those days), whereas today even a Baptist President of the United States, along with many secular liberals, sees positive gains from putting young and disadvantaged children in school uniforms, and highly recommends the practice. How is it, editorialists ask, that with vastly less funding, Catholic school systems deliver results superior to those demonstrated in tax-supported public schools? Discussions of "intangibles" regularly note the full and raw palpability of their consequences.

On an utterly different level, consider the shock received by many modern rationalists, believers in the Enlightenment, reason, and science, when, under attack by postmodernists who describe science as a phallic attack upon the earth's *fragile* ecology, reason as nonholistic delusion and right-brained distortion of humanism, and the Enlightenment as a mythic celebration of male arrogance and a naive, precritical mask of illicit power, they discover in the Pope of Rome, quite suddenly, the world's most prominent defender of reason and its prerogatives. The Jewish and Christian faiths require a robust confidence in the power and validity of human inquiry; the thirst of the human mind for understanding, light, and truth; and the hunger of the intellect to set aside false gods, falsehood, and false assumptions while trying to hone in faithfully on the true. If these drives of the human soul are in vain, then Judaism and Christianity are pointless. They are addressing the wrong animal.

Again, those thinkers today, unbelievers as well as believers, who see that systematic relativism makes it strictly impossible for human beings to condemn Nazism and its abominations, therefore consider it a moral obligation to attack moral relativism, root and branch, and to defend a nonarbitrary, nonsubjective standard of right and wrong, a kind of rudimentary set of universal rights—or, at least, universal wrongs. For it is sometimes easier, clearer, and more economical to proceed in such matters by a kind of universal *via negativa*: Thou shalt not commit genocide, practice torture, rape, enslave other human beings, impose harsh labor upon children, violate the conscience of individuals. One does not have to be a believing Jew or Christian to hold to such a *via negativa* or to uphold a universal declaration of human rights. On the contrary, some of the most eloquent voices in formulating such responses, theoretical and practical, to the relativism and nihilism of the early twentieth century—to Nietzsche, De Man, Sartre, and others—were atheists and agnostics who described themselves as secular humanists. Albert Camus described one of them in his novel *The Plague* as a secular saint. In circles known to me, I held Sidney Hook (for all his faults) as one such, but there are many. Are not such persons and such defenses of reason and universal principles in human affairs signs of what once was called "the laws of nature and nature's God"?

As a penultimate illustration, consider the news from physics, biology, and genetics. Taking the last first: in 1972, a journalist could write that what is aborted in a human abortion is "only a mess of matter from a woman's body," not much more than the menstrual flow or an unwanted appendix; but genetics has now made it clear that, on the contrary, whatever else it is, the aborted has a genetic code altogether different from the woman's, a code that is unique and individual. This genetic datum, scientists may make haste to note, does not settle what legal status ought to be assigned to the aborted. But at least three things about it are clear: it is a unique individual being, it is human both by genetic analysis and (from just a few days on) by resemblance, and it is gendered, more frequently female than male. To those who placed upon the infant in the womb the value that Catholics did in 1972, this news is not hard to take. Comfort of this sort comes frequently to Catholics in our time. We hold the view that if there seems to be a conflict between the findings of science and the findings of Catholic theology, it must be based either upon bad science or upon bad theology, or upon both, for one and the same Creator is the source of truth in both, and there are not two truths. The bad news is that it may take generations to sort out what the truth is, and who went wrong and why.

Meanwhile, of course, the side likely to be ridiculed in our time, and deemed heterodox by the right-thinking, is not the side of science. *Inherit the Wind* did not make Clarence Darrow seem like the fool and the

244 · *Michael Novak*

shifty one, and cannot be said to have done evenhanded justice to the mind and spirit of William Jennings Bryan. And even today, only in economics do liberals use the term "Darwinian" as a pejorative; otherwise, they utter it with a reverence perhaps not wholly critical.

Finally, those who hold that creation is as strewn with signs of design as the night sky with the Milky Way or the universe with galaxies may find much more echo of their religious beliefs in the physics of the end of the twentieth century than they did in the physics promulgated with the arrogance of youth in the nineteenth. That physics is a different mode of inquiry than theology, and works by different methods and different standards of evidence, pursuing questions of a rather different meaning and range, is by now far clearer than it was two or three generations ago. Both theologians and scientists have had their moments of arrogance and nonsense; both have learned humility, at least a bit. Evangelical Christians today, likely as others to have a graduate degree in the sciences, will tell you freely that a day in Genesis is not twenty-four hours, and that the point of the biblical narrative is not to add to physics as a science but, rather, to make a theological claim about the dependence of all things upon the Creator—and not only "in the beginning," but at each successive instant of time. And physicists—Paul Davies is one—will tell you freely today that many of the questions raised by the ancients, in the pre-Christian as well as in the Christian age, have respectable and respectful analogues in the advanced speculations of physics, not only in astrophysics and subatomic physics but also in the relations of physics and biology. I am thinking of his *God and the New Physics* (1983), as well as his more recent *The Mind of God* (1996), *The Cosmic Blueprint* (1987), and *Are We Alone?* (1995).

Science is not faith, but in both there is today a shared wonder and sense of awe; in both, too, there is engagement, by different methods, in analogous problems of order and chaos, randomness and design, determinism and freedom, and mind and matter. (Is it "everything is mind, never matter," or "everything is matter, never mind?") And what is time? And how, then, shall we think of eternity? Is it an unimaginably long time, a time before time, beyond the limits of time (and in what sense of "limits"), or . . . ? The uses of mathematics today verge on pure poetry, and the exigencies of canons of simplicity take the breath away. Physics, these days, breathes the air, nearly, of the metaphysics of old. (What's missing is the intuition of—and judgment on—existence, a content that is not graspable as a scientific concept but is implicit in scientific judgments of fact.)

A touch of metaphysics here may be more than some readers can bear, but for those who can follow me—or whose curiosity is piqued to read further elsewhere (in Maritian's *Existence and the Existent*, for example)—let me note that a philosophy of existence is of a different order from a philosophy of being, in which being is understood as part of the Great Chain of Being, a set of linked, graduated concepts. The philosophy of existence can be said to have been given self-consciousness for the first time by Thomas Aquinas. Its central spiritual movement is wonder at the coming-into-being of existents and of their continuance in existence.

The fact of existence is recognized neither as a concept is grasped nor (in that respect) in an intuition or act of insight but, rather, through a reflection—a sort of backward glance or reflexion—on what is occurring in a particular act of judgment, that is, a judgment that something is a fact, is existing, *is*. The jump from being a mere concept, a possibility, a bright idea, to being in fact true, to existing among other existents, to standing out from the nothingness of mere possibilities and being thrust into actuality is the great, and most decisive, jump. The act of judgment in which one decides whether in a particular case this jump has, in fact, occurred is no simple act, but complex and searching and deeply demanding of the subject who exercises it. (Many a professor boasts of having a poor memory, but nary a one has boasted of having a poor judgment. Such a confession would be too undercutting; for to a man without good judgment, what sense of reality remains?)

Both the act of existing and the act of judging are highly privileged acts in the Catholic tradition of philosophy, and are vital to certain key theological understandings. It was one of the glories of Flannery O'Connor that she grasped the importance of these two activities in daily human life—in two different senses of the word "activities": existing and judging—and in the work of Maritain and St. Thomas. This recognition is one of the chief sources of luminosity in her tales of simple people.

One feature much cherished in the Catholic tradition is its longevity. Another is its breadth. Take the longevity first. To be Catholic is to share in being Jewish, and thus to have a heritage going back to Genesis. (A Jew does not have to be Christian, but a Christian has to be Jewish; apart from Judaism, Christianity doesn't make sense.) To be Catholic is also to inherit, as one's own, the history of Greece and Rome. In a recent polemic, for example, a secular liberal writer observed that several prominent writers who stressed the idea of "character" are all Catholics, and suggested in this confluence some nefarious (gunpowder?) plot. He might just as well have noted that Catholics learn the concepts of "character" and "virtue" by studying Plato, Aristotle, Seneca, and Cicero—just as Thomas Jefferson, James Madison, and George Washington did. A classical education is the proud inheritance of Catholic youth, even in these dark times.

As for breadth, it goes without saying that the point of the name "Catholic" is "universal," inclusive of the whole world and all cultures—the opposite of "tribal," but not without appreciation for what is distinctive in each culture and each tradition. These days, about half of all Catholics come from Africa, Asia, and Latin America (the "Third World"); no church—or community—is as universal in its circumference. But the range of personality types encompassed within the Church—the people of God, as we say, in order to stress the people at the grass roots—is also universal. Simply to cite some recent Western (especially American) personalities: Catholic life reaches all the way from Cardinal Spellman to Dorothy Day, from Brendan Behan and Graham Greene and Heinrich Böll to Phyllis Schlafly, from Daniel Berrigan to Henry Hyde, from Mario Puzo's "Godfather" to Charles Peguy's Jeanne d'Arc, from Joan Didion and Margaret Atwood and Joyce Carol Oates to Tom Clancy and Ted Kennedy and Tom Hayden. It is bigger and rowdier than a Canterbury pilgrimage, and peopled as variously as Dante's *Divine Comedy* and Michelangelo's Sistine Chapel—ceiling,

walls, and all. Every type of sinner and saint has place in it. When
England was Catholic, it was still a merry place, and had a good red
wine. The Jansenists of France and the parts of Ireland they influenced
had a touch of Puritanism, but left to itself, Catholic tradition sins in the
opposite direction: Catholicism, Chesterton quipped, is a thick steak, a
glass of stout, and a good cigar. It is a sacramental church, alive with
and alert to the senses, delighting each sense in turn in the most sacred
moments of its worship. Through the senses, Catholic faith goes to the
soul, and virtually alone among the great religions, it holds to the resurrection of the body as well as the soul. No other religion is so body-
centered while maintaining the primacy of the spirit. (This is the real
significance of the seemingly odd Catholic insistence on the assumption
of the body of the Mother of God into God's presence—enjoying first
what is promised to all).

It will be said—it is often, in fact, said—that the undoing of the
Catholic Church will be its decidedly out-of-fashion teaching on sexu-
ality. We will see. The chances seem higher that a grand reductio ad
absurdum is even now being enacted, before our eyes, in the sexual habits
of the enlightened persons of our century and the century just beginning.
The modern ethic, Albert Camus wrote, will be chiseled on a million
tombstones: *He [she] fornicated and he read the papers.* Better yet, as Peggy
Noonan wrote: "An American liberal is a woman [man] who believes
that, as a non-negotiable bottom line, she [he] has a right to screw anyone
or anything any time or any place she [he] wishes to." In terms a bit
more judicious and genteel, Judge Robert Bork explicates the premises
that make such an entitlement seem plausible to those long lines of Americans slouching over the horizon toward Gomorrah.

The only tragedy, for a Catholic, is not to have been a saint. That
will be the tragedy of nearly all of us. That is why our favorite prayer,
throwing ourselves upon Our Lady, sounded over and over like the
beating of a billion hearts, says "pray for us sinners." At the heart of
our faith lies the sinner, and deeper yet, the mercy of God.

There is no higher position in the Church than saint. A Pope who is
no saint is just a failed Christian, maybe worse for the scandal of the

thing. A priest, the same. These are hard vocations; we should pray for those called to them, a kind of crucifixion.

Sainthood has from the first moments been open to women, and women have raced with men to go further in the love of God and the service of human beings, especially the neediest and most neglected. For the enlightened of our generation, of course, sainthood is not enough. They would rather have the honors and preferments and (as they think) the powers.

I like the age we live in very much. It is a wonderful time to be alive. But it is not in all respects a sane world, and some of the least participant in common sense seem to be the talking classes, who in the world of symbols and communication and "culture" have unequaled power. Against the attraction of such principalities, the Catholic people and the Catholic faith—and the sacramental life by which we are admitted into communion with our Creator and Redeemer, and live by Him and in Him and with Him, and He in us—exert a balance. Dante described this gravitational field in the last lines of *Il Paradiso*: "the Love that moves the sun and all the other stars." And so it is. An inheritance that has no price.

And in case you do not know it, here is the most beautiful line in all the hymnody of the West, and perhaps all humanity. It is for this line that we designate millennia from His birthday: *"Ubi caritas et amor, ibi Christus est!"* Perhaps you need to hear it hanging on the cold morning air high in the Gothic arches of a stone monastery, in the echoes of Gregorian chant, when its sound seems to mingle in the sunlight, and spring and Easter come. But the most important thing is when it changes your life.

A Life of Privilege
Roger McCaffrey

S OME OF the reasons I remain a practicing Catholic are too personal to relate—even for money. Suffice it to say that a multitude of small signs from on high, and one or two miracles of grace, have kept me on track. I have never so much as considered actually leaving the Church. There are too many reasons for staying.

Catholicism is "a country of the heart and mind," as Anne Muggeridge says. The borders are the same for all, but the places we live in, the people we visit, and the culture we imbibe are as different in any two Catholics' lives as they are in any two Manhattanites'. The life of any practicing Catholic is more than "mere" faith and prayer.

And mine hasn't been boring. First things first. My wife, Priscilla, is classically lovely and devoted, and a Catholic. One minute with her would persuade you of my good fortune. I'm from a large, cohesive clan that views the world with the same rather skeptical Irish-Catholic eyes. If Priscilla's side—eight sisters and a brother—is included, the "family" grows to humongous; my children have seventy cousins, and the meter is still running.

The advantages to this are obvious, but might come as a surprise anyway: I'm connected to society, and even to most elements of my professional life, via brothers and sisters, in-laws, and, of course, parents. I trust them implicitly. I can depend on them. Life is completely different if you don't have family. You feel isolated, perhaps defensive; you certainly worry about the future a lot more—that is, old age.

It's been a rich life so far. When my children, and their seventy cousins, mature, it will be even richer. And Catholicism, the orthodox kind, is absolutely central to it all, the binding glue. I cannot picture life without it. I cannot picture my family stripped of their faith.

Nonetheless, I remain Catholic not simply because of a superb family or because I enjoy ritual or prayer (which is hard work, when it is real) or Gregorian chant. Rather, as Cardinal Newman put it when asked why in the end he was a Catholic: I have a duty to be.

And I don't relish the prospect of hanging around, because in one crucial area, I feel like a stranger in my own country. Masses, everywhere, are almost a parody. Unctuous, cliché-driven priests dominate parish life. Edgy women and laymen in coats and ties (maybe) buzz around the sanctuary as though it were a 7-Eleven. Only yesterday we treated the sanctuary as the holy of holies.

As a result of our alienation, Priscilla and I attend the traditional Latin Mass, a deviation barely tolerated by the Church establishment. It is an increasingly popular alternative in two-thirds of America's dioceses. Which is good, because the Latin Mass has become nothing less than the center of our lives. And ultimately, receiving the Sacraments, preeminently the Eucharist (not to mention confession), keeps me Catholic.

But there's another consideration, too. My big secret. My Catholicism is personified in a wife and family, and also friends and mentors, whom I can trust with my life, my wife, my children—even as society and the moral order collapse all around us. They are my private society. I depend upon them, and always have, more than they can ever know. Where would I be without the ten or twelve most important people in my life? I doubt I would have gotten very far. And, since most of them are or were Catholics par excellence, what do I owe the Church that made them? Everything. Surely basic human loyalty, as a start.

I'm the son and grandson of exemplary Catholics. My paternal grandfather, Neil McCaffrey, Sr., made his mark as a premier Church goods salesman, back when salesmen—*men*—went to the customer every day. He got to know New York clergy and nuns, to put it mildly. He died when I was seven; I remember him vaguely. I remember him praying with grandma. His tattered prayerbook is now mine.

His son Buddy—my father, Neil McCaffrey, Jr.—was the product of the most complete training an American boy could have: New York's minor seminary, Cathedral, in the glory days. The archdiocese's seminaries, as *by-product*, gave us a raft of impressive civic leaders and intellectuals, and once set the standard for the others. Of course, New York seminaries minted thousands of fine priests. They guided many millions of souls and for a generation positioned the Church near the center of a nation's life, notwithstanding America's Protestant elite.

Both grandmothers, daily Mass-goers, impressed me at the tenderest age. To think of them was, and is, to think of the rosary murmured in the living room after dinner, or of trudging to Mass, holding Grandma's hand, on a cold winter morning. It must have been pretty important because it was incredibly boring, yet no one got up to leave: such were my thoughts at age four or five.

By the time I started grammar school, going to church meant a little more: watching grown-ups faint at the 10:45 on Sundays. This was stupefying, and a tremendous sign of the importance of the occasion. Every weekend, life for a boy in any New York parish was thus enriched. With people fasting for three hours (and some since dinner the previous night) before they could receive Communion, the ushers would carry out at least one, sometimes two or three, pale-faced parishioners from packed churches. Were they *dead*? There was always that exhilarating possibility. One of the reasons I long for the old days is so that my sons can have the same thrill I had.

My father's mother, Anastasia Waterman, was the daughter of a rather profane, sometime-millionaire insurance salesman. It appears that his claim to fame was that he drank with Babe Ruth and Mayor Jimmy Walker, but his wife and daughters were pious. Anastasia passed that faith on to her daughter, whom she groomed for the Franciscan nuns who taught millions of Catholic children in the Northeast, us included. There was scarcely a family occasion from the mid-1960s onward, I might add, that didn't include a Franciscan nun or two. Their presence really dampened the level of cynicism distressingly, though we generally permitted them to stay for dessert.

My mother's mother, a first-generation Italian, Grace Russo, died a few years ago at age ninety-five, razor-sharp to the end. "Heaven help me" were her last words. She was always saying that. She walked three miles to daily Mass, well into her eighties. Her husband, a convert, died with the Sacraments, although we always inquired, when we were small, why he didn't go to Mass with Grandma. Anyway, he made up for some of that, because he abhorred Franklin Roosevelt. It was a distaste he passed on to his children, one of whom, Joan, met my father at a Catholic Center (ubiquitous when New York was Catholic) in Pelham, a suburb of New York City, where they both grew up. Dad detested FDR, too. But it wasn't her GOP credentials that tipped the scales. "I could see the light of faith in her eyes," said my father about his betrothed. "When I think of your father," said one writer Dad published and befriended, "I think of your mother. I have never thought of them separately."

They did work as a team, though "work" doesn't adequately describe raising six kids in the 1960s and 1970s. It took its toll on my heroic mother—*that* I remember vividly; I also remember her good cheer through our miserable and dangerous teen years. I tried to be a good kid, if only because she'd have been heartbroken otherwise. But she and my father knew what they were doing. In fact, most of the chief influences on me, with the exception of Priscilla, grew up in a self-confident Church that dominated several of America's great cities for a couple of lovely decades. I was awed as a boy to hear stories from people like Grandma of entire baseball stadiums filling up in the 1950s with Knights of Columbus worshipping the Blessed Sacrament. It was a Church that mass-produced obedient, relatively happy souls from its parishes Sunday after routine Sunday. They were not fluent in Latin; it didn't matter.

By contrast, my own life has been defined by the crisis and astonishing self-doubt in the Church, and by the moral revolution in the West. Both phenomena kicked into high gear after Vatican II.

My parents, very much involved in the moral/psychological combat for their children's souls, nonetheless were happily diverted by a wide variety of friendships that they invited their teenage kids to enjoy. Lots of authors—some became treasured friends of mine—paraded through our house on Washington Avenue, but not only Rightists. For all my folks' conservatism, their friends crossed party lines in every possible way: Murray Rothbard libertarians, Manhattan liberals, even one or two strange creatures called WASPs, and yes, of course, Catholics. Catholics Who Didn't Vote for JFK. (There were a few.)

Three or four of my father's best friends were the latter. One evolved from the Right's most promising intellectual to an icon of the Left. Dad was deeply saddened (*that* kind of liberal he couldn't appreciate). Two more friends—priest soulmates—became part of the chancery machine. The first friends my folks lost after Vatican II were Catholics. Hilarity in the living room was replaced with stiff exchanges of goodwill in cards at Christmastime. I looked up at my father's funeral—a traditional Latin requiem—and was struck at one unintended effect of Vatican II: half his pallbearers were Jewish.

They could easily all have been. None, however, was under any illusion about Joan and Neil McCaffrey's traditional Catholic convictions. One I rank as a mentor. "Neil and I were—and are—brothers," says writer Vic Gold, a sentiment I share about him. "And I thank God for having, in his mysterious way, brought him into my life." Ditto again. Vic's sense of moral outrage at the galloping decadence and cultural depravity has always been a beacon. So, in a way, has his deadly wit. There isn't a nostrum that appears in *Time* or *Newsweek*, or on the lips of politicians, that Vic hasn't anticipated by a decade. I'll never forget the days after Reagan was shot. Would John Hinckley have the book thrown at him? We all wondered. No, said Vic blandly, he'd probably write one, and do the TV talk show circuit.

So, for all my Catholic activities, a couple of trusted friends or associates aren't remotely Catholic. I wish I had some clever way to show how they are Christian without realizing it, or something. But the fact is, they are far from the Church. I don't know why God has arranged this. It's strange—their decency, combined with their lack of faith. . . . I can trust them like brothers, but they're unbelievers. I'm afraid I derive no ecumenical charge from this. My faith isn't threatened, but it isn't enhanced.

Priscilla has had a hand in nearly everything I have done professionally. When I told her that for the first time, she couldn't understand how a mother who has spent all her time with the children can possibly have had that definite a role in her husband's career. But it's there in her serious counsel and abundant prayers. It's there in her deeper understanding of human nature and religion. And, alas, it's there in her IQ. I think it's higher than mine, and that can confuse a fellow. Whatever, she is responsible for making my life productive and happy since 1983. Without her to confide in, I would have taken more than one wrong turn.

But my dependence on the Church and its citizens hardly ends there. All my possessions and worldly success, such as they are, come one way or another from Rome. All my basic training, right down to the last prepositional phrase . . . all my self-discipline . . . not to mention my alleged talent—all it of it was bequeathed me through foot soldiers of the Church. Beginning with the old nuns—who get such lousy press—and led by a redoubtable commander in chief, the principal of Our Lady of Perpetual Help School, Sister Therese Carmel. She ran the best grammar school in Westchester. God bless her, the old (we figured her for fifty-five or sixty) battle-ax was very un-Franciscan: she scared the hell out of us all, patrolling the halls and forbidden parts of the grounds, gleefully confiscating hundreds of thousands of dollars' worth (I later realized) of baseball cards from helpless boys who meant no harm to anyone, more or less. (Today, we could probably sue Sister for damages. Or perhaps a class action suit against the entire Franciscan Order? Hmm.)

By the time I entered high school, a Jesuit played a big role in my development: Fr. Vincent Miceli, the son of Italian immigrants, who was more Sicilian than American, despite being raised from the cradle in New York City. I met him at home. When rivals undermined his book contract for *The Gods of Atheism*, which was originally to be published by Loyola, my father snatched it up for Arlington House. His publisher gave this thirteen-year-old a chance to meet the estimable Miceli, who acted as though there's no such thing as a bad boy. I revered him; so did many a teen taught by Miceli during his early years in Alabama. "You don't have to like the Ten Commandments," he once told me wryly. "You just have to obey them." On another occasion, looking for comfort, I confided to him that I was nagged by doubts that I'd get to Heaven. "Maybe you won't," he replied. (Why waste words?)

Conversation with Miceli was never dull. Among the hundreds of topics: what happened to Garry Wills (friend of Miceli and my father), what happened to Curt Flood, what happened to Bill Buckley, what happened to the Yankees, what happened to Pope Paul VI, why Reagan wasn't conservative enough. Rarely was there disagreement, and from those dinners a friendship developed between us from which I derived much more than Father did. As a counselor and spiritual guide, he was without peer.

When he invited me, after college, to help him launch his television and radio apostolate, I threw in with him, eschewing full-time politics as a profession. It was to be a fateful decision, changing the course of my life entirely. As a direct result, in my travels I met Priscilla.

Miceli personified all the best qualities of the old Jesuits with his boundless energy and productivity. He taught at both the Angelicum and the Gregorian in Rome, and at St. John's, Fordham, and Loyola/New Orleans. He wrote extensively—for everything from the *New York Times* to *L'Osservatore Romano*. An excellent moralist and spiritual guide, he was also a shrewd popularizer of theology and philosophy. Two of his books remain in print several years after his death, which came on the Feast of Corpus Christi (he'd regard that as a high honor), June 2, 1991. That day, a young New Yorker named Vincent Miceli—no relation— having been ordained a priest the day before by Bishop Thomas Daily of Brooklyn, celebrated his first Mass. Graham Greene couldn't come close to that symbolism.

Dietrich von Hildebrand has also influenced my life, more through his books and essays on the Church than by personal magnetism. He was a friend of my parents and I'd met him a few times, most memorably at two secret Tridentine Masses celebrated for the elderly philosopher in his suburban New York apartment, circa 1972. He was a passionate defender of the traditional rite, despite his reputation as a liberal (he surely wasn't a Thomist) during the pontificates of Pius XI and XII. The latter developed a keen appreciation of von Hildebrand's works, and Pope Pacelli called the German "the twentieth-century doctor of the Church." I was a fascinated spectator, both at his apartment and when he and his wife, Alice, visited my folks in Pelham. Von Hildebrand related, at one point, his conversation with Pope Paul VI, with whom he was reluctantly granted an audience at the end of Vatican II. The Pope, who later gave von Hildebrand an award for service to the Church, kept this meeting short, clearly uninterested in the philosopher's concerns about the direction of the Church.

Watching von Hildebrand pray his ardent thanksgiving after Holy Communion was enough to intimidate any slothful soul, and I definitely qualified at sixteen. Whether he was simply talking to himself or was in ecstasy, I don't know, but in either case, this was a man who had profound faith and love of the Church, a true soldier of Christ. Knowing him gave life to his books, and I devoured a couple as a teenager. At the University of Dallas, I wrote my theology thesis on *Liturgy and Personality*, von Hildebrand's gem on the meaning of Mass for individual souls, which blends psychology and theology in a way that probably hadn't been done before and hasn't been done since. My Cistercian thesis reader sent a stinging note when he returned the paper: "My advice," wrote Fr. David Balas, who lacked the admiration for von Hildebrand that I had, "is to stop reading extremists and start to study theology." Poor von Hildebrand: considered beyond the pale by conservatives in the 1940s and 1950s, and a dangerous reactionary by liberals in the 1960s and 1970s. I felt quite the moderate.

Another of his books, *The Devastated Vineyard*, which I kept on my reference shelf as a young man, attempts to explain what caused the collapse of the Church after Vatican II, continuing along the lines of *Trojan Horse in the City of God*, which was written as the Council ended and warned of emerging modernist tendencies. The new edition of *Trojan Horse*, in fact, earned the endorsement of John Cardinal O'Connor. The book reinforces the view that Vatican II was used as a pretext to change the Church, a view that has shaped my Catholic publishing ventures. (To complete that shaping, I had only to meet the traditionalist author Michael Davies, and read his early works on Archbishop Marcel Lefebvre and the Church since the Council. He put to rest any lingering doubts, which flourished for a few months in college, about my ultraconservatism.)

A decided influence on me, post University of Dallas, has been Pat Buchanan. You don't think he needs an introduction? I beg to differ. His public persona and the real Buchanan are two different animals.

Peggy Noonan, Reagan's speechwriter, said of Buchanan even before he ran for president: "He's been through the wars. . . . He is, prematurely, one of the grand old men of the movement." Long before I knew him, this is precisely the way I viewed Buchanan, whose style I tried to make my own. His book on growing up Catholic in the halcyon 1940s and 1950s had crystallized my choicest prejudices about the 1960s and 1970s. When I heard that he was launching a newsletter in 1989, I sought him out. Our only previous meeting had been in 1981, when we dined with our mutual friend Victor Lasky—whose books on JFK and Watergate vindicated Richard Nixon, Pat's patron—and Buchanan commanded me, "Go see *The Great Santini*," one of his favorite flicks. Needless to say, I obeyed. Even drove into the wrong part of town to do it. Since then, when he's recommended a book or a friend ("You really should give— base line we —a call . . ."), I do so within hours. Buchanan, like my father and like most (but not all) serious people, isn't loquacious. When he talks, ultraconservatives like me listen.

I wasn't interested in making money on his newsletter, by the way; I simply wanted to work for Pat. It turned out he wasn't interested in making money, either, and he phased the publication out to run for president in December 1991. I joined the campaign, and naturally took Priscilla up to New Hampshire for the historic announcement. The morning of the big day, with the hotel packed with salivating journalists, one of them—one of the brightest, and a Catholic who wrote for the *Washington Post*—saw me at breakfast before the speech. "I've just read Pat's

258 • Roger McCaffrey

speech," he said. "It's radical. No Republican has ever given a speech like this." I said, "That's why I like the man."

Prior to the presidential campaign, I'd fly down to Washington each month to help put together the newsletter, and then sometimes join Pat and his superb wife, Shelley, for a meal. I discovered in Pat the epitome of a Catholic gentleman, full of warm memories of his past, and devoid of bitterness. He was brutally beaten by the press in the two years I worked for him. Never did I see him nurse a grudge, or even lose his cool. A class act, and the smartest politician, Catholic or not, I've ever encountered.

✝

An underrated factor in the lives of most Catholics, certainly mine, is the priest closest to them. Make that priests, plural; these friends, parish clergy or professors, who have come mostly through publishing projects, are one of the great blessings of my life. A dozen of them, because of their example and counsel over the years, hold it in their power to dissuade me from any decision or opinion (except investing).

To meet them as men who face the same stresses as any business executive—but without the golden parachutes, and no choice but to leave the priesthood if they don't like their boss at the chancery—has been a revelation. There are no tougher men than good priests. Mentally tough. Up at dawn, seldom out sick, facing loneliness day in and day out, dealing with the problems presented by that most difficult human animal, the religious zealot. In short, knowing them and hearing their problems has given me the sort of feeling that comes only after realizing that your own complaints are trivial.

✝

As a teenager, I read James Burnham's book *Suicide of the West*. Burnham, who converted to Catholicism in his final days, was Trotsky's prize pupil in the Americas, and retained some of the Machiavellian proclivities of the modern even as he desiccated contemporary liberalism during the second half of his life. He dismissed *all* political movements as ideologies.

That disturbed me; conservatism—or at least the brand I bought—wasn't an ideology. It was a way of life, and a close cousin of my Catholicism. So I went in to consult Dad, locating him behind a cloud of pipe smoke in his study.

Logically, wouldn't Burnham have to disqualify his own politics as an ideology? Dad agreed, then said something that has never left me: "Sometimes I'm conservative. But, as a Catholic, sometimes I'm liberal, sometimes reactionary, sometimes radical. It depends." That put me on a track far wider than the supply-side conservative's but much narrower than Rembert Weakland's. After orthodoxy, sheer prudence is the key to everything, for a Catholic. For me: *How* can I pass on "the pearl of great price," to use Christ's words, to my children? How do I protect them—and, for that matter, other family and friends if they need help—from the ravages of sin? *What are the best ways?* Do I not owe them the best, and God, too?

Luckily, the Church herself has taught us, through Scripture and tradition. There are varying spiritualities, of course. But, as Cardinal Newman says, "Reverence for the old paths is a chief Christian duty. We look at the future indeed with hope; yet this need not stand in the way of our dwelling on the past days of the Church with affection and deference." "What we have heard and known," says the Psalmist [Ps. 77], "and what our fathers have told us, we will not hide from their sons."

Why am I still a Catholic? It's my duty. "Thus saith the Lord. Stand ye in the ways, and see, and ask for the old paths, where is the good way, and walk therein, and ye shall find rest for your souls." The old paths. The Church of Rome.

The Making of a Rebel Catholic
William A. Donohue

WHEN I was a kid growing up on Long Island in the 1950s, it seemed only natural that the Yankees, Dodgers, or Giants would win the World Series. There were other teams, of course, but they existed mostly to satisfy the crowds in other cities during the summer and to prepare the way for another New York victory in the fall. It also seemed natural that most people were Catholic. To be sure, I knew that there were Protestants, Jews, and others, but most of the people in my neighborhood were, quite naturally, Catholic.

Being a Catholic, then, meant doing what most other people did. And that meant going without meat on Friday, going to confession on Saturday, and going to Mass on Sunday. I guess a lot of Catholics ate fish on Friday, but in my family it was pizza or pasta. The most difficult part of giving up meat came when I attended a sporting event on a Friday night (usually professional wrestling) and wanted desperately to have a hot dog. But like all my friends, I either abstained or waited until midnight before indulging. It was just the natural thing to do.

Confession was a bit terrifying, but it did instill a needed sense of guilt. After all, I knew I had done some things wrong and needed to repent. Now this was in a day and age when guilt was not seen as a vice; rather, it was seen as a natural attribute: it came with the territory of confessing to wrongdoing.

My family liked to sleep late, so we usually went to the 12:45 Mass on Sunday, unless I was scheduled to be an altar boy at an earlier Mass.

Being an altar boy was not hard work, but it did place a burden of responsibility on me that was occasionally worrisome. I just knew that I had to do everything right. But again, it was only natural that this should be so. After all, Mass was the most serious part of my life.

It was only natural for Catholic boys and girls in my neighborhood to attend Catholic schools. Public schools, it seemed, were for Protestants. Indeed, until adulthood I did not know that there was such a thing as a private Protestant school. I knew there were Jewish schools, but I had never heard of a Protestant school.

It was only natural that the nuns I had in school wore habits. The nuns I had were, like any other teachers, of varying competency and kindness. Because I was frequently in trouble (I *always* got a "U," or unsatisfactory, in conduct), I did not endear myself to many of the nuns. But there was one nun who understood me, and that was Mother Alexis.

I really loved Mother Alexis, my seventh grade teacher. She was young and pretty and incredibly kind to me. I was a smart aleck, and she dealt with me in a manner other than the usual punitive approach. Oh, sure, my poor mother was summoned to meet her on a regular basis—just as she had always been summoned to meet with my teachers—but Mother Alexis knew me and got me to behave and perform in class better than any other teacher. I'll never forget her.

It shocked a lot of people, students and teachers alike, when I applied to Pius X for high school. Here I was, the wildest kid in the class, seeking a seat in a high school seminary. In the seventh and eighth grades, I really felt that I had a vocation and wanted to become a priest. That's why I was disappointed to learn that I was fourth on the waiting list to attend Pius X. As it turned out, I wound up in a military boarding school run by the Christian Brothers. My mother felt that the school would provide me with the kind of environment that would act as a heady tonic to my dysfunctional family life: my father had left my mother, my sister, and me when I was just a few years old, and never contributed to our welfare.

I hated high school. It was the military part of it that I despised. In trouble all the time, I was often barred from going home on weekends like the other kids; this was the kind of punishment accorded to wise guys like me. Unfortunately, my conduct hurt my schoolwork, and that left me at the bottom of the class. I continued my crazy ways in college, only to get thrown out after one year.

+

At age nineteen I entered the Air Force. Back in 1966, everyone I knew who was thrown out of college (and I knew quite a few in that category) wound up in the Army, Navy, Air Force, or Marine Corps. None of us tried to, or wanted to, avoid military service.

It was in the Air Force that I grew up. But I also grew away from the Church. Not that I ever turned on the Church; I just got lazy. I went to Mass on occasion, but more often than not I just slept in on Sundays. Almost all my Catholic friends did the same, so it seemed the natural thing to do.

After a stint in the Air Force, I attended New York University for my B.A., the New School for Social Research for my M.A., and then went back to NYU for my Ph.D. This time I was on the fast track: in 1970, when I got out of the Air Force, I had one year of college. In 1975, I sat for my Ph.D. orals and two years later took a position as a college professor, having completed all the work for my doctorate save the dissertation.

+

My undergraduate and graduate years gave me an opportunity to study with teachers and students who were mostly non-Catholic. What I missed most was the emphasis on moral values, never mind a focus on the spiritual dimension of life. Practically every lecture and classroom discussion had a materialistic bent, so much so that a presentation of a value-laden position was summarily challenged. And when the conversation dealt with religion, there was nothing but outright disdain.

The same professors and students who boasted of their tolerance and open-mindedness were incredibly intolerant and narrow-minded when religion was discussed. Indeed, with regard to the Catholic Church, it was not uncommon to hear things said that would have quickly been branded as bigoted had they been said about any other segment of our society.

What I found most interesting about this was that almost none of the professors or students had really forsaken religion altogether; rather, they had found in Marxism an ersatz religion. Marxism was given a messianic cast, a vision of redemption that was held with the grip of religious fervor. Heaven, or Utopia, as they called it, was achievable on earth, via the teachings of Karl Marx. And woe to those who disagreed! It is no wonder that the late French sociologist Raymond Aron once labeled Marxism "the opiate of the intellectuals."

While going to school full-time, I took a part-time job as an athletic coach at a wealthy Catholic elementary school in Manhattan. The following year I reversed things and went part-time to school and worked full-time. Working at St. Lucy's School in Spanish Harlem was one of the greatest experiences of my life.

When I first went looking for full-time work, I pursued a number of jobs as an accountant, since I had been trained as an accountant in the Air Force and had quite good computer skills. But every job interview I had didn't work out once my prospective employer discovered that I was attending graduate school, studying sociology. They suspected that I wasn't serious about being an accountant (which I wasn't), and that ended the interview.

Taking the advice of my friends, I learned not to divulge my graduate student status to my interviewers. Then the job offers came rolling in, and they were good ones. But my heart wasn't in it. My tenure as an athletic coach working with young boys convinced me that I wanted to be with kids. So teaching naturally recommended itself as a suitable field. However, the problem was that I had never taken any education courses, and was thus screened out of the public school jobs. That's when it hit me—there was always a possibility of landing a Catholic school job.

Had I done what most people would have done—namely, put my

name on the waiting list with the Archdiocese of New York—I might never have become a teacher and might never have had the career I've had. It just never occurred to me to contact the Archdiocese, so instead I wrote to fifty-nine schools plucked out of the Manhattan, Bronx, and Queens phone directories that began with the name "Saint." I wrote to schools named after saints that I never heard of before.

The first school I heard from was St. Lucy's. Located in a tough area, its students mostly Puerto Ricans and African Americans, this poverty-stricken school was so bad that no one on the Archdiocesan waiting list wanted anything to do with teaching there. So when my application was received, it didn't take long to hire me. I simply had no competition.

I taught the first grade in 1973, responsible for every subject, including religion. Teaching religion triggered my serious journey back to the Church. It made me rethink Catholicism and made me want to appreciate the greatness of the Church. This feeling intensified in the next three years as I moved up to become homeroom teacher of the seventh and eighth grades, teaching religion (along with social studies) to grades five through eight.

My St. Lucy's experience taught me the value of Catholic education better than anything I had previously known or encountered. Here were kids from families without fathers (I could relate to that) who were trying to overcome an environment that was hardly conducive to learning. But despite tremendous odds, they succeeded, and they succeeded for two reasons: they had great moms and they went to a great school.

There was a public school right across the street from St. Lucy's. Every day I would walk from the subway past the two schools, observing the incredible differences between them. The public school kids were dressed shabbily and were hanging out in a rather unorganized fashion. My kids from St. Lucy's were well dressed in their neat uniforms and were engaged in organized activities. When the bell rang, my kids knew to line up and keep quiet.

St. Lucy's was not without problems, but we had none of the really bad problems that the school across the street had. There were occasional fights, but there were no gangs and there were no drugs. The public school was so bad that it was shut down by the City of New York after a series of rapes and gang incidents.

St. Lucy's worked because the mothers who sent their kids there wanted it to work and because the inculcation of Catholic values that the teachers gave the kids had real-life consequences. I didn't need to read the voluminous reports that demonstrated the superiority of Catholic schools—I saw the results firsthand. Catholic schools worked because they outlined for the kids a set of parameters, grounded in their faith, that their otherwise open-ended experiences didn't provide.

The truth is that Catholic schools in the ghetto have done more to provide for upward mobility than any other single force. And yet those who claim to champion the interests of the poor typically resist any voucher-type plan to assist them. It is this kind of hypocrisy that confirmed my feelings about the liberal-Left professors and students who surrounded me.

✝

Teaching at St. Lucy's intensified my interest in Catholicism, but it also made me question some of the things going on in the Church. To be specific, I couldn't for the life of me figure out why the Church would approve religion textbooks that were devoid of religion. The books are better today (though they still need much improvement), but the books I had to work with in the 1970s were a sham.

The typical religion textbook used in the elementary schools in the 1970s was suitable for classroom use in most public school ethics courses. The references to Jesus, Mary, the Church, and the saints were minimal. The books were so mushy, trendy, and touchy-feely do-goody that few atheists would have objected. I mean, didn't everyone believe in peace and love and all that? But where was the context? Where were the principles, the foundation that anchored all these wonderful sentiments? Where were the teachings about moral wrongs? If sin or evil existed, you would never know from by reading one of those books.

My unhappiness with the religion books had an interesting outcome. In 1976, I was asked by my principal to represent St. Lucy's at an

Archdiocesan educational program. About seventy nuns and priests (I was one of only a few laypersons) attended the session. We were asked by the moderator what problems we were encountering teaching religion. I unloaded. I held up a copy of the eighth grade religion book and blasted it for its vacuousness. My tirade split the audience, but it also got me elected chairman of the Religious Education Council of the Archdiocese of New York, something I neither sought nor wanted.

In my new role, I was asked to propose some programs that might be useful to religion teachers in the Archdiocese. It seemed only natural that I follow through on what got me to this point, so I arranged to have the publishers of the religion textbooks show up and present their material.

When the program began, the publishers were delighted, thinking that this was a great time to hawk their literature. But I let them have it, chastising them for publishing irresponsible books. Again, the crowd reaction was mixed, but I accomplished what I wanted. It's hard to tell whether I helped to move the publishers to produce more responsible books, but I like to think I might have nudged them just a little.

After teaching at St. Lucy's, I took a position at La Roche College in Pittsburgh, a small Catholic college in the city's North Hills section. That is where I met my wife, Valerie. Valerie was a Lutheran, and that posed some problems at first, but when our two daughters were born in the 1980s, she cooperated without reservation in raising them in the Catholic faith. And in 1996, Valerie herself became a Catholic.

I had many good years at La Roche, but they were not like the ones I had at St. Lucy's. Like so many Catholic colleges, La Roche was a Catholic school in name only.

It always bothered me to hear administrators tell prospective students and their parents how Catholic La Roche was, and then observe these very same persons speak critically of Catholicism when the students and parents left. What they wanted was a check, and they knew how to con it. And yes, these same people talk endlessly of how greedy the 1980s were.

Teaching at La Roche convinced me that what Catholic colleges need more than anything else is an affirmative action plan to recruit committed Catholic faculty and administrators. Every search committee I served on placed a premium on hiring blacks and women, but not one ever mentioned the value of hiring a practicing Catholic. I will never forget the time when I showed enthusiasm for a candidate who wasn't shy about saying that he wanted to teach at a Catholic school: the dean exploded, saying she hoped he didn't think we were too Catholic.

It also bothered me that virtually all the Catholics who were invited to speak on campus, and virtually all the Catholic programs that were sponsored, were of the social justice and peace variety, which, for the uninitiated means they were of Left orientation. There was great interest in doing something for the poor and the homeless, but no interest in doing something for the unborn. And their idea of peace could be summed up in one word—surrender.

I know there are phony Catholic conservatives, too, and I have no use for them either. But it wasn't that crowd that opposed a monsignor as the new President of La Roche, simply because he was a monsignor, or that favored a Protestant woman as President, simply because she was a woman (her religion meant nothing). No, it was the head of the founding order of nuns who took that position—without, it should be noted, ever having met either the monsignor or the Protestant woman. Fortunately, in the end she didn't prevail; a coalition of liberal and conservative Catholics succeeded in getting the monsignor the job. He has turned things around, and the college is on the way back to regaining its Catholic identity.

✠

After my tenure at La Roche (which was interrupted by a yearlong fellowship at the Heritage Foundation), I was selected President of the Catholic League for Religious and Civil Rights. Without doubt, it has done more to deepen my faith than any other experience, and has certainly done more to make me proud to be a Catholic.

The Catholic League was founded in 1973 by Father Virgil Blum, a Jesuit professor at Marquette University. Its principal objective is to defend individual Catholics and the Institutional Church from defamation and discrimination. The League, which was modeled somewhat after the successful Anti-Defamation League of B'nai B'rith, was located in Milwaukee from 1973 to 1990, when Father Blum died. Then the headquarters moved to Pennsylvania for a few years before finally being relocated to New York. I took over as President in July 1993 and I am proud to say that our membership has grown from 27,000 to 350,000 in just four years.

✣

I knew there was anti-Catholic bigotry before I took this position, but I had no idea of the extent and variety of it. Throughout the large part of American history, much of the bigotry was aimed at individual Catholics, and it often coincided with ethnic prejudice. Indeed, even today, as a recent study by the National Council of Christians and Jews showed, the number one prejudice in America is held by non-Catholics against Catholics, outstripping the prejudice against African Americans, Muslims, Jews, Native Americans, Hispanics, and other groups. Though there is still discrimination against Catholics in some segments of society, the problem of anti-Catholicism these days has less to do with attacks on individual Catholics than it has to do with attacks on the Institutional Church.

Anti-Catholicism today comes from many sources: activist organizations, the artistic community, commercial establishments, schools and colleges, government, and the media. Some of it comes from the familiar sources associated with the Klan, and, of course, there are publishing outlets that specialize in anti-Catholic literature. But the most dangerous and consistent form of anti-Catholic prejudice comes from the elites.

It is a mantra among the educated class that tolerance is their virtue and intolerance is the bane of the uneducated. The studies that have been done on tolerance seem to support this claim; however, my own published research on this subject reveals that only one of the studies exhibits the kind of rigor associated with serious social science research. In any event, as Arthur Schlesinger, Sr., and many other honest scholars have indicated, anti-Catholicism is the last respectable prejudice among intellectuals. From where I sit as President of the Catholic League, this is a truism that has stood the test of time.

Contemporary anti-Catholicism seeks to undermine the authority of the Catholic Church. This is done in the classroom; in movies and on television; in plays, songs, and art; in cartoons, books, and op-ed pieces; and in government programs. Quite simply, many sectors of the establishment bear an animus against the Church. The question is why? And why aren't other religions fingered for the same abuse?

Anti-Catholicism in the late twentieth century is a function of clashing conceptions of liberty as expressed by the Catholic Church and elites. The Church holds that freedom means the freedom to do what is right, and our elite culture holds that freedom means the freedom to do what we want. Elites, therefore, are right to point to the Catholic Church as an obstacle to their realization of liberty. They want a sky's-the-limit interpretation of liberty, one that is suitable to the unencumbered self they so cherish. But the Church ties what is morally right to its conception of liberty, and embraces an understanding of the self that is integrally associated with God and His laws. The two perspectives couldn't be more contradictory.

The reason why the Catholic Church is selected for abuse has everything to do with the fact that the Church tenaciously holds to moral truths in a day and age when mainline Protestantism has become assimilated to the dominant culture. In short, if I were an angry activist seeking to promote radical egalitarianism or a radical conception of moral relativism, I sure wouldn't attack those religions that have already yielded. No, I would lash out at the Catholic Church.

It is a tribute to the Catholic Church, then, that it is still chosen as the institution to discredit by those bent on nihilism. If for no other reason, this makes me proud to be a Catholic: Why would I ever want to be an ally of those who seek to deny the verity of moral absolutes?

✦

In my lifetime, there have been several persons who have had a great impact on my Catholic thinking, but none more than my mother. Her sustained devotion to the Church, and especially to Our Blessed Mother, has left me with a resource that is simply indispensable and indescribable. There was no one quite like her.

Of the public figures who have influenced me, mention must be made of Bishop Fulton J. Sheen. When I was growing up, he was the Catholic I most identified with; my family watched his TV show so attentively that no one was allowed to speak while he was on. In many ways, I thought of Sheen as the Church, so visible and erudite was he.

As an adult, I have come to love Pope John Paul II. A first-rate intellectual and a first-rate leader, he is the greatest living moral resource in the world. In particular, his encyclical *Veritatis Splendor* has had a great effect on me. The Holy Father's explication of Church teachings on moral absolutes is more than a work in moral theology, it is the grandest statement on liberty ever written. It makes John Stuart Mill's 1859 essay "On Liberty" look juvenile by comparison.

I have also come to love Mother Teresa. She epitomized the best of Catholicism, helping the indigent and the dispossessed without ever blowing her own horn. She knew the difference between compassion and sentimentality, and it put her at odds with many of those who fancy themselves crusaders for the poor. The attacks on her by embittered atheists and socialists is testimony to her courage and a telling statement on how ideologically corrupt the radical Left really is.

Though I don't know any one of them well, I have also been inspired by the Sisters of Life. Just being in their presence is a humbling experience: they are emblematic of the very best of the religious, quietly serving the Church and touching people in a way that no one else can. More than any other order, they exude a holiness and grace that is hard to describe.

Father Benedict Groeschel is as close a male analogue to Mother Teresa as I know. Selfless, bright, and courageous, Father Groeschel services the poor in a way that no bureaucracy could ever do. He pulls no punches and has a great sense of humor, making all of those in his company feel special.

Father Richard John Neuhaus is not only the premier Catholic intellectual in America; he is also a considerate and thoughtful person. His writings have had a great impact on me, and his publication *First Things* is a treasure of good writing and sober commentary. It is a great bonus to the Catholic Church that he became one of ours in the late 1980s.

In my role as President of the Catholic League, I have had several opportunities to get to know John Cardinal O'Connor. He has a reputation as a tireless warrior for the Church, and it is one that he has justly earned. Never afraid of controversy, Cardinal O'Connor will not be intimidated from speaking the truth, and in that regard I hold him as a model to be emulated.

I have only recently gotten to know Anthony Cardinal Bevilacqua, but I think the Church is indeed lucky to have him. A clear thinker with a focused approach, Cardinal Bevilacqua has a soft side to him that never stands in the way of the tough calls he has forthrightly made. He has impressed me as few others have in recent years.

The chairman of the board of directors of the Catholic League is Father Philip Eichner. He is one of the brightest persons I have ever met. He is also one of the most effective leaders I have ever met. Moreover, Father Eichner has done more to support the Catholic League than any other person. He has his pulse finely tuned to the Church's tempo and more fully understands Catholicism in its entirety than anyone I know. But more than that, he is a very special person, one whom I admire second to no one.

Finally, if I had gotten into that high school seminary, the kind of priest I would have wanted to become is the kind of priest Monsignor John Woolsey has become. Responsible for upending the morally irresponsible sex education program that some New Yorkers wanted in the early 1990s, Monsignor Woolsey is a man's man, a brilliant example of how a mixture of brains and guts can get the job done. Like Father Eichner, he has been extraordinarily kind to me.

✛

I believe that the day will soon come when being a Catholic will be in vogue once again. Having been on the defensive for some time, the Catholic Church will experience rising opportunities, and the laity will be called upon to play an increasingly important role in the Church. As Cardinal Bevilacqua has said, the laity are 99.992 percent of the Church, and with leaders like him, it is just a matter of time before our strength is realized by everyone, Catholic and non-Catholic alike. That's why it's a great time to be a Catholic. It's only natural that things should work out this way.

A Safe Place: Upon Entering the Catholic Church at the Two-Minute Warning

Dr. Bernard Nathanson

I T WAS Ash Wednesday. When I set out for the 7 A.M. Mass, a pitiless wind was sweeping its way down the main streets of this unforgiving megalopolis and a crepuscular light was sounding the tocsin for the night crawlers (the homeless, the night-shift workers, perhaps even the vampires among us) to return to the shadowy country of the Chthonic. I walked the two blocks to my parish church, holding the collar of my battered trench coat tight against my throat, my mother's admonition not to forget to wear my scarf and gloves—articles I have not owned or used for thirty years—flashing like a neon beer sign in my sleepy brain. I stood outside the new door (the lumber was still orange and fresh, the stone walls of the church chipped and weathered), and I wondered briefly how I had come to this place at this time in my life. Never mind. I entered the church, practiced anew my right-knee genuflection (I had been bending the left knee until the kindly parish priest jokingly asked if I were left-handed, and I replied that mancinism was *not* one of the sins I had managed to amass in the course of my long, lonely life), and slipped easily into my customary place in the back of the church. My sanctuary, my safe place.

When I had been discussing conversion with my mentor—an Opus Dei priest of formidable intellectual powers and seemingly limitless patience—I had once protested that although I had read widely in the history, theology, philosophy, and politics of the Church, I knew almost nothing of those simple customs, traditions (I termed them the "me-

chanics" of Catholicism), and habits of the Faithful. He countered by
reminding me that those were merely the "furniture" of the room—first
we had to come to a resolution of when and how and why I should
enter the room; later we would deal with the "furniture." At the first
several Masses I attended at the endearing little parish church around
the corner, I had taken a seat near the front and invariably was left
standing while the rest of the Faithful were either sitting or kneeling,
and vice versa; the priest (with whom I meet regularly now, privately)
took me by the elbow after a Mass. In his characteristically kindly way,
he said, "Maybe, Doctor, it would be better for the next little while if
you took a seat in the back so you could watch what the others are
doing." I had never heard sounder advice, and now—even though I am
familiar with the exquisitely moving choreography of the Mass—from
habit I still sit in the back of the church.

At my first confession I had tightly clutched a paper, given to me by
my mentor, that scripted the order of things for that Sacrament and
provided me the cues. But as I entered the confessional I realized—to
my growing horror—that it was pitch dark in there, and I was unable
to make out a word of the script. I fumbled a few moments, the priest
prompted me, but I was suffering a fulminating case of stage fright by
this time. Finally he breathed heavily through the screen and asked if I
were a recent convert. When I replied that I was, he muttered something
to the effect that he wondered how any priest could baptize a convert
so poorly prepared. How could I tell him that it was one of the great
princes of the modern church who had baptized and confirmed me? So
I mumbled something about a failing memory and a touch of stage fright,
and with that he helped me through to the end.

Conversion is a solemn, momentous experience—but it has its lighter
moments (*vide supra*—or is Latin *completely* forbidden even when re-
counting one's experience with the Experience?). I believe that it is a
part of the boundless grace of God that we are provided with a sense
of humor, the ability to laugh at ourselves, in blinding contrast to the
eschatological sunburst of nascent Faith and the gift of Grace. George
Santayana once said that humor is an affirmation of our dignity.

Walker Percy, a physician-novelist and a convert to Catholicism in his twenties, wrote that the proper answer to the question "Why are you a Catholic?" was (and is) "What else is there?" Percy amended that answer by stating that a smart-mouthed question deserves a smart-mouthed answer, and in his autobiography (*Signposts in a Strange Land,* 1991) concedes that the question—in the appropriate context—truly deserves a thoughtful, comprehensive answer, which he goes on to provide. His answer puts to shame what follows, but I shall struggle to provide my own answer, graceless as it may be.

On a bitterly cold Monday morning in December 1996, I formally entered the Catholic Church. I had been on the cusp of doing so for at least four or five years, and for the last two years had been attending Mass regularly although not participating in the Eucharist. I had consistently sensed that without the Eucharist, the surrounding rituals and ceremonies were attractively complex apparatuses—but without batteries. On those Sundays when the time came for the Eucharist, I would remain on my knees, conscious of the line of eager worshipers forming to receive Him, Body and Blood. I was aware that I was an outsider in this sodality, that I was condemned to remain such until I had shed my existential dystopia and slipped easily and gratefully into the body of Christ. An interviewer for a Catholic newspaper recently asked me if it was a jolting experience to proceed from a stiff-backed Jewish atheist posture to full participation in the Catholic corpus, and I replied that, no, it was more a barely perceptible speed bump than a jarring encounter with a concrete barrier. I was wrong, of course. Planets realigned themselves, the laws of gravity and motion were suspended, the spiritual sun of the Body and Blood of Christ stood still to displace my ego at the center of my cosmos, and the laws of metaphysical mechanics were rewritten as I received my First Communion on that fateful December morning.

In those two years in which I had worshiped as an empathizer but not yet a full participant in the joyous ceremony of the Mass, I was struck by a number of what seemed to me unique and remarkable practices—for instance, the welcoming of one and all to the Mass, with no measuring glances from the clergy or the worshipers. It was as if they were saying to me, *please join with us in this solemn occasion to celebrate our Lord and His work.* There were no requirements here, no green card, no expensive tickets to buy, nothing but an unconditional welcome, a feast of sensory and spiritual input that—conflating in some as yet un-described area of the brain (or heart, or both)—managed to quench a hitherto unslakable thirst in the very nuclei of the cells of my body and mind.

And there was that moment in the Mass when each turned to his neighbor—most likely a stranger—and shook the proffered hand, mur-muring "Peace be with you" or responded "And with you." It was a moment of human contact, of touching, of warm flesh upon flesh—as welcome to me as the heat and security and utter safety of a mother's enveloping love. Since I had spent a good portion of my life pursuing the love and security my mother had withheld from me (through no fault of hers, God rest her decent, generous soul) in my childhood, that moment in the Mass often enough brought me to the verge of tears—and still does.

And there was—always—the mystery at the heart of the service: the Incarnation and the Eucharist. Malcolm Muggeridge—another convert like me (he became a Catholic in his seventh decade)—has described the Incarnation as the Master Drama of this universe. I have little of the Euclidean certainty that St. Mug had: for me, a humble catechumen, a spiritual novitiate, the Mass and the Sacraments are the vital organs, and I am Andreas Vesalius poring over the venous and muscular systems of the body while simultaneously gasping in awe at the apparently limitless wonder of the whole organism.

The Catholic Church and I are an odd couple indeed. As a boy living on the Upper West Side of Manhattan (a well-to-do-Jewish ghetto), I regarded Catholics as aliens, as practitioners of a dark art. I recall a German-American Catholic family who lived on the northern corner of our block; they exemplified the sinister sense of mystery surrounding those auslanders. The sons in the family were pale, beefy, and ram-bunctious. We smaller, weaker Jewish boys *(yeshivabuchers)* regarded them as threatening "aliens" (children are so naturally xenophobic) and avoided them assiduously. Even my mother and father issued a stern set of instructions to me and my sister, forbidding any social intercourse at all with the "foreign Papists" (my parents were first-generation Americans, my mother's family having emigrated from eastern Poland to Canada and thence to the United States, and my father's family from eastern Germany to Canada, and finally to the United States). As I reflect back over the decades, I wonder what the "foreign Papists" were told about *us*. What instructions were issued to those children by *their* parents?

I attended a fashionable (and academically superior) grammar and high school, and my closest friend was a tall, gangling, melancholic boy named Tom Mix (really!). The student population of the school was probably 98 percent Jewish; the instructors were all non-Jews. Major Jewish holidays were unofficial school holidays (I do not count the B-list days, such as Shevuoth, Succoth, and Simchas Torah), and invariably we would make elaborate plans on how to spend the A-list holidays, such as Rosh Hashanah and Yom Kippur, fruitfully (the options were outdoor sports, movies, excursions to amusement parks such as Coney Island), with a bare minimum of synagoguery; after twenty minutes of prayer and worship on the A-list holidays, a mysterious epidemic would sweep through the preteen male population in the synagogue: lower abdominal pain, slight nausea, dizziness, light-headedness, and visual blurring. We would sneak down the aisles of the shul to emerge on the blessed sidewalk miraculously cured (forget antibiotics!), then race down the block to the nearest movie house, or take the subway to the old Polo Grounds or Yankee Stadium.

I recall one Saturday when Tom Mix was my invited guest to my home; he and I and two or three of my Jewish classmates were sitting around learnedly discoursing on how to spend the next A-list holiday most fruitfully. When his time came to speak, Tom looked at us a little mournfully and murmured, "Well, I have to go to school that day. You see, I'm Christian."

An awkward, painful silence followed. We Jewish boys had only the most inchoate, unformed, but vaguely fearful concept of the Christian. I recall hastening to fill the silence with some supreme inanity, some bit of trivia to cover what I perceived as an inexcusable gaffe. The conversation resumed, somewhat stilted; my relations with Tom Mix were irreversibly altered thereafter.

When I asked my father that fateful question about Christians—What *is* a Christian, and why are they different from us?—my father (the medical professor and fount of all knowledge) artfully deflected my probing questions by pronouncing that Christians believed that Jesus Christ was the Messiah come to earth as the Old Testament had predicted; that He was regarded as divine; that Christians bowed and groveled before icons of Him and His Mother, who had become pregnant with him in some utterly inexplicable (and medically impossible) manner; and that it was all pagan nonsense (but to his credit, he would consistently concede that Jesus Christ was a great teacher of morality). He added a coda to his little sermon, a doggerel he had been taught by *his* mother and stepfather (both ultra-Orthodox Jews). It began "Yuschka Pandrik ligt in die erde. . . ." Yuschka Pandrik was an unspeakably derogatory term in Yiddish for Jesus Christ, and the remainder of the sentence states that He lies in the earth. The doggerel was set to a crude tune, and as my father began singing it to me, my mother and baby sister wandered into the room. Soon they were all singing it and I was giggling, though I understood little or nothing of it—only that somehow Christianity and Jesus Christ stood for the persecution of the Jews down through the ages.

As if religious persecution and mass slaughter began and ended with Christians persecuting Jews, with Jews persecuting Christians, with Romans persecuting and massacring Christians, with Hindus and Muslims performing vile acts of bigotry on each other! Where were the stories of Protestants persecuting Catholics in England and Ireland down through the centuries? Of whites and blacks, or of white frontiersmen, and even white governments, destroying the Native American culture and heritage? Gustavus Meyer, a scholar in the field of bigotry, once wrote:

> Committees composed of broad-minded men of all faiths have been formed to combat bigotry. This can be done most effectively by a *full* knowledge

of the facts. To understand the phenomena of the present it is vital to grasp the past, with which there are the closest interrelation. Precedents informing inherited notions, legends and prejudices are . . . the precursors of terrific outbreaks of bigotry. Cloaked over as this may appear at times, it is nonetheless a fateful undercurrent. A period may come when it is used with powerful and ghastly effect, as in Hitlerized Germany and subjugated countries, not only against the people of one religion, but the spirit of persecution has there been extended to all religions, and to religion itself. (*History of Bigotry in the United States*, 1960, p. 164)

And thus I entered my adolescent years skeptical of religion, contaminated by bigotry in an unusually vicious form, and heavily armored in the breastplates and blinding visors of prejudice and ignorance.

At Cornell University, I had a room in a comfortable private home in a pleasantly bucolic part of Ithaca called College Town. Joe N., a blond, slight Catholic boy with a severe orthopedic disability (he had suffered from polio as a child, and walked with a pronounced limp) had a room across the hall from me. Joe was an engineering student, had an engaging grin, and loved nothing more than to speak proudly of his girlfriend at home. He was devoutly Catholic when he arrived at Cornell but, removed from the sheltered environment in which he had come to young adulthood and thrust into the moral vacuum of a major secular university with a remarkably permissive political climate (I myself briefly flirted with an organization known as the Young Communist League in the World War II days), his determination to remain decent and faithful shredded visibly, semester after semester. By the time I left Cornell to enter medical school in Canada, Joe was involved in a squalid affair with a swarthy, undeniably attractive waitress at the local "greasy spoon," and was simultaneously wringing his hands over the thought that his beloved, loyal girlfriend back in New York City might be pregnant. He was actively pursuing the abortion alternative. I do not know what became of Joe (we had absolutely no communication with each other from the time I left Cornell), but I recall musing over how fragile an element faith was, how fragile a foundation on which to build one's life. I also recall, to my limitless shame, the baleful, perverse sense of satisfaction I enjoyed as I witnessed the fragmenting of the nucleolus of young Joe's life. I pray for him and his girlfriend now, even though I know nothing of their fate, and pray for forgiveness of my own shameful sinning in that revolting, Godless mise-en-scène.

My life and times through the years of medical school, residency, political activism in the pro-abortion arena, and as director for years of a monstrous abortion mill here in New York City are matters of public record, and I shall not bore the reader with yet another dreary recitation of mea culpas. It remains to be said that I was brilliantly successful, earning indecent amounts of money practicing my professional specialty (obstetrics and gynecology), and was afflicted with a fulminating case of acquisitive fever: lavish homes, trendy autos, beautiful trophy wives, wine cellars, stables of horses, and fearfully expensive schools and tutors for my son. Life's final irony: as one ages and the acquisitive fever ebbs, another fever replaces it—the fever to disacquire, to divest, to confront death unburdened with the trinkets and ornaments one had expended such effort to acquire in the halcyon years. As Bernard Berenson aged into his nineties, he wrote:

> Happy is the man who finds pleasure and satisfaction in his job, and does not hanker and strive to get a financially and socially and politically more remunerative one that will procure him neither pleasure nor satisfaction. . . . They may even attain all material reward and appreciated positions, but internally the sense of failure haunts them. So the religions which advised contentment with the lot to which the Lord had called them were right. . . . (*Sunset and Twilight*, 1963, p. 427)

Berenson, perhaps the world's foremost authority on quattrocento painting, and who had made and lost millions in the commerce of art, had been born a Jew, was baptized a Catholic in his early years, latterly professed Episcopalianism, and was buried as a Jew. The final words of that passage quoted above, written when he was ninety-two years old and living in retirement in Florence, are these: "Few obey them [the advices of the religious regarding the ephemeral nature of material acquisitions] and few are happy within, no matter how showy without."

Now—for me—the lash of desire has been stilled, permanently.

I cannot recall precisely the moment I knew, in some undefined, visceral sense, how unspeakably shallow, how revoltingly irrelevant, my life had become. Malcolm Muggeridge describes his own epiphany as viewing his volcanic and lustful past: "as sins which clutter up [my] life like seaweed in the Sargasso Sea" (*Confessions of a Twentieth-Century Pilgrim*, 1988). With the failure of my third marriage; with my pathetic attempts to revisit youth through cosmetic surgery, body-building, tinting of hair, and vestments more suitable to a postgraduate student than an aging boulevardier; and through devoting an unseemly portion of my waking hours to what Saint Augustine termed "scratching the itching sore of [his] lust," I was dwelling in the suzerainty of the demons of sin, oblivious to all but the seemingly endless carnival of pleasures, the party that never ends (or so the demons would have you believe). I was, as Berenson described it in the last year of his life, "in the deepest winter of my discontent. I see everything as frosty, uninviting, ungenial and myself as a pillar of ice, the ice of a moraine, not of a high glacier" (*Sunset and Twilight*). I had at my disposal a veritable arsenal of anodynes: whiskey (somehow that never really worked for me: I would become nasty, then deeply introspective, finally unbearably sleepy but unable to sleep); food—there are eighteen thousand restaurants in New York City, and the spectrum of choice is virtually limitless; companionship—my address book when I was between wives, and even within marriage, would have made Don Juan sick with envy; drugs—a physician has the unique privilege of healing himself with anything in the pharmacopeia, ranging from tranquilizers to hypnotics; books—my own library was composed of some ten thousand volumes, and I had read nearly all of them.

Why did I choose—from this wealth of guaranteed, proven, money-back-if-not-satisfied anodynes, the company of a youngish priest who had bailed out of the secular world at the zenith of his career on Wall Street to take up the cloth? I do not, to my everlasting shame, even recall how I met him—but somewhere in the deepest recesses of my restless mind, in some dark alleyway, in an unfamiliar byway off a rusting gyrus in the left parietal lobe of my increasingly bubbling-hot brain, a chord resonated—and I found myself virtually pleading with this man to talk to me, to soothe me, to tell me the most secret secret of his always calming, steady presence. And—mirabile dictu—he responded as if the script had already been completed and we were simply performing the ineluctable third act of the drama. The only anodyne worth pursing was the one that nullified all the rest: the search for God, the proprioceptive reality that Jesus Christ was in me to the tips of my very fingers and toes, the unbreakable promise of forgiveness for the Sisyphean moral baggage under which I had been weighted for too many years. Find the lapidary certitude of everlasting life.

We talked, and talked, and talked. It was a marathon conversation lasting some five years or more. In the beginning I was desperate (though careful never to show him how truly desperate I was) but curious; toward the middle of this Goethean drama I was more interested than curious; at the end (miraculously, the frequency of the talks decreased as I became more and more convinced) I was walking freely and contentedly into the welcoming arms of the one true Church.

The Church and I had proven wrong one of the most revered Euclidean axioms: that parallel lines never meet in space. For years before my baptism I had held a farrago of views on the moral and ethical state of this society that bore a striking similarity to those of the Church. I was not a Roman Catholic, but to hear my views on politics, ethics, morality, and the crumbling of the pillars of certainty, one would have come away convinced that I *was* indeed a Roman Catholic. The parallel lines intersected at my baptism, and I shed a quiet tear that wintry morning to mark that improbable intersection.

As a former mayor of the city of Dis, I will answer your question, Why am I a Catholic? I give you in all seriousness, and with no "smart-mouthedness," Dr. Walker Percy's only half-facetious answer: What else is there?

Why Are You a Catholic?
Walker Percy

THE QUESTION, Why are you a Catholic? arouses in me, I'll admit, certain misgivings. One reason, the first that comes to mind, is that the prospect of giving one's "testament," saying it straight out, puts me in mind of an old radio program on which people, mostly show business types as I recall, uttered their resounding credos which ended with a sonorous Ed Murrow flourish: *This—I believe.*

Another reason for reticence is that novelists are a devious lot to begin with, disinclined to say anything straight out, especially about themselves, since their stock in trade is indirection, if not guile, coming at things and people from the side, so to speak, especially the blind side, the better to get at them. If anybody says anything straight out, it is apt to be one of their characters, a character moreover for which they have not much use.

But since one is obliged by ordinary civility to give a response, the temptation is to utter a couple of sentences to get it over with, and let it go at that. Such as:

I am a Catholic, or if you like, a Roman Catholic, a convert to the Catholic faith. The reason I am a Catholic is that I believe that what the Catholic Church proposes is true.

I'd as soon let it go at that and go about my business. The Catholic faith is, to say the least, very important to me, but I have not the least

283

desire to convert anyone or engage in an apologetic or polemic or a "defense of the Faith." But a civil question is entitled to a civil answer, and this answer, while true enough, can be taken to be uncivil, even peremptory. And it hardly answers the question.

One justifies the laconicness as a reaction to the current fashion of confessional autobiographies written not only by showbiz types and writers and politicians but by respectable folk as well, confessions which contain not only every sort of sonorous *This—I Believe* but every conceivable sexual misadventure as well. The sincerity and the prodigality of the conversions seem to be understood to be virtues.

There is also a native reticence at work here. It has to do with the disinclination of Americans to discuss religion and sex in the company of their peers.

When the subject of religion does arise, at least in the South, the occasion is often an uncivil one, a challenge or a provocation or even an insult. It happens once in a while, for example, that one finds oneself in a group of educated persons one of whom, an educated person of a certain sort, may venture some such offhand remark as

Of course the Roman Catholic Church is not only a foreign power but a fascist power.

or, when in a group of less educated persons, perhaps in a small town barbershop, one of whom, let us say an ex-member of the Ku Klux Klan—who are not bad fellows actually, at least hereabouts, except when it comes to blacks, Jews, and Catholics—when one of them comes out with something like

The Catholic Church is a piece of shit.

then one feels entitled to a polite rebuttal in both cases, in the one with something like, "Well, hold on, let us examine the terms *power, foreign, fascist*"—and so on, and in the case of the other responding in the same tone of casual barbershop bonhomie with, say, "Truthfully, Lester, you're something of a shit yourself, even for white trash"—without in either case disrupting, necessarily, the general amiability.

Yet another reason for reticence in matters religious has to do with the infirmity of language itself. Language is a living organism and as such is subject to certain organic ailments. In this case it is the exhaustion and decrepitude of words themselves, an infirmity which has nothing to do with the truth or falsity of the sentences they form. The words of religion tend to wear out and get stored in the attic. The word *religion* itself has a certain unction about it, to say nothing of *born again, salvation, Jesus*, even though it is begging the question to assume therefore that these words do not have valid referents. And it doesn't help that when religious words are used publicly, at least Christian words, they are often expropriated by some of the worst rogues around, the TV preachers.

+

So decrepit and so abused is the language of the Judeo-Christian religions that it takes an effort to salvage them, the very words, from the husks and barnacles of meaning which have encrusted them over the centuries. Or else words can become slick as coins worn thin by usage and so devalued. One of the tasks of the saint is to renew language, to sing a new song. The novelist, no saint, has a humbler task. He must use every ounce of skill, cunning, humor, even irony, to deliver religion from the merely edifying.

In these peculiar times, the word *sin* has been devalued to mean everything from slightly naughty excess (my sin was loving you) to such serious lapses as "emotional unfulfillment," the stunting of one's "growth as a person," and the loss of "intersubjective communication." The worst sin of all, according to a book I read about one's growth as a person, is the "failure of creativity."

One reason the poet and novelist these days have a hankering for apocalypse, the end of the old world and the beginning of the new, is surely their sense that only then can language be renewed, by destroying the old and starting over. Things fall apart but words regain their value.

A boy sees an ordinary shell on the beach, picks it up as if it were a jewel he had found, recognizes it, names it. Now the name does not conceal the shell but celebrates it.

SMART-MOUTHED ANSWER

Nevertheless, however decrepit the language and however one may wish to observe the amenities and avoid offending one's fellow Americans, sometimes the question which is the title of this article is asked more or less directly.

When it is asked just so, straight out, just so:

"Why are you a Catholic?"

I usually reply,

"What else is there?"

I justify this smart-mouthed answer when I sense that the question is, as it usually is, a smart-mouthed question.

In my experience, the question is usually asked by two or three sorts of people. One knows quite well what is meant by all three.

One sort is perhaps a family acquaintance or friend of a friend or long-ago schoolmate or distant kin, most likely a Presbyterian lady. There is a certain type of Southern Presbyterian lady, especially Georgian, who doesn't mince words.

What she means is: How in the world can you, a Southerner like me, one of us, of a certain class and background which encompasses the stark chastity of a Presbyterian church or the understated elegance of an Episcopal church (but not a Baptist or Methodist church), a Southern Christian gentleman, that is to say—how can you become one of *them*, meaning that odd-looking baroque building down the street (the wrong end of the street) with those statues (Jesus pointing to his heart which has apparently been exposed by open-heart surgery)—meaning those Irish, Germans, Poles, Italians, Cajuns, Hispanics, Syrians, and God knows who else—though God knows they're fine people and I love them all—but I mean there's a difference between a simple encounter with

God in a plain place with one's own kind without all that business of red candles and beads and priest in a box—I mean, how can you?

The second questioner is a scientific type, not just any scientist but the sort who for certain reasons has elected a blunt manner which he takes to be allowed by friendship and by his scientific mien—perhaps a psychiatrist friend with their way of fixing the patient with a direct look which seeks to disarm by its friendly directness, takes charming leave to cut through the dross of small talk and asks the smiling direct question: "Why *are* you a Catholic?" But there's a question behind the question: I mean, for God's sake, religion is all very well, humans in any culture have a need for emotional bonding, community, and even atonement—in the sense of at-one-ment—I myself am a Unitarian Universalist with some interesting input of Zen lately—but I mean, as if it were not strange enough to elect one of those patriarchal religions which require a Father God outside the cosmos, not only that but that He, this Jewish Big Daddy, elected out of the entire cosmos to enter the history of an insignificant tribe on an insignificant planet, it and no other, a belief for which, as you well know, there is not the slightest scientific evidence—not only that, but of the several hundred Jewish-Christian religions, you pick the most florid and vulgar of the lot—why *that?*

Yet another sort could be a New Age type, an amorphous group ranging from California loonies like Shirley MacLaine to the classier Joseph Campbell, who, as wildly different as they are, share a common stance toward all credos: that they are to be judged not by their truth or falsity, sense or nonsense, but by their mythical liveliness. Here the question is not challenging but congratulatory, not: "Why are you a Catholic?" but "So you are a Catholic? How odd and interesting!"

Episcopalians are too polite and gentlemanly to ask the question—and are somewhat inhibited besides, by their own claim on the word *Catholic.*

Jews, whatever they may think of the Catholic Church, are too intuitive to ask the question, having, as they do, a sense of a commonality here which comes of being an exotic minority, which is to say: never

mind what I think of your religion or you of mine; we've both got
enough trouble at least to leave each other alone.

So the question remains: "Why are you a Catholic?"

Asked from curiosity alone, it is a civil question and deserves a civil
answer.

Accordingly, I will answer here in a cursory, somewhat technical, and
almost perfunctory manner which, as unsatisfactory as it may be, will at
least avoid the usual apologetic and polemic. For a traditional defense of
the Catholic claim, however valid it may be, is generally unavailing for
reasons both of the infirmity of language and the inattentiveness of the
age. Accordingly it is probably a waste of time.

My answer to the question, then, has more to do with science and
history, science in its root sense of knowing, truth-seeking; history in
the sense that, while what is true is true, it may be that one seeks different
truths in different ages.

The following statements I take to be commonplaces. Technically
speaking, they are for my purposes axioms. If they are not perceived as
such, as self-evident, there is no use arguing about them, let alone the
conclusions which follow from them.

Here they are:

☩

The old modern age has ended. We live in a postmodern as well as a
post-Christian age which as yet has no name.

It is post-Christian in the sense that people no longer understand
themselves, as they understood themselves for some fifteen hundred
years, as ensouled creatures under God, born to trouble and whose salvation depends upon the entrance of God into history as Jesus Christ.

It is postmodern because the Age of Enlightenment with its vision of
man as a rational creature, naturally good and part of the cosmos which
itself is understandable by natural science—this age has also ended. It
ended with the catastrophes of the twentieth century.

The present age is demented. It is possessed by a sense of dislocation, a loss of personal identity, an alternating sentimentality and rage which, in an individual patient, could be characterized as dementia.

As the century draws to a close, it does not yet have a name but it can be described.

It is the most scientifically advanced, savage, democratic, inhuman, sentimental, murderous century in human history.

I will give it a name which at least describes what it does. I would call it the age of the theorist-consumer. All denizens of the age tend to be one or the other or both.

Darwin, Newton, and Freud were theorists. They pursued truth more or less successfully by theory—from which, however, they themselves were exempt. You will look in vain in Darwin's *Origin of Species* for an explanation of Darwin's behavior in writing *Origin of Species*. Marx and Stalin, Nietzsche and Hitler were also theorists. When theory is applied, not to matter or beasts, but to man, the consequence is that millions of men can be eliminated without compunction or even much interest. Survivors of both Hitler's holocaust and Stalin's terror reported that their oppressors were not "horrible" or "diabolical" but seemed, on the contrary, quite ordinary, even bored by their actions, as if it were all in a day's work.

The denizens of the present age are both sentimental and bored. Last year the Russians and Americans united to save three stranded whales and the world applauded. It seemed a good thing to do and the boredom lifted for a while. This was not true, unfortunately, of the million Sudanese who died of starvation the same year.

Americans are the nicest, most generous and sentimental people on earth. Yet Americans have killed more unborn children than any nation in history.

Now euthanasia is beginning.

Don't forget that the Germans used to be the friendliest, most sentimental people on earth. But euthanasia was instituted not by the Nazis

290 · Walker Percy

but by the friendly democratic Germans of the Weimar Republic. The Weimar Republic was followed by the Nazis.

+

It is not "horrible" that over a million unborn children were killed in America last year. For one thing, one does not see many people horrified. It is not horrible because in an age of theory and consumption it is appropriate that actions be carried out as the applications of theory and the needs of consumption require.

Theory supersedes political antinomies like "conservative" *vs.* "liberal," fascist *vs.* Communist, Right *vs.* Left.

Accordingly, it should not be surprising that present-day liberals favor abortion just as the Nazis did years ago. The only difference is that the Nazis favored it for theoretical reason (eugenics, racial purity), while present-day liberals favor it for consumer needs (unwanted, inconvenient).

Nor should it be surprising that for the same reason liberals not only favor abortion but are now beginning to favor euthanasia as the Nazis did.

Liberals understandably see no contradiction and should not be blamed for favoring abortion and euthanasia on the one hand and the "sacredness of the individual," care for the poor, the homeless, and the oppressed on the other. Because it is one thing for a liberal editor to see the poor and the homeless on his way to work in his own city and another to read a medical statistic in his own paper about one million abortions. A liberal may act from his own consumer needs (guilt, sentimentality) and the Nazis may act from theory (eugenics, racial purity), but both are consistent in an age of theory and consumption.

The Nazis did not come out of nowhere.

It may be quite true what Mother Teresa said—if a mother can kill her unborn child, then I can kill you and you can kill me—but it is not necessarily horrifying.

America is probably the last and best hope of the world, not because it is not in the same trouble—indeed, the trouble may even be worse due to the excessive consumption in the marketplace and excessive theorizing in academe—but because with all the trouble it preserves a certain innocence and freedom.

This is the age of theory and consumption, yet not everyone is satisfied by theorizing and consuming.

The common mark of the theorist and the consumer is that neither knows who he is or what he wants outside of theorizing and consuming.

This is so because the theorist is not encompassed by his theory. One's self is always a leftover from one's theory.

For even if one becomes passionately convinced of Freudian theory or Marxist theory at three o'clock of a Wednesday afternoon, what does one do with oneself at four o'clock?

The consumer, who thought he knew what he wanted—the consumption of the goods and services of scientific theory—is not in fact satisfied, even when the services offered are such techniques as "personal growth," "emotional maturity," "consciousness-raising," and suchlike.

The face of the denizen of the present age who has come to the end of theory and consumption and "personal growth" is the face of sadness and anxiety.

Such a denizen can become so frustrated, bored, and enraged that he resorts to violence, violence upon himself (drugs, suicide) or upon others (murder, war).

Or such a denizen may discover that he is open to a search for signs, some sign other than theorizing or consumption.

POSTMODERN SIGNS

There are only two signs in the postmodern age which cannot be encompassed by theory. One sign is one's self. No matter how powerful the theory, whether psychological or political, one's self is always a leftover. Indeed, the self may be defined as that portion of the person which cannot be encompassed by theory, not even a theory of the self. This is so because even if one agrees with the theory, what does one do then? Accordingly the self finds itself ever more conspicuously without a place in the modern world, which is perfectly understood by theorizing. The face of the self in the very age which was itself designed for the self's understanding of all things and to please the self through the consumption of goods and services—the face of the self is the face of fear and sadness because it does not know who it is or where it belongs.

The only other sign in the world which cannot be encompassed by theory is the Jews, their unique history, their suffering and achievements, what they started (both Judaism and Christianity) and their presence in the here-and-now.

The Jews are a stumbling block to theory. They cannot be subsumed under any social or political theory. Even Arnold Toynbee, whose theory of history encompassed all other people, looked foolish when he tried to encompass the Jews. The Jews are both a sign and a stumbling block. That is why they are hated by theorists like Hitler and Stalin. The Jews cannot be gotten around.

The great paradox of the Western World is that even though it was in the Judeo-Christian West that modern science arose and flourished, it is Judeo-Christianity which the present-day scientific set of mind finds the most offensive among the world's religions.

Judaism is offensive because it claims that God entered into a covenant with a single tribe, with it and no other. Christianity is doubly offensive because it claims not only this but also that God became one man, He and no other.

One cannot imagine any statement more offensive to the present-day scientific set of mind. Accordingly it is Hinduism and Buddhism, which have no scientific tradition but whose claims are limited to the self, its existence or nonexistence, which are far less offensive to the present-day scientific set of mind, are in fact quite compatible.

The paradox can be resolved in only two ways.

One is that both the Jewish and Christian claims are untrue, are in fact nonsense, and that the scientific mind-set is correct.

The other is that the scientific method is correct as far as it goes, but the theoretical mind-set, which assigns significance to single things and events only insofar as they are exemplars of theory or items for consumption, is in fact an inflation of a method of knowing to a totalitarian worldview and is unwarranted.

SEMITIC ARTHURIAN

Now that I have been invited to think of it, the reasons for my conversion to the Catholic Church, this side of grace, can be described as Roman, Arthurian, Semitic, and semiotic.

Semitic? Arthurian? This is funny, because what could be more un-Jewish than the chivalric legend of Arthur? And who could be more un-English than the Old Testament Jews?

Or are they? Or could it in fact have been otherwise? My first hero and the hero of the South for a hundred years was Richard I of *Ivanhoe*, who with his English knights in the First Crusade stormed the gates of Acre to rescue the holy places from the infidel. But earlier than that there was the Roman emperor Marcus Aurelius. If one wished to depict the beau ideal of the South, it would not be the crucified Christ, but rather the stoic knight at parade rest, both hands folded on the hilt of his broadsword, his face as grave and impassive as the Emperor's. In the South, of course, he came to be not the Emperor or Richard but R. E. Lee, the two in one.

Bad though much of Southern romanticism may be, with Christianity and Judaism and Roman valor seen through the eyes of Sir Walter Scott, how could it have been otherwise with me? After all, the pagans converted by Saint Paul did not cease to be what they were. One does not cease to be Roman, Arthurian, Alabamian. One did, however, begin to realize a few things. The holy places which Richard rescued and whether he thought about it or not were, after all, Jewish, and he probably did not think about it because his Crusaders killed Jews every which way on the way to the Holy Land. Yet Scott succeeded in romanticizing even the Jews in *Ivanhoe*. But did the European knight with his broadsword at Mont St. Michel make any sense without the crucified Jew above him?

A modern Pope said it: whatever else we are, we are first of all spiritual Semites. Salvation, the Lord said, comes from the Jews.

In a word, thanks to the Jews one can emerge from the enchanted mists of the mythical past, the Roman and Arthurian and Confederate past, lovely as it is. For whatever else the Jews are, they are not mythical. Myths are stories which did not happen. But the Jews were there then and are here now.

✝

Semitic? Semiotic? Jews and the science of signs? Yes, because in this age of the lost self, lost in the desert of theory and consumption, nothing of significance remains but signs. And only two signs are of significance in a world where all theoretical cats are gray. One is oneself and the other is the Jews. But for the self that finds itself lost in the desert of theory and consumption, there is nothing to do but set out as a pilgrim in the desert in search of a sign. In this desert, that of theory and consumption, there remains only one sign, the Jews. By "the Jews" I mean not only *Israel*, the exclusive people of God, but the worldwide *ecclesia* instituted by one of them, God become man, a Jew.

It is for this reason that the present age is better than Christendom. In the old Christendom, everyone was a Christian and hardly anyone thought twice about it. But in the present age, the survivor of theory and consumption becomes a wayfarer in the desert, like Saint Anthony, which is to say: open to signs.

I do not feel obliged to set forth the particular religious reasons for my choosing among the Jewish-Christian religions. There are times when it is better not to name God. One reason is that most of the denizens of the present age are too intoxicated by the theories and goods of the age to be aware of the catastrophe already upon us.

How and why I chose the Catholic Church—this side of grace, which leaves one unclear about who does the choosing—from among the Judeo-Christian religions, Judaism, Protestantism, the Catholic Church, pertains to old family quarrels among these faiths and as such is not of much interest, I would suppose, to the denizens of this age. As for them, the other members of the family, the Jews and the Protestants, they are already all too familiar with the Catholic claim for me to have to repeat it here. It would be a waste of their time and mine. Anyhow, I do not have the authority to bear good news or to proclaim a teaching.

A Peddler's Words
William McGurn

W HY A Catholic? To a mind corrupted by long, misspent years in the information racket, it ought to have been an easy assignment, which is exactly what I thought—one or two nights in front of the word processor, a cup of black coffee beside me, banging out fine sentences strung together with flawless precision and interrupted only by the occasional but illuminating allusion to Blake or Augustine. Ours, after all, is the age of the newsman: CNN's "expanded" headline coverage twenty-four hours a day; the *Wall Street Journal* on your doorstep before breakfast; and the Internet, with which every potential Unabomber can have his fifteen minutes of fame. Never before have we had so much information and so little time to read it. For those of us who provide it, this means continually feeding the beast, and so week after week, with dreary regularity, I labor at my screen until I have patched together 600 words on the latest burning issue—a newly imprisoned dissident in China, a demonstration-turned-violent in Korea, still more complaints from the U.S. Trade Representative about the trade deficit with Japan—all to be surrendered to the Production Department in three or four hours' time. When Judgment Day arrives and the rest of the world is gazing heavenward, my colleagues and I will no doubt be found at our screens, frantically trying to put together a two-column sidebar on "What the Second Coming Will Mean for the Bond Market."

Often I arrive in the morning expecting to write about missile sales in the Middle East, only to find that the flavor of the week is labor rights in Indonesia. The one thing I have learned is not to worry all that much, because it all rather evens out; inevitably, next week the urgencies will be reversed, and anyway, stories are not so different as they might seem. It works rather like one of those improvisation nights where actors are given a scene, characters, and a situation, then fumble around for a few minutes before channeling their plot down the well-worn lanes of the tried and true ("What is required now from the [fill in the blank] government is some gesture of goodwill that will permit the [fill in the blank] peace process to move forward . . .").

In this light, a few words on the Catholic faith oughtn't to have been too taxing, with the added enticement that, since it is my own faith at issue, it permits me to speak with some measure of genuine authority. Months after the initial solicitation, however, I find it not quite so easy as I had supposed; long after the coffee beside my Macintosh had been drained and I had rearranged everything on my desktop several times, it was not just a matter of no words, it was a matter of no thoughts. In trying to summon up something persuasive, I recalled Cardinal Newman's line that though everyone has a reason, not everyone can give one. Yet the consolation vanished when I reflected that this was not a affliction from which Newman himself suffered: his *Grammar of Assent* and *Apologia Pro Vita Sua* are two of the best-argued reasons anyone has ever given. In the end, alas, mine are more prosaic. To begin with, my choice of religion was not, originally, my own: I became a Catholic because my parents had me baptized one. And if I might still be found before the Church altars, I have to suppose that it is because my transgressions have not yet attracted sufficient attention for me to be booted out.

It's more complicated than that, of course (further confirmation of Newman's point about reasons). It may be worth lingering over the point. James Joyce thought Newman the finest writer of English prose ever produced, but I'm not sure Newman would have cut it in the news business. There are no throwaway lines in Newman, no false notes. His brilliantly argued *Grammar of Assent* was meant to show that the human mind, though rational, cannot be limited to the kind of syllogisms favored by logicians and mastered, we must confess, by generations of Catholic apologists, much less by the sloganeering that passes for news analysis. I suppose what Newman was getting at is that just because you cannot prove a proposition on paper doesn't mean you can't know it to be true, and that your coming to know something to be true in just this way is perfectly reasonable. If, for example, someone you know has been accused of theft and you yourself have noticed items missing, you will be less inclined to accept his protests of innocence. If, however, this same person has proved more than worthy of trust in the past, you will be inclined to think him innocent and be ready to say so. Something similar is at work with faith. I'm not sure many of those who fill the pews each Sunday are there because they have read one of Saint Thomas's Five Ways. They are there, it seems to me, because the sum total of their lives—their experiences, learning, and intuition—appears to them to confirm the fundamental message delivered from the altar with each sacrifice of the Mass.

The essence of that assent, at least for a Christian, can be boiled down to two broad propositions. First, why a God? Second, conceding a God, conceding even a Christ, why a *church*—and why one that has the conceit to call itself *the* Church? These are the perennial questions, asked by all men in all ages and all languages, whether it be an Aristotle setting out his First Cause, a Pilate putting to death another troublesome Messiah, a Thomas Aquinas meditating on the divine essence, a Chairman Mao Zedong emptying his China of missionaries, or a John Paul storming the Berlin Wall. Though the answers they give are surely different, it is striking that the question remains so persistent. In contrast to our Scholastic philosophers, I am not sure that God's existence really can be "proved," however much sense the idea of a God makes to me. What I am sure of, however, is that those who deny Him cannot ignore Him. For a Being said not to exist, the Almighty makes an astounding, one might even say miraculous, number of appearances in the writings of those who most passionately deny Him. It may help explain why such works are so conspicuously lacking in humor.

For me, the concept of God was never particularly difficult. My father tells me that when he first explained the facts of life and asked if I had any questions, I inquired whether Eve had a belly button, which strikes me as insightful for a six-year-old (I'm afraid it's all been downhill since then), and decidedly more to the point than most of what is put out today by the National Conference of Catholic Bishops or the World Conference of Churches. Because it has always seemed so natural, I have long found debate about the existence of a God tedious. In the course of my travels, I have not infrequently bumped up against Christians heartened to find that one religious heart beats in a mostly secularist press. Among my journalist colleagues, by contrast, the reaction inclines more to astonishment. Both miss the point. Whether there is a God is debatable. But if He does exist, He does so whether we ignore or embrace Him. One way or the other, He is a fact radically unaffected by our position on Him.

The newsroom, to be sure, has its own orthodoxies, saints, and dogma, though naturally without the humility necessary for genuine wisdom or charity. Malcolm Muggeridge once remarked that the native shivering in the bush before a painted stone was closer to the truth than Bertrand Russell, and it remains true of Russell's counterparts today, the kind of people who deny revelation but look to the *New York Times* because it is "authoritative." Music alone persuades me of a Creator, perhaps because I am a rank amateur. Even those of us who do not know music recognize a bad note when we hear one, and are capable of appreciating the greatness of a composition that vastly exceeds our puny understandings. Clearly there is some harmony that transcends our individuality; you don't have to understand Chopin to enjoy a symphony. I watch my sixteen-month-old daughter respond to the beat of a nursery rhyme and find myself awed by the intelligence in her eyes, the quiver of recognition in her frightfully tiny body, the shared, unstated link with humanity, past and present, that it bespeaks.

The philosophers will tell you that this is the teleological argument, and that it is not conclusive. Of *course* it is not conclusive. Were it conclusive, there wouldn't be any debate. I merely find it persuasive. And as I grow older, it occurs to me that the design we see or don't see is a matter of angle. A field of wheat seen from ground level seems random and haphazard. From an airplane, however, that same field reflects a series of clearly discernible patterns, because man has an ordering mind: rows, ridges, and rectangles. Place a particular grain of this same wheat under a microscope, moreover, a completely different design emerges: of cell structure, tissues, organs, and so forth. Artists know this instinctively, that the way to see something is not straight on, like a passport photograph, but by exaggerating features or taking us to a neglected perspective, whether it be the flat, sturdy faces of Grant Wood's *American Gothic* or Icarus obscurely falling to sea in the corner of a Brueghel canvas.

Consequently, the God of philosophers has not been difficult. What *is* difficult is the God of my church, or, as I understand it, the Church of my God. What a mass of contradictions is this Church! Within its walls rage some of the most bitter and divisive battles mankind has known, with the special bitterness of family quarrels run amok. From without, the medieval certainty with which it delivers its judgments on the practices of our day can suggest a never-ending replay of the Galileo case. Even among fellow Christians the Catholic Church arouses suspicions. In certain circles, I am well aware, there exists the theological understanding that Rome is itself an obstacle to the Christian God, and (in the case of some strains of Evangelical Protestantism) an instrument of Satan. How tempting it is to dismiss all these contrary apprehensions as due to ignorance and misinterpretation, and yet . . . and yet, it is not hard to understand how those who hold them arrive at the points they do. Enough times I have read it in their eyes, when some inadvertent piece of evidence betrays my Roman affiliation. Though they may be looking at me, it is clear their attention has suddenly been fixed elsewhere, as though a bag lady had somehow burst in on a business meeting, insisting she was my mother. Initial shock at the interruption shortly yields to astonishment at the familiarity. And the eyes say what the mouth may be reluctant to speak: "You *know* this woman?"

Add to this inauspicious mix a church apparatus woefully unequipped for the age. Each day in my office, the fax machine spews forth dozens of press releases aimed at catching an editor's eye via appeals to favored catchwords: "new," "latest," "modern," and so on. The Church, in sharp contrast, exults in the anachronistic. It speaks in a defunct tongue and elevates dead men and women to sainthood. It insists that the wafer the priests press to my tongue in response to a 2000-year-old command is in fact, the Body and Blood of Jesus Christ. In a world where the Madonna of Caravaggio, Titian, and Fra Angelico has been superseded by the Madonna of MTV and Chastity is Cher's lesbian-activist daughter, it remains administered by celibates. And over this peculiar lot there presides a Pope—the last of the earth's absolute monarchs, the *Washington Post* loses no occasion to remind us (when it is not comparing the operations of the Vatican to those of the Soviet Kremlin)—who may no longer wear the a three-tiered crown but whose titles remain as fantastic as that claimed by any bonze: Pontifex Maximus, Lion of Judah, Paramour of Yahweh, and so on and on. And it cheerfully propagates the most implausible contradictions: Felix Culpa ("happy sin"), Virgin Mother, Good Thief.

At times its history might seem an exercise in the repudiation of Paul's Second Letter to the Corinthians. Even as orthodox a Pope as John Paul II has proposed that the Church atone for the sins of two millennia. The Chair of St. Peter might today be occupied by a saint—a full third of the Popes have ultimately been canonized—but it has burned its share as well. For every Aquinas a critic might point to a small-minded book burner; for every Mother Teresa, an overfed Mother Superior; for every John Paul, an Alexander VI. "Catholic" countries reflect these contradictions: the millions of abortions in Poland; the thousands of prostitutes in the Philippines; the drunkenness that continues to plague Ireland; the marital infidelity associated with Latin America. In this way good people have come to view Catholicism as a synonym for laxity and hypocrisy. Here I speak with the misbegotten authority that comes from having heard the cock crow many times in my own life.

What could anyone find persuasive in such a church? Surely the question admits of only one answer: that it is still here, open for business. We are an age that disbelieves in miracles, yet what could be more miraculous than the continued existence, the continued *attraction*, of a Church that has survived not only ,persecution from without but also from within, accumulated centuries of pride, mendacity, and—most debilitating of all—mediocrity? The miracle is not the Faith: The Faith is a proposition that is either true or false. The miracle is the Church, the Western world's oldest institution. Surely the Evangelicals who attribute this persistence to the Devil are closer to the truth than the folks of the Worldwatch Institute, who see it as mere superstition. I once put it to the philosopher Sidney Hook why in his own works he identified Christianity exclusively in Catholic terms when some of the Protestant faiths might be more congenial to his rationalistic outlook. He responded, "In this I agree with Marx, that Protestantism is but the last outpost on the road to atheism." Coming from a professed atheist, a man who once wrote a newspaper column castigating a doctor for having saved his life despite his orders, his answer seared itself in my memory.

If I have an advantage here, it doubtless owes itself to the peculiar church in which I grew up. Mine was a childhood that straddled both the pre- and postconciliar Churches: When I made my First Communion in suburban New Jersey, it was in a parish of *Going My Way* self-assurance: new brick buildings including a school, a convent, a rectory, a friary, and a church. The mock-leather kit all we boys received included plastic rosary beads and a missal featuring photographs of the Tridentine Mass. No sooner had I gotten the book, however, than it was made redundant by the new Mass, the priest of my missal, in his lacy white surplice and his back to the congregation, replaced by a priest with sideburns driving a red sports car. One by one the religious brothers and sisters who taught my classmates and me became ever more unrecognizable as they became more ordinary. First they abandoned the names they took upon joining the orders, so that Sister Angelita became Sister Maureen; Brother Jerome, Brother John, and a whole host of others remain confused in my memory because, after a quarter-century, the two names for each person have become jumbled in my mind. After they had changed their names, they began to shed their habits. By the time they had finished these outward changes, they must have realized that there was no longer anything that separated them from the world. So they followed the process to its ultimate conclusion and began leaving their orders.

The principal of my grade school, Sister Regina Agnes, left her convent and later appeared among the protesters outside my father's FBI office in New York. My eighth-grade teacher, Brother Jeffrey, showed up at our graduation in a three-piece corduroy suit of bright mauve, which was taken (as it was no doubt intended) as an announcement of his departure from the Rule of St. Francis. In fact, upon reflection I calculate that with one or two exceptions, every religious whom I had as a teacher ended up abandoning his or her vocation, which development I have sufficient egotism not to regard as evidence of any overwhelming character failing on my part. Of the priests I knew at St. Anthony's, it was the pastor who worked hardest to tear down the parish he had spent so much time building. And the priest I liked reentered my life recently in the form of a newspaper headline saying that he was being sought in connection with charges of having molested a boy from the same parish, a boy at whose marriage he would later officiate. I knew of no such things, but have to say that such evidence as exists inclines to the boy's version of events.

Disappointment, therefore, I can understand, and have tasted. Likewise with anger. What I cannot for the life of me fathom, however, is how confirmation of sin is supposed to be an argument against a church whose greatest task this day is to persuade people to recognize it by its rightful name.

In the media in which I toil, these inevitable scandals—a bishop runs off with his secretary, a clerk skims from the collection plate, a nun has an abortion—is treated as evidence that the Church does not really take its own teachings seriously. Yet at least in this one area the Church appears to be quite literally practicing what it preaches: that we are all sinners in need of God's mercy and redemption. I have not been able to come up with a single Pope who has interpreted the Creed's statement of "one holy, catholic, and apostolic Church" to mean a perfect church;

to the contrary, the only two people the Church has in its 2000 years recognized as free from the stain of sin are Mary, the Mother of Our Lord, and Our Lord Himself, who reminded us that even the just man sins seven times a day. How curious that in an age that looks favorably on rich churches, poor churches, gay churches, artist churches, socialist churches, and conservative churches, there should not be among them a church catering to sinners!

I suspect, moreover, that the conspicuous presence of sinners among our ranks is less a difficulty for the Faithful than we are led to believe. For most of those sad, weary faces that file into church each Sunday, it is not scandal that disillusions. It is humdrum. A saint who snores is always going to be a harder test of faith than a Mafia don who prays. Such trials as the Faithful endure are not because their priests are world-weary Cardinal Richelieus but because they are so . . . ordinary, the Father Mackenzies darning their socks in the rectory quiet. Likewise, the lack of transcendent beauty. How many of the Faithful would gladly embrace a violent martyrdom in a distant land rather than endure the pinpricks of a thousand "Kumbayas."

Curiously, it is the Church's acknowledgment of these imperfections that allows it to survive. For modernity by its nature is incapable of such an admission: a world that denies the transcendent ends up manufacturing its own fantasies. Everywhere our age insists on clean lines and minimalism, from the soulless Bauhaus boxes of Mies van der Rohe to the sharp metal chairs of Philippe Stark. Everywhere the modern aesthetic searches for an unconsummated purity in form, in material, in soul. Until recently this sort of thing was confined to the wealthy, because it is expensive. But capitalism (which I support, for other reasons) has now democratized it for the masses, and the Good News is proclaimed in every late-night infomercial: middle-aged mothers restored to bikinis; senior citizens relieved of their wrinkles; the fat made thin, the bald made bushy, the white made tan and the dark made white. Life becomes a *Baywatch* set where every body that appears on the beach—for however fleeting a second—is a perfect 10.

In this brave clean world, the Catholic Church, with its incense and oils, looms as grotesque. Yet the modern's denial of sin leads to its own grotesqueries. With the Berlin Wall having fallen and the order it represents now a synonym for backwardness, it is difficult to recall the promise once held out by Communist societies ("communism = socialism + electrification" was one such formulation). How soon the bloom came off these particular roses! In a recent best-selling book by Chairman Mao's former physician, the author opened his story with an account of the challenge he faced in preserving the Chairman's body after death, such preservation having become required in Communist societies. In the course of his investigations, the doctor learned from Russian and Vietnamese counterparts that bits and pieces had fallen off both Lenin and Ho Chi Minh in the past, which made him feel much better about the manufacture of a wax dummy that stands in for Chairman Mao's corpse whenever it is undergoing one of its frequent renovations. And here I must part company with Saint Thomas, who teaches that the Almighty's nature precludes a sense of humor.

Within America, the twists of fate have been more ironic. Though the Church continues to be attacked as "un-American"—as a 1989 *Philadelphia Inquirer* editorial put it—the nature of that attack, not to mention the nature of those doing the attacking, has shifted 180 degrees. For most of the American history, the Catholic Church has been regarded by a pilgrim America as a cross between Scripture and mummery, a cult that plied its trade on the ignorant and superstitious. It was Maria Monk and her awful tales. Yet the most extraordinary thing has happened. Over the course of the last three decades, when the tales of many real priests and nuns would make Maria Monk blush, the church lampooned regularly in our press is not the Whore of Babylon but the Church of Impossibly Strict Standards, a change that says more about the America in which the Catholic Church finds itself than about the Church's relative position within it.

Naturally this shift leaves many of our Protestant brethren, especially those in the Evangelical community, scratching their heads in confusion. On the one hand, they continue to retain grave doubts about the Roman Church and especially the papacy. On the other hand, they can see that at a point in history when the civilization and principles they hold most dear have been most under attack, the most vigorous voice raised in defense belongs to a Pope of Rome. Hence the growing political alliance, not always easy but very real, between orthodox Catholic and Christian Evangelical.

For Bible Belters are more broad-minded than the children of progress. They also don't face nearly as great a dilemma. For these latter, the difficulty is that a Catholic Church that they hold to be irrelevant must at the same time be relentlessly attacked as public enemy number one. Needless to say, both propositions cannot be true, and the tension makes for an immensely entertaining spectacle. In the newsroom, for example, if you are prepared to acknowledge yourself a Christian, much less a Catholic, you must accept that you will be regarded as practically an imbecile. Yet as I sit back and watch, I see that it is the Church that sets the terms for the world, and not vice versa. It was Gorbachev who came to Rome hat in hand, not vice versa; it was the Vice President of the United States who was forced to back down on his plans to enshrine a worldwide right to abortion at the U.N. conference in Cairo, not the Pope; it was the Pope who in the Philippines drew 4 million people for a Mass, the largest gathering in history—not Woodstock, not Hitler at Nuremberg, not the Red Guard rallies in Beijing. In a particularly fit penance, it is the press that must cover it all.

In a business built on bylines, what is most maddening to my colleagues is how little our coverage matters to Rome. In reading *His Holiness*, the recent papal biography by Carl Bernstein and Marco Politi, I was not surprised to learn that John Paul seldom reads newspapers. It is to this as much to the interventions of the Holy Spirit that I attribute his extraordinary popularity, and when I learned it, my estimation of the man, previously high, went up several more notches. In the United States no leader gives a speech before consulting focus groups and trying to figure out what message the people want so he or she may then begin trying to supply it, whether it's Bill Clinton speaking earnestly about "a bridge to the twenty-first century" or Newt Gingrich countering with "family values." As a delusion it is a particularly contemporary one—had Abraham Lincoln had focus groups in his day, he might have saved himself from being shot, but we would have today a Confederate States of America—and the cynicism of the American electorate reflects it.

The Catholic Church takes a different approach, one that would be poisonous on Madison Avenue. For it sees itself as charged with telling people what they need to hear, whether they like it or not: to resist the uncritical embracing of the new that often passes for being modern. In an interview with the Jewish-born Jean-Marie Cardinal Lustiger of Paris in the mid-1980s, when I asked him whether it was not something of a contradiction to have a man so wedded to tradition on the Chair of St. Peter at the closing of the twentieth century, he repeated a distinction he had used with another American reporter a few weeks earlier. "Do not confuse a modern man with an American liberal. They are not the same thing."

G. K. Chesterton summed it up by saying the Church's job is to preach the unpopular virtue. In our own time this is to remind people that being contemporary is not simply to give in to the latest fad. I think here of Paul VI, whose decision on behalf of *Humanae Vitae* rent the church and is held in derision in most fashionable circles. In retrospect we can see that the fiercest attacks were mounted not by married people but by the clergy. In many ways I suppose it is because they, too, are manifestly human: If you were a priest comfortably ensconced in a nice university or a suburban parish, how much more pleasant it might be to substitute "Do as you think best" for "Go and pick up your cross." With their characteristic predilection for mechanics, opponents of *Humanae Vitae* have represented it as simply a ban on artificial contraception. Yet even a cursory reading reveals that the thrust of that document was less about contraception than about the contraceptive society, a society whose outlines Paul VI had even then discerned, where whim became not only possible but ipso facto moral.

Twenty-five years later, John Paul would complete this thought in his own indictment of the "culture of death." And it is given added force because of the sheer consistency of John Paul's person with his message. Yet the meek have their own power. On a recent visit to St. Peter's, the day before my family was to meet this present Pope at a special audience to which we had been invited, I paused in front of the unadorned tomb of Paul VI and reflected how much more compelling *Humanae Vitae* is for having been issued by a weak Pope like him, a Pope who died heartbroken at the chaos he perceived within his own ranks. Who today can read Paul's concerns about "the wide and easy road" society was opening up and not believe that he was a prophet?

Not even the Church pretends its message is easy. I feel safe in saying that I speak for many Catholics when I say that the truths it propounds can be deucedly inconvenient, robbing even indulgence of its pleasure, like cheating on a diet. Love the sinner and hate the sin, we are taught, when all my impulses run in the opposite direction. It is at such times I have wished, and wished hard, for a little license, not an outright liberation but a weekend furlough. "Lord, make me chaste—but not yet" is the prayer that makes Augustine believable, for the acknowledgment of prayer ultimately robs indulgence of its one attraction: pleasure. Yet it is in these gritty moments, when we catch a glimpse of leering selves in the mirror, that we may find a bit of truth, suddenly calling to mind a snatch from a long-forgotten catechism, and by grabbing onto this part, we may, with goodwill and effort, be led back to the whole. It is often forgotten that part of the Church's arrogance is that when it speaks, it speaks to all men, not just those within its fold.

The claims upon which these teachings rest may be fantastic, based on a particular interpretation of Christ's words to Peter. Yet it is equally inescapable that a literal and figurative Church was in short order built on Peter, and that the gates of Hell, much less the gates of *Time* magazine, have yet to prevail. In light of some of those who have run the Church, this might be thought, as I have suggested earlier, something of a miracle in itself. For the claim itself cannot be glossed over. It is this claim that defines the Church, this claim that makes it "the" Church even to its enemies, this claim that lies at the heart of the choice it forces people to make. And it is a claim that admits of no middle ground, only yea or nay. Once answered, it puts all other questions—about the Virgin Mary, about papal infallibility, about *Humanae Vitae*—into a radically different perspective. Is the Catholic Church what it says it is?

My own answer to that question, for better or for worse, is the Communion I take on my lips each week. In this I perceive I am not different from the people next to me. For most of us, the road to Christ is not Damascus but Emmaus, with the Risen Lord falling in by our sides unrecognized, waiting for us to figure it out. The point is that the Lord is ever there, and even in the worst of times gives us signs if we are disposed to recognize them: a Slav comes to the Chair of St. Peter; an electrician in the Gdansk shipyards stands up; a nun founds an order in the slums of Calcutta that is devoted to the poorest of the poor; a weak and demoralized Pope, against the advice of his own chosen panel, offers up a document that will either prove the salvation of the civilization it represents or provide its epitaph. In places like the newsroom, these are all dealt with as contradictory and isolated happenings, yet it is not hard to see that, viewed through the eyes of the Faithful, they take on an exhilarating continuity. It is a continuity, moreover, that we find ourselves linked to in each sacrifice of the Mass. What tired sinners like me find in our Church is not an infallible list of answers to our particular predicaments but a touch of the transcendent, a glimpse of things hoped for but not expected to be seen.

This was the vision, after all, that guided the Church for 2000 years, a vision that could exert a powerful influence even on a crusty old agnostic like H. L. Mencken. "The Latin church," he once wrote, "which I constantly find myself admiring, despite its frequent astounding imbecilities, has always kept clearly before it the fact that religion is not a syllogism but a poem." Oils, vestments, candles, wine, water, bread— truly these are implausible things in the age of the silicon chip. No less implausible is faith in a Messiah born of a Virgin Jewess in an obscure part of Roman Palestine. But the only thing more preposterous than faith in an unseen God is faith in a visible mankind, who over his several millennia on this orb has amassed a pathetic record of cruelty, barbarism, and fanaticism in nearly every place at nearly every time, from Attila the Hun to Slobodan Milosevic, without learning much along the way. The ridiculous spectacle of Sister O'Grady removing *The Catcher in the Rye* from a high-school bookshelf pales when placed against the impotence of the United Nations in Bosnia, the lugubrious intonations of Carl Sagan, or the emergence of a U.S. Assistant Secretary of State as the world's largest condom salesman.

What this world needs to recover most is a sense of the transcendent whose metaphors are the Sacraments, inspiring the imagination to understand where the pure intellect comes up short. It is a need, moreover, that we in the Fourth Estate feed with our front pages and their desperate, unrequited pursuit of the new. Tragedy in Rwanda! Market Crashes! Market Soars! President Blank Defeated! President Blank Elected! Top Aide Resigns over Affair! The joke is on us, for the more relentless the quest for the scoop, the more readers feel they have heard it all before. In this absurd world, where the imagination has become parched, the Gospel words ring out with a freshness and vigor undimmed by frequent retelling. "Never man spake like this man," explained the officers of the high priests for their failure to arrest Christ as assigned. These words live in our hearts, but the reason we might hear them today, whether in a back province of China or the front row of St. Patrick's Cathedral, owes itself to a Church that traces itself back to a fisherman named Simon.

None of these is a reason for being a Catholic, much less becoming one, but that is because the process of becoming a Catholic is not, as popularly presented, checking off the boxes in a catechism. It is, as my fellow newspaperman Charles Moore has eloquently written, more like falling in love. Trying to list the individual reasons makes them suddenly flat and ridiculous; the activating reason is the sum total of these reasons—Newman's *Grammar of Assent*—which is greater than its constituent parts. Quite often the bits and pieces that go into that decision, that confirm for us decisions we have made, are small enough things in themselves, a mélange of the universal and the particular. In this century we have had ample evidence of man's attraction to error. But we might also want to appreciate his particular affinity for truth, and the priceless aura of serenity we sense among those who have it even when we ourselves do not. It is for this reason that Hollywood insists on putting its nuns in habits.

Have I ever experienced a moment equivalent to that of born-again Christians, where I felt some vision of God? The answer is, first, decidedly no; second, that I never expect to; and third, that in what no doubt is my narrow-minded way, I rather distrust people who say they have. What I do have are unexpected little epiphanies of utter contentment: of watching the shining faces of a choir of Filipina maids at my parish in Hong Kong; of early morning Mass before an obscure side altar in St. Peter's, with no one but a priest and altar boy; of a 1985 meeting in a Gdansk apartment with a group of men whom none of us could then know would a few years hence constitute the first free Polish government, my eye drawn to the swollen bellies of their pregnant wives and the glorious rebuke it represented to the shabbiness around them; of a Christmas Eve service in Manila where, at the moment the wooden bambino was held aloft, I felt a sudden communion with a yet unknown infant lying in an orphanage in China; and, finally, of a candle I lit seven months later with my wife at the Grotto of my beloved Notre Dame, with that same infant, our new daughter, in her arms. And all of these moments the more luminous for the unparalleled joy I behold in a mother and father now enjoying their grandchildren after lifetimes spent trying to inculcate in their children, by dint of example, the importance of putting God first. I fear these are not terribly original reasons (I confess I should find them less convincing if they were), and I appreciate that other, more discriminating minds might well remain unmoved. But the question to me implies the answer.

My Church is not without its hard edges. At times it can be uniquely unlovely. If, however, one takes Christ's words to Peter at face value, one could see how the task has been discharged in a way that might be expected from a human institution entrusted with a divine enterprise: inspiring the most sublime works of art, producing saints of extraordinary holiness, yet somehow managing to survive the fools, fakes, and mountebanks into whose hands the endeavor has periodically fallen. Cognizant of my own sins, I remain grateful for a Church whose doors remain open. If I stay, however, it is not because it accepts me for what I am. It is because it understands what I might yet be.

About the Contributors

MARY CUNNINGHAM AGEE is a former high-powered executive at Seagrams and Bendix Corporation, who now devotes herself to charity. She runs The Nurturing Network, a national organization that helps young women facing the crisis of unwanted pregnancy. She grew up in Hanover, New Hampshire, and attended Wellesley College. Agee also has a master's degree from Harvard Business School. Her book, *Powerplay*, stayed on the *New York Times* bestseller list for ten weeks. Agee lives in Napa Valley, California, with her husband, Bill, and their two children.

MARIO ANDRETTI is widely regarded as one of the greatest race car drivers of all time; he is a four-time Indy car champion, United States Auto Club National Dirt Track Champion, winner of the International Race of Champions title, and Driver of the Quarter Century. He remains Indy Car racing's all-time leader in pole positions won, laps led, and his record of career victories is second only to A. J. Foyt's. He holds the world closed-course speed record of 234.75 miles per hour, set July 31, 1993. With his fifty-second Indy car victory at the Phoenix 200 in April, 1993, Andretti became the first driver to win races in four decades. This race also marked his one hundredth major career victory.

WILLIAM BENTLEY BALL has led counsel in First and Fourteenth Amendment cases in twenty-two states and in ten Supreme Court Arguments. He was national chairman, Committee on Constitutional Law, Federal Bar Association, 1970–1974. He serves on many advisory boards as well as on legal journals. He is on the board of Visitors for Thomas Aquinas College, The Catholic League for Religious and Civil Rights, and a member of the Fellowship of Catholic Scholars. Currently a partner of Ball, Skelly, Murren and Connel Law Firm, he teaches as an adjunct professor at the Dickinson School of Law, and writes for journals such as *First Things*, *Crisis*, *Human Life Review*, *Commonweal*, and *America*. He has received numerous public service and honorary degrees. He lives in Harrisburg, Pennsylvania, with his wife, Caroline, and they have a grown daughter.

MARK BAVARO was born in East Boston in 1963. He attended Danvers High School and Notre Dame University, where he played football as a tight end from 1982–1985. He went on to play for the New York Giants from 1985–1990 and also donned the Philadelphia Eagles uniform for two seasons. He now lives in Topsfield, Massachusetts, with his wife, Susan, and their two children.

NICHOLAS BURNS is a career diplomat with the United States Department of State. During the past fifteen years, he has served in a variety of senior positions in Washington and overseas, most recently as the State Department Spokesman for Secretaries of State Warren Christopher and Madeleine Albright. Mr. Burns graduated from Boston College and the Johns Hopkins School of Advanced International Studies, and received a certificate from the Sorbonne. He lives in Vienna, Virginia, with his wife, Libby, and their three daughters.

JOHN E. COONS went to law school, practiced a bit, and taught law for forty years at Northwestern and Berkeley. He and Marylyn Bowles married in 1956. Their four sons include a musician, banker, public high school teacher, and worker-student (formerly a rock singer). Their daughter teaches in an inner-city Catholic school.

BOB COUSY is the color commentator for the Boston Celtics. After playing basketball at Holy Cross College, he joined the Boston Celtics in 1950, and was coach at Boston College from 1963–1969. He was head coach for the Cincinnati Royals and the Omaha Kings before becoming a sports broadcaster. He is the author of *Basketball Is My Life*. He was national director of Big Brothers from 1964–65. Named to the Basketball Hall of Fame in 1971, he lives in Worcester, Massachusetts, with his wife, Missy.

SUSAN DODD is the author of three novels and two short story collections. Her education includes degrees from the School of Foreign Service at Georgetown University, the University of Louisville, and Vermont College. She has received several awards, including the Iowa School of Letters Award for Short Fiction, the Friends of American Writers Award, and a Fellowship from the National Endowment for the Arts. She has taught at Vermont College, the Iowa Writers' Workshop, and Harvard University, and is currently teaching writing at the graduate level at Bennington College. Her books include *No Earthly Notion*, *Mamaw*, and *The Mourner's Bench*. She lives on Ocracoke Island in the Outer Banks of North Carolina.

WILLIAM A. DONOHUE is president of the Catholic League for Religious and Civil Rights and an adjunct scholar at the Heritage Foundation. In the Catholic League journal, *Catalyst*, he publishes accounts of injustice corrected, citing an instance of public anti-Catholic bias and the reply (usually an apology) from the offender. He has published three books: *The Politics of the American Civil Liberties Union*, *The New Freedom: Individualism*, and *Collectivism in the Social Lives of Americans*. Mr. Donohue received his Ph.D. in sociology, and has taught at St. Lucy's School in New York and La Roche College in Pittsburgh.

ANDRE DUBUS has written eight books of fiction, his most recent being *Dancing After Hours*. He received a B.A. from McNeese State College, and an M.F.A. from the University of Iowa. He received the PEN/Malamud Award and fellowships from the National Endowment for the Arts, Guggenheim, and MacArthur Foundations. Mr. Dubus taught at Bradford College, and has been a visiting teacher at the University of Alabama and Boston University. In July 1986, he was struck by a hit-and-run driver, and as a result of the accident, lost one leg and is paralyzed in the other. He is currently working on a collection of personal essays. Dubus lives in Haverhill, Massachusetts, and has six children.

MARY ANN GLENDON is the Learned Hand Professor of Law at Harvard University, writing and lecturing on comparative and constitutional law and legal theory. She has written nine books, including *The Seedbeds of Virtue*, *Rights Talk*, and *The Transformation of Family Law*. In 1994, she was appointed by John Paul II to the Pontifical Academy of Social Science. A year later, she was named to the Holy See's Central Committee for the great Jubilee 2000, and headed the Holy See's delegation to the United Nations Women's Conference in Beijing. Ms. Glendon received her B.A., J.D., Masters of Comparative Law from the University of Chicago and studied European Law at the Universite Libre de Bruxelles. She and her husband, Edward Lev, live in Chestnut Hill, Massachusetts. They have three daughters.

FR. ANDREW M. GREELEY was ordained a Catholic priest in 1954 and remains a priest in the archdiocese of Chicago. A professor of social science at the University of Chicago and sociology at the University of Arizona, he is a research associate at the National Opinion Research Center. Author of nearly one hundred books, both nonfiction and fiction, including several bestsellers, he is currently at work on three new novels. Fr. Greeley attended St. Mary of the Lake Seminary and received his M.A. and Ph.D. from the University of Chicago.

JOHN HASSLER, Regents Professor Emeritus at St. John's University, Minnesota, has published eleven novels. His first, *Staggerford*, was chosen as Novel of the Year in 1977 by Friends of American Writers and *Grand Opening* was selected as Best Fiction of 1987 by the Society of Midland Authors. His other novels include *Simon's Night*, *The Love Hunter*, *North of Hope*, *The Dean's List*, and *A Green Journey*, which was adapted for television. After forty-two years as an English teacher in various Minnesota high schools and colleges, he has retired to write. He lives with his wife, Gretchen, in Minneapolis and is completing his memoirs.

FR. THEODORE M. HESBURGH, C.S.C., led Notre Dame for thirty-five years—the longest term among active college presidents. He also served on many boards and commissions, and was the first priest to be a director of Chase Manhattan Bank and a trustee of the Rockefeller Foundation. He has held fifteen Presidential appointments. He won the AAUP's Meiklejohn Award, recognizing his crucial role in blunting the attempts of the Nixon administration to quell campus disturbances in 1970. He has written two books, including the bestselling *God, Country, Notre Dame*.

KATHLEEN HOWLEY is descended from Galway farmers who immigrated to Boston in 1914. She is a freelance journalist who writes for the real estate section of the *Boston Globe*. Prior to the *Globe*, she wrote three weekly columns for the *Boston Herald*, including "Charlie on the MBTA," a feature that chronicled life on the city's subway system. She has gained recognition as a writer of religious articles. After receiving her journalism degree, she moved to West Africa to work on a newspaper development project in Monrovia, Liberia's capital. She lives on the oceanfront in Cohasset, Massachusetts, and is working on her first novel.

WILLIAM X. KIENZLE left the priesthood after twenty years of service and became a writer of mysteries such as *The Rosary Murders*, *Death Wears a Red Hat*, and *Masquerade*, among others. He is known for his novels featuring Father Robert Koesler, a liberal priest whose knowledge of Catholicism and church law assists him in solving crimes. Mr. Kienzle attended Sacred Heart Seminary College, St. John's Seminary, and the University of Detroit.

BOWIE KUHN is active in sports, business and legal work, but is best known for being commissioner of baseball from 1969 to 1984. He is currently president of the Kent Group and Sports Franchises. He is on the finance committee of Domino's Pizza, Inc. He is the author of *Hardball: The Education of a Baseball Commissioner*, published in 1987. Kuhn has a B.A. cum laude from Princeton, and took a law degree at the University of Virginia. He worked as a lawyer and became a partner at several firms; he was senior partner at Myerson & Kuhn and a partner at Willkie, Farr & Gallagher. He is on the board of directors for the

Baseball Hall of Fame & Museum and the International Tennis Hall of Fame, and is a trustee of New York Medical College and Jacksonville University.

ROGER McCAFFREY founded his own publishing house and two Catholic magazines for which he serves as editor and publisher. He is the president of Roman Catholic Books, which reprints popular Catholic classics by English-language authors. He is also a mail-order marketing consultant. Mr. McCaffrey has coauthored two books, *Player's Choice: Major League Baseball Players Vote on the All-Time Greats* and *An Executive's Complete Guide to Licensing*. Born in Pelham Manor, New York, he received his B.A. in theology from the University of Dallas. He and his wife, Priscilla, have three children.

WILLIAM McGURN is senior editor for the *Far Eastern Economic Review*. Born in California, he grew up in Bergen County, New Jersey. In 1980, he graduated from Notre Dame with a bachelor's degree in philosophy and a year later received a master's degree from Boston University's College of Communications. McGurn's journalism career began as assistant managing editor of *The American Spectator*, and he subsequently worked on a variety of publications, including *This World*, *The Wall Street Journal/Europe*, *The Asian Wall Street Journal*, and *The National Review*, where he was Washington Bureau chief. He is a member of the Council for Foreign Relations and author of the recent book *Perfidious Albion: The Abandonment of Hong Kong*. McGurn lives in Hong Kong with his wife, Julie, and their daughter.

DR. BERNARD NATHANSON is a former abortionist turned pro-lifer. The son of a Jewish doctor in Ottawa, he attended Jewish private schools, then Cornell University, and completed his medical training at McGill University. For thirty years he directed the United States' largest abortion clinic and founded what was to become the National Abortion and Reproductive Rights Action League. He joined the pro-life movement in 1989, and in 1996 he was baptized a Roman Catholic. Dr. Nathanson is the author of *The Hand of God* and *Aborting America*. He has been married three times and has a son, Joseph. He lives in Manhattan.

MICHAEL NOVAK is a founder of the Catholic journal *Crisis* and won the Templeton Progress in Religion Prize in 1994. He attended Stonehill College A.B. Summa Cum Laude, B.T. cum laude Gregorian University, Rome, and received his M.A. from Harvard University. He has been associate professor of philosophy and religious studies at Old Westbury College and a visiting professor at U.C. Santa Barbara, Syracuse University, and the University of Notre Dame. He is the author of numerous works of fiction and nonfiction, including, *The Tiber Was Silver*, *Belief and Unbelief*, *Will It Liberate?*, *The Catholic Ethic*, and *The Spirit of Democratic Capitalism*. Currently he is a fellow at the American Enterprise Institute. He is married and has three children.

WALKER PERCY is the author of six novels and two nonfiction works, which run the gamut from mysteries of theology and existentialism to psychology and semiotics. Born in Alabama in 1913, he lost both parents as a teenager and was raised by an uncle. Trained as a doctor at Columbia's College of Physicians and Surgeons, he contracted tuberculosis while working as a pathologist, and during his recovery, he decided both to become a writer and to convert to Catholicism. His novel *The Moviegoer* won the National Book Award in 1962, and *Love in the Ruins* won the National Catholic Book Award in 1971. Mr. Percy died in 1990.

MARIA SHRIVER is a national news correspondent for NBC, and has served as anchor for a number of NBC news programs. She is a contributing anchor for *Dateline NBC* and anchors *First Person with Maria Shriver*, a series of prime-time NBC news specials. Shriver has reported on a variety of topics, interviewing newsmakers ranging from world leaders to unforgettable everyday people. She has been honored with numerous awards, including a first-place Commendation Award from American Women in Radio and Television and an Emmy Award. Before joining NBC News, she served as a co-anchor of *CBS Morning News*, national correspondent for Group W's *PM Magazine*, and a producer for Westinghouse Broadcasting. She began her career as a newswriter/producer for KYW-TV in Philadelphia. Born in Chicago, she received a B.A. from Georgetown University. She lives in Los Angeles with her husband and their four children.

WILLIAM E. SIMON served as Secretary of the Treasury under Presidents Nixon and Ford, and was the first administrator of the Federal Energy Office. After leaving government, Mr. Simon launched a series of successful business enterprises, including the Wesray Corporation and WSGP International. He has been an active member of the U.S. Olympic Committee, serving as president and treasurer, and was inducted into the U.S. Olympic Hall of Fame in 1991. A graduate and trustee of Lafayette College, he donated a chair in political economy and provided funds for the construction of two new buildings at the college. He is currently chairman of the board of William E. Simon & Sons, Inc., a private merchant bank, and is president of the John M. Olin Foundation, which provides grants to support and promote a wider understanding of the free enterprise system. In addition, he has authored two bestselling books, *A Time for Truth* and *A Time for Action*.

KATHLEEN KENNEDY TOWNSEND is the first woman lieutenant governor of Maryland. Townsend is the daughter of Robert F. and Ethel S. Kennedy. Before her election in 1994, she gained experience as deputy assistant attorney general in the U.S. Department of Justice. She has taught at the University of Maryland–Baltimore County and the University of Pennsylvania. She was the first executive of the Maryland Student Service Alliance, a public-private partnership founded to inspire young people to serve their communities. Townsend lives in Baltimore County, Maryland, with her husband, David, and three of their four daughters.

About the Editors

KEVIN RYAN is professor and director of the Boston University Center for the Advancement of Ethics and Character. He was born in Larchmont, New York, in 1932, attended Catholic grammar and high schools, and took his bachelor's degree at St. Michael's College of the University of Toronto. After graduation, he enlisted in the navy, gained a commission, earned wings as an airborne air controller and served aboard four aircraft carriers. After the service he took a graduate teaching degree at Columbia Teachers College and was a high school English teacher. He attended Stanford University for his Ph.D. and during that period married his wife, Marilyn, in 1964. He took his first university position at the University of Chicago two years later. Before coming to Boston University in 1982, he taught on the faculties of Harvard, the University of Lisbon, and Ohio State University. Ryan has written and edited seventeen books, primarily on education and character formation.

MARILYN RYAN was born on a dairy farm in Washington State in 1940. She attended the University of Washington and majored in English. In 1960, she was Washington State chairman for "Youth for Kennedy," and in 1961 she was a summer intern for Senator "Scoop" Jackson. Immediately after graduating from college, she went on one of the early cultural exchange programs to the USSR, sponsored by the YMCA. Following this trip, she took a position as an English teacher in Nyack, New York. She met her future husband during that first year of teaching.

Raised in a nonreligious family, Marilyn attended various churches as a girl. Before she married in 1964, she became a Catholic, returning to the faith of her Slovenian grandparents. After her marriage and a move to California, she worked for *Sunset Magazine* and later taught high school English. Her first child, Hilary, was born in 1967, shortly after the Ryans moved to Chicago, where Kevin had taken a professorship at the University of Chicago. Alexandra was born four years later. Long interested in public policy, Marilyn took a graduate degree in political science at the University of Chicago. The Ryans moved to Columbus, Ohio, in 1975, where their third child, Justin, was born. Shortly after settling in Columbus, they became involved with PreCana work at the Ohio State Newman Center. Based on this work, Marilyn and Kevin wrote *Making a Marriage*. In recent years, Marilyn has busied herself launching her family, helping Kevin with his writing, gardening, and doing occasional writing. The Ryans have two grandchildren, Julia and Nicholas Briggs Tucker.